BLACKLINE MAPS OF WORLD HISTORY

The Complete Set Expanded
with Unlabeled Maps
5000BC – The Present

Created by
TERRI JOHNSON

BRAMLEY BOOKS
www.bramleybooks.com

A Division of Knowledge Quest, Inc.
San Antonio, Texas

BLACKLINE MAPS OF
WORLD HISTORY

The Complete Set Expanded
with Unlabeled Maps
5000BC – The Present

This book contains over 200 hand-drawn maps along with companion unlabeled maps pertaining to the time period from 5000BC to the present. Suggestions for their use are contained under the Introduction and Lesson Plan sections, but may be used differently to tailor fit the individual needs of your home school or classroom. DISCLAIMER: Note that the dates and scales are approximate, but should be adequate for the maps' purpose as a history supplement. Be aware also that one may discover discrepancies in area or boundary lines depending upon the resource used. If for any reason you are dissatisfied with this product, you may return it for a full refund of your purchase price. Please return complete packet in new condition along with your invoice or original receipt to the origin of purchase.

Permission to Reproduce

Knowledge Quest, Inc. grants the right to the individual purchaser to reproduce the maps herein for noncommercial, individual use. Reproduction for an entire classroom, school, or school system is strictly prohibited. Please call (210)745-0203 or e-mail orders@knowledgequestmaps.com for information on quantity sale discounts. No part of this publication may be reproduced for storage in a retrieval system, or transmitted in any form, or by any means, electronic, mechanical, recording, or otherwise without the prior written permission of the publisher. For information regarding permission, write to Knowledge Quest, Inc. at the address below.

How to Order More Copies
Please send check or money order for $45.00 + S&H to: (use enclosed order form)

P.O. Box 789
Boring, OR 97009
(877)697-8611

Visit us online to order by credit card and to view our growing selection of maps, timelines and more. History makes sense using maps and timelines!

TABLE OF CONTENTS

TABLE OF CONTENTS, CONTINUED...

TABLE OF CONTENTS, CONTINUED...

MODERN TIME PERIOD

INTRODUCTION

It only makes sense to study geography alongside history. In history, we learn about times, places and people. Each aspect of historical study is important in its own right, but they cannot be studied exclusively of one another. For example, when you study the Norman Conquests, you learn that it took place between 1066 and 1087AD and that it was the Normans of France who crossed the English Channel to conquer Britain. After reading about this event in history, why not have the student look at a map or globe to find out where it took place? Better yet, have him label and color a map drawn specifically of that region and for that time period in history. When children have visual cues, it helps to cement fact into their minds.

These maps were created for this purpose and may be posted to a bulletin board upon completion or assembled into a history notebook. Our students compile the completed maps into a notebook along with narrations from the history books we have read and pictures of historical events that the children have drawn and captioned. When we have completed a unit of history study, the children then have their own "book" which they have made which tells the story of the history that they have learned and summarized. The maps make nice colorful entries into their notebooks.

Some areas of these maps have been purposely left unlabeled. This allows the teacher and student to discuss the map briefly before coloring it. There are a few questions included for each map under the "Lesson Plans" section which follows. The student may be asked to label a certain body of water or a bordering country. He may be asked to draw in a river or identify a city, color-code a key or draw a compass rose. The teacher should be willing to help with spelling or with answers if the child does not know them. This is meant to be fun and interactive and not a test or drill. Learning geography comes with familiarity and repetition. In fact, if the student incorporates all of these maps into his study of world history, he will begin to memorize geographical facts which will remain with him for a lifetime.

To gain the most benefit from these blackline maps, it would be advantageous to have on hand a globe, wall map, or an atlas for reference. The student may be asked to look up something on the globe and then label it onto the blank map. Also, have available some decent art supplies. As your student matures, he or she should be expected to present to you upon completion a neatly colored or pencil shaded map. For variety, allow the student to experiment with watercolors for a different effect; or let her use glue and glitter on a major route. No matter what their age, children should always be encouraged to do their "best".

We hope these maps enhance your study of history and make learning geography an enjoyable and interactive learning experience for your student(s).

Terri Johnson

The Ancients
5000BC ~ 400AD

Lesson Plans

Discussion Questions:

1. First Cities and Early Civilizations – Page 14
   - Point to the cities that you have learned about in your history studies so far.
   - Do you know the name of the long body of water on the lower left side? It is called the Red Sea. Label it on your map.
   - The land of Mesopotamia means "between the rivers." Point to it on your map.
   - Which sea on your map looks the largest? Do you know its name? It is called the Mediterranean Sea. Label it.
   - *Unlabeled map exercise: Find and label the first cities of the ancient world. In which modern day countries were these cities located?*

2. The Sumerians of Mesopotamia – Page 16
   - Point to the Tigris River. Point to the Euphrates River. On which river is the city of Ur located? Which word in the title means "between the rivers"?
   - Do you know the name of the body of water into which the two rivers empty? It is called the Persian Gulf? Label it on your map.
   - What is the name of the sea at the top of your map? It is called the Caspian Sea. Label it.
   - *Unlabeled map exercise: Draw ziggurats at the locations of Sumeria's four major cities. Label all bodies of water, including the two main rivers.*

3. Ancient Egypt – Page 18
   - Do you remember seeing that body of water with the long inlets on an earlier map? What is its name? Label it.
   - Point to the Nile River. Can you see where it connects to the Mediterranean Sea? What are all those connecting lines? They are the branching rivers which are flowing down into the sea and it is called the Nile Delta. Delta is the name given for the deposited land at the branching mouth of a river. *(See dictionary for a more detailed definition).*
   - *Unlabeled map exercise: Find and label the major cities of Ancient Egypt. Draw the division between Upper and Lower Egypt and label these two kingdoms, as well as all bodies of water shown on this map.*

4. The Island of Crete – Page 20
   - Go back to your first map "First Cities and Early Civilizations" and see if you can find Crete on that map. Label it on that map if possible.
   - Do you see that little edge of land in the bottom left hand corner of your current map? Can you guess what continent that might be? Label "Africa" on your map.
   - *Unlabeled map exercise: Draw in the city of Knossos. Label all land shown on this map – modern-day names are adequate.*

5. Ancient India – Page 22
   - The ocean to the south and east of India bears the same name. Label it on your map.
   - About how many miles or kilometers separate the two cities of Mohenjo-daro and Harrappa?
   - *Unlabeled map exercise: Using your ruler for greater accuracy, draw in the cities of Mohenjo-daro and Harrappa. Label all bodies of water.*

6. The Rise of Babylon – Page 24
   - Do you recognize these two rivers? Name and label them on your map. Which river is the city of Babylon located on? Consult your Mesopotamia map on Page 12 for help with the answer.
   - You cannot see it on this map, but tell which country is located on the left side *(west)* of the Red Sea?
   - *Unlabeled map exercise: Draw in and label the four major cities of the Babylonian Empire. Label surrounding countries and bodies of water.*

7. Egypt's Middle and New Kingdoms – Page 26
   - Label the seas at the top *(north)* and right *(east)* sides of your map.
   - Notice the Key on the bottom left corner. What is it for? How is it helpful to you in understanding this map of Egypt? Why is it called a "key"? Look up this word in the glossary on page 9.
   - Do you remember what those branching rivers are called?
   - *Unlabeled map exercise: Label the cities that were thriving during this period in Egypt's history. Label the pyramids as well as the Valley of the Kings.*

8. The Assyrian Empire – Page 28
   - Name and label all three seas on your map.
   - Point to and name all three rivers.
   - Find and label Crete.
   - *Unlabeled map exercise: Label the five major cities of the Assyrian Empire. Label the surrounding kingdoms (i.e. Israel, Egypt, etc.) and bodies of water.*

9. China's Shang Kingdom – Page 30
   - Point to the Yellow River. Point to the Yangtze River. Find out the name of the southernmost river by consulting your globe or world map? *(One of its many names is Xi Jiang.)* On which river are all of the villages located?
   - Trace the rivers in blue. Color the fertile land surrounding the Yellow River in green.
   - *Unlabeled map exercise: Draw in and label the major cities along the Yellow River. Label the seas and the surrounding countries.*

10. The Israelites Leave Egypt – Page 32
    - What is the name of the sea to the north on your map? Label it.
    - What is the name of the river system on which Goshen is located? *(Nile Delta)*
    - Follow with your finger the possible path the Israelites followed when fleeing Egypt. In what country did they eventually settle?

- What are those two narrow bodies of water at the bottom of the page? This is a zoomed in view of a sea that should be very familiar to you by now. If uncertain, refer to your globe or look back to previous maps for the answer.
- *Unlabeled map exercise: Label all major cities and landmarks along the route taken by the fleeing Israelites.* **Extra challenge:** *Do some research on your own about the Exodus from Egypt and draw in the route that you find to be the most probable route taken by the Israelites, as well as the date that you believe it happened. Use Bible commentaries, study Bibles and other historical resources to aid you in your search. Have fun with this.*

11. Classical Greece – Page 34
- Point to the Aegean Sea. Which sea is that to the south of Greece?
- Label the island to the south of Greece. If uncertain, refer back to your 4th map on page 16.
- How far is it between the cities of Marathon and Athens *(26 miles or 40 kilometers, thus the name Marathon for the length of the race)*? Based on this information, draw your own scale on this map *(hint: it can be longer than 40K, but does not have to be.)*
- *Unlabeled map exercise: Draw in all major cities in Ancient Greece. Also find and label the city of Troy. Label all surrounding countries and waterways.*

12. Phoenicia's Trading Empire – Page 36
- Find Greece and label it.
- Find Egypt and label it.
- Point to Crete.
- Here is another Key. How is it helpful to you in understanding this map?
- *Unlabeled map exercise: Find and label all major cities of the Phoenician Empire. Draw in the trade routes routinely traveled by the sea merchants.*

13. Ancient Africa – Page 38
- Locate Egypt on your map. Color this country green. We know much about Egypt because the Egyptians left behind so many artifacts, but Egypt is only a small portion of a very large continent called Africa, where many people groups have lived since very ancient times.
- Point to the Sahara Desert. What is a desert? Color this large area brown.
- *Unlabeled map exercise: Label all rivers and surrounding oceans. Label the Sahara Desert, as well as Bantu, Kush, Nubia and Egypt. Find and label the city of Cairo.*

14. Israel's Divided Kingdom – Page 40
- Where had the Israelites been living before they settled in Israel?
- They used to live near the Red Sea. Now they live by a sea that rhymes with the Red Sea. Do you know its name? Label the sea alongside the Kingdom of Judah the "Dead Sea". Label the body of water further north the "Sea of Galilee".
- Israel at this time is no longer a united country. It has become divided in two. Make sure to color the two kingdoms different colors.
- *Unlabeled map exercise: Label the two kingdoms in Israel. Find and label all cities and surrounding countries. Label the sea to the west of Israel.*

15. **The Persian Empire** – Page 42
    - Name and label the three seas *(hint: one is called a gulf)* and the three rivers.
    - What is the name of the country that Persia conquered to the far left of your map, just east of Greece? *(Lydia)*. Label it on your map. What is its modern day name? Refer to your globe to find out.
    - *Unlabeled map exercise: Find and draw in the two major cities of the Persian Empire. Label all rivers and surrounding seas.*

16. **The Conquests of Alexander the Great** – Page 44
    - How many cities did Alexander the Great name after himself? The one in Egypt became the most well known. Label all five Alexandrias on your map and then complete the key.
    - Using a blue or black marker or crayon, draw in the Nile River. Do not forget the delta.
    - *Unlabeled map exercise: Label all of the cities by consulting an historical atlas that depicts the Conquests of Alexander the Great. How many cities were named after his horse? Label all surrounding seas.*

17. **India's Mauryan Empire** – Page 46
    - Using a wall map or globe as your reference, draw in the Ganges River. It is acceptable if it is not exact. Trace over this river as well as the other rivers with a blue marker or pencil.
    - *Unlabeled map exercise: Label the kingdoms of the Mauryan Empire. Label the ocean to the east and the sea to the west. Label the island to the south.*

18. **The Qin Empire of China** – Page 48 *(Qin is pronounced "Chin")*
    - What is the approximate distance between the Yellow and Yangtze Rivers?
    - *Unlabeled map exercise: Label the rivers and the Great Wall of China. Research and mark the date of its beginning. How long did it take to build?*

19. **The Republic of Rome** – Page 50
    - What does the country of Italy look like? What does it look like it is doing to the island of Sicily? *(Many people think it looks like a boot kicking a ball)*.
    - Point to Rome. This is where one of the greatest empires began. Point to Carthage. On what continent is this city located? *(Africa)*
    - *Unlabeled map exercise: Label the surrounding islands and seas. Find and draw in the cities of Rome and Carthage. How far apart were these two cities?*

20. **Rome v. Carthage** – Page 52
    - Draw a line showing how Hannibal and the Carthagians snuck in the "back door" of Italy and into the Republic of Rome. *(Cross over the Strait of Gilbraltar into Spain, then through the Alps into Italy)*
    - Referring to a previous map, label the three islands shown here.
    - What is the name of the country you might recognize to the lower right *(SE)* of Italy?
    - *Unlabeled map exercise: Draw in the cities of Rome and Carthage. Label the countries and mountain range that Hannibal and the elephant army had to pass through to arrive on the northern side of Italy. Label all bodies of water.*

21. Palestine During the Time of Christ – Page 54
   - Point to any city names or places that are familiar to you. Tell what you remember happened there.
   - Label the large sea on the left side of the map.
   - *Unlabeled map exercise: Find and label the cities of Jesus' birth and childhood. Draw in as many cities as you can in which Jesus taught and ministered. Label the countries and bodies of water surrounding Judea.*

22. The Roman Empire – Page 56
   - What else can you find to label or draw onto this map? *(Ireland, Italy, Greece, Sicily, Crete, Red Sea)*
   - The lower part of Britain that you see was also part of the Roman Empire. Make sure to color it the same color as the rest of the empire.
   - *Unlabeled map exercise: Label all of the countries that were incorporated into the Roman Empire. Draw in the cities of Rome, Pompeii, Thessalonica and Constantinople. Label the bodies of water and draw in Hadrian's Wall in Britain.*

23. Barbarians Invade the Roman Empire – Page 58
   - Label all countries and bodies of water that you know on this map. (Refer to the previous map "The Roman Empire".)
   - What is the name of the continent that encompasses the main portion of this map?
   - *Unlabeled map exercise: Draw in the cities of Rome and Constantinople. Mark the names of the barbarian tribes and the direction from which they traveled when they invaded Rome. Label the mountain range that divides Europe from Asia. Label all bodies of water.*

pppp

Glossary of Terms Used

Artifact – a simple man-made object that provides evidence of an ancient culture.

Continent – one of the seven great land masses of the world – *Europe, Asia, Africa, North America, South America, Australia and Antarctica.*

Delta – deposited land at the branching mouth of a river.

Desert – a large area of land where there is very little water and plants do not grow.

Empire – a kingdom which has been extended by military might to include countries which were originally independent.

Gulf – an area of sea partly surrounded by land, larger but with a narrower opening than a bay.

Inlet – a narrow arm of the sea or of a river.

Island – a piece of land, smaller than a continent, entirely surrounded by water.

Key – something to help you decipher a code.

Kilometer – a unit of distance measurement equaling 1,000 meters.

Mile – a unit of distance measurement equaling 1,760 yards.

Ocean – the large bodies of salt water which comprise the majority (over 2/3) of the earth's surface.

Republic – a form of government in which the head of state is an elected president rather than a monarch.

River – a stream of fresh water flowing into another body of water.

Sea – a body of water smaller than an ocean, partly or completely enclosed by land.

Geographical Regions Covered

Red Sea	Mediterranean Sea	Mesopotamia
Tigris River	Euphrates River	Persian Gulf
Caspian Sea	Nile River	Crete
India	Indian Ocean	Babylon
Egypt	Assyria	China
Yellow River	Yangtze River	Greece
Aegean Sea	Phoenicia	Africa
Sahara Desert	Dead Sea	Israel
Persia	Italy	Carthage
Roman Empire	Palestine	Britain
Europe		

Teacher or parent, you may choose to use these terms and geographical regions listed to put together an end of the year quiz. However, if you follow the lesson plans throughout the year, you may not feel that this is necessary.

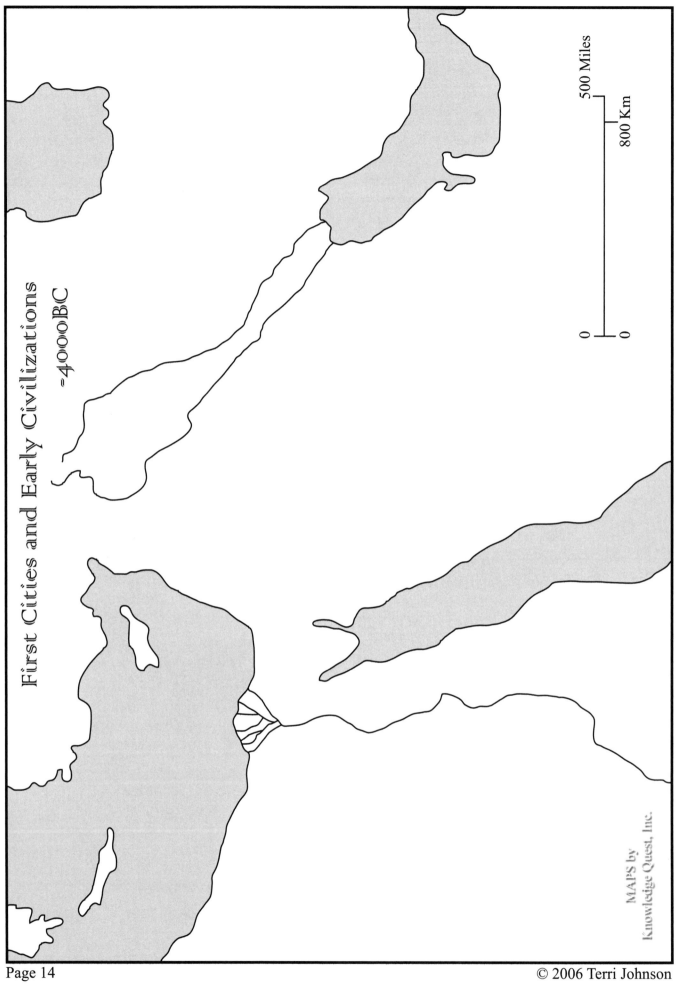

First Cities and Early Civilizations

~4000 BC

500 Miles

800 Km

0

0

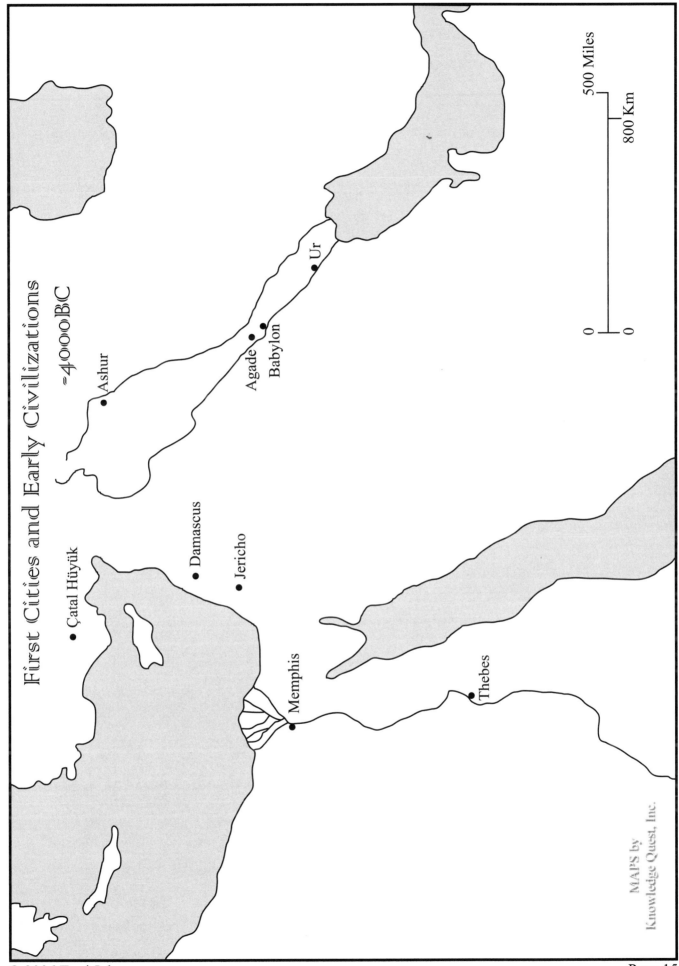

First Cities and Early Civilizations
≈4000 BC

Çatal Hüyük

Ashur

Damascus

Jericho

Agade
Babylon

Ur

Memphis

Thebes

500 Miles

800 Km

0

0

MAPS by
Knowledge Quest, Inc.

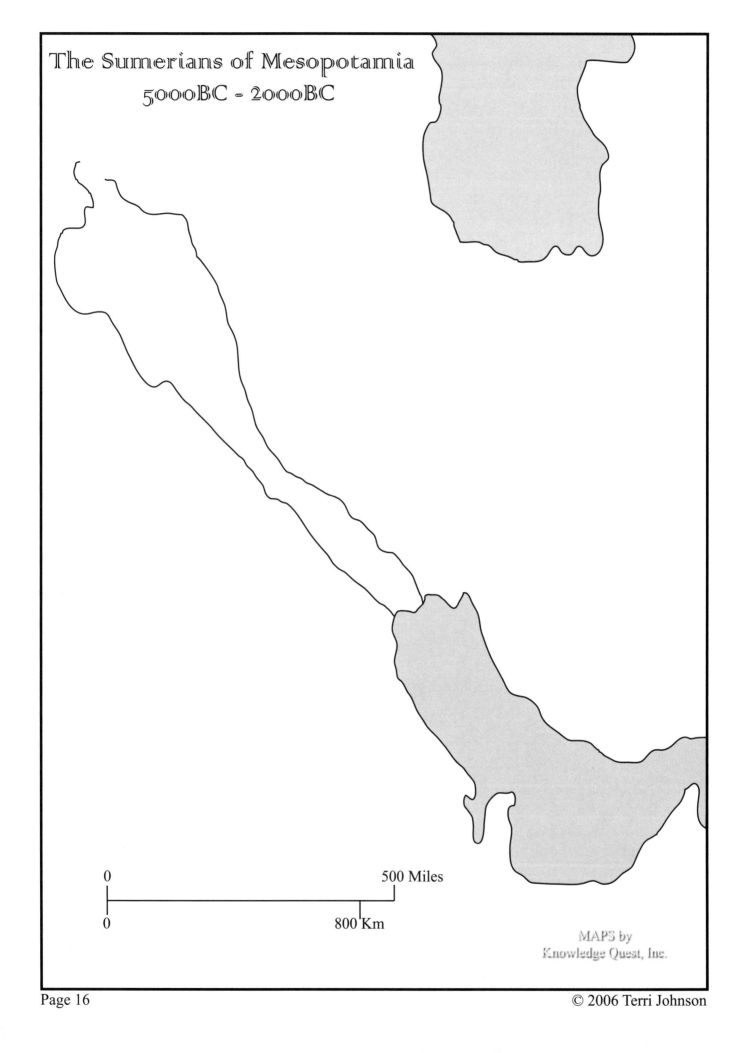

The Sumerians of Mesopotamia
5000BC ~ 2000BC

0   500 Miles

0   800 Km

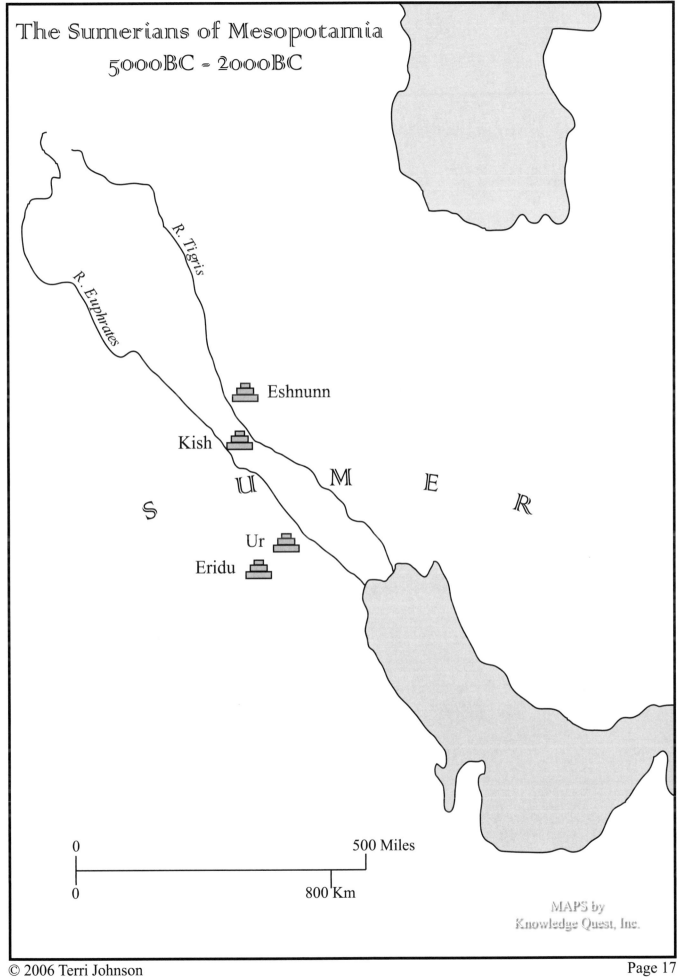

The Sumerians of Mesopotamia
5000BC - 2000BC

R. Tigris

R. Euphrates

Eshnunn

Kish

S U M E R

Ur

Eridu

0   500 Miles

0   800 Km

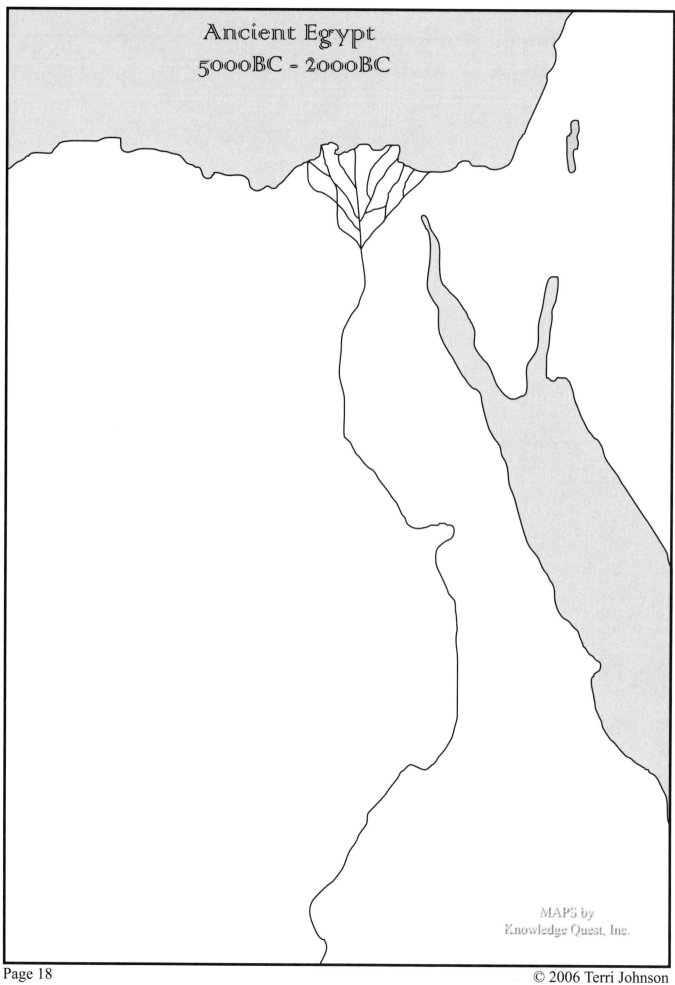

Ancient Egypt
5000BC - 2000BC

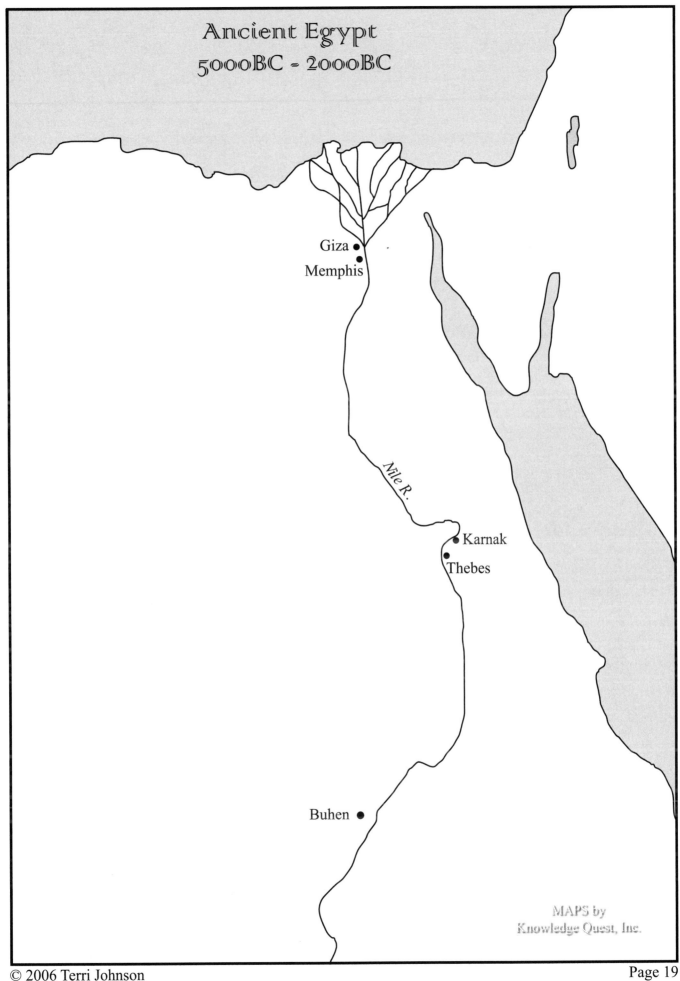

Ancient Egypt
5000BC - 2000BC

Giza

Memphis

Nile R.

Karnak

Thebes

Buhen

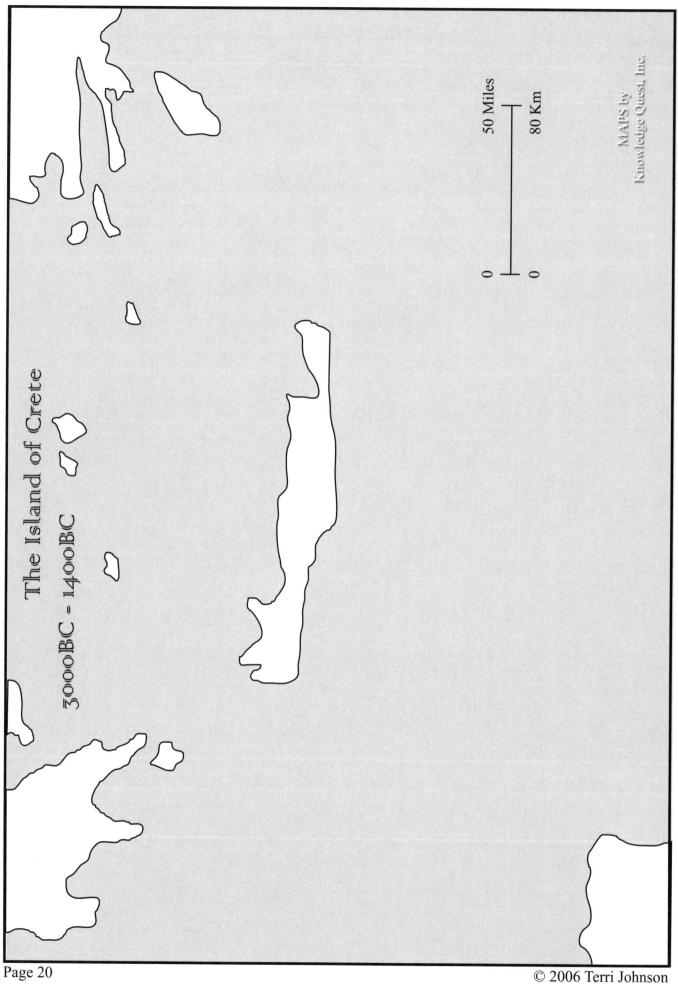

The Island of Crete

3000BC – 1400BC

50 Miles

80 Km

0

0

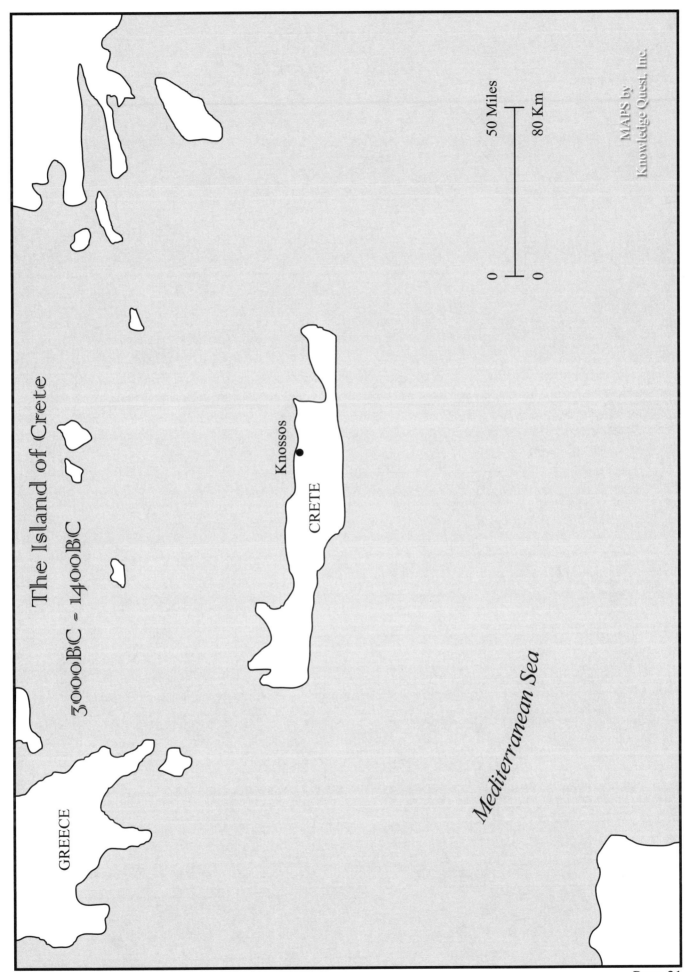

The Island of Crete

3000BC - 1400BC

GREECE

CRETE

Knossos

Mediterranean Sea

50 Miles

80 Km

0

0

MAPS by
Knowledge Quest, Inc.

© 2006 Terri Johnson

Page 21

Ancient India
2500BC ~ 1500BC

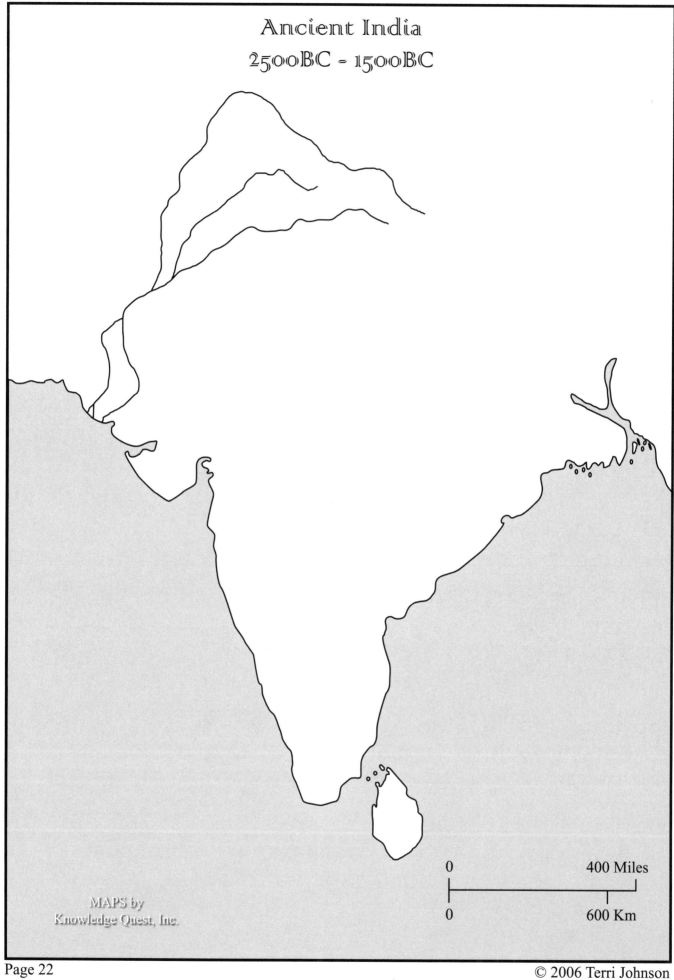

0 — 400 Miles

0 — 600 Km

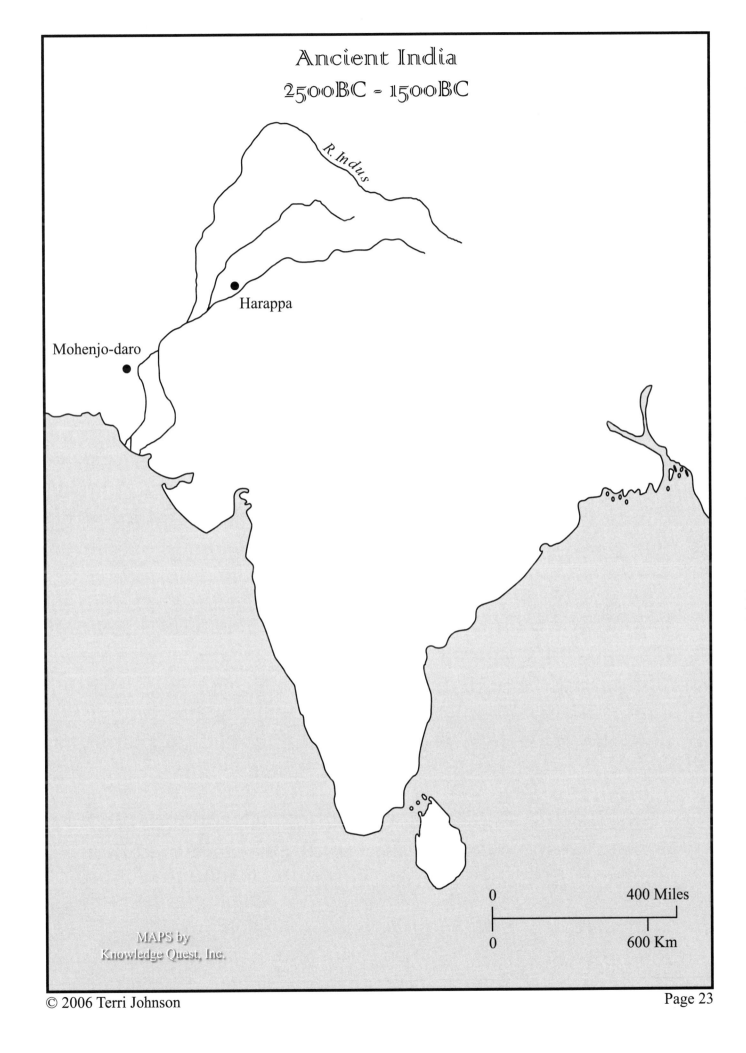

Ancient India
2500BC - 1500BC

R. Indus

Harappa

Mohenjo-daro

0   400 Miles

0   600 Km

MAPS by
Knowledge Quest, Inc.

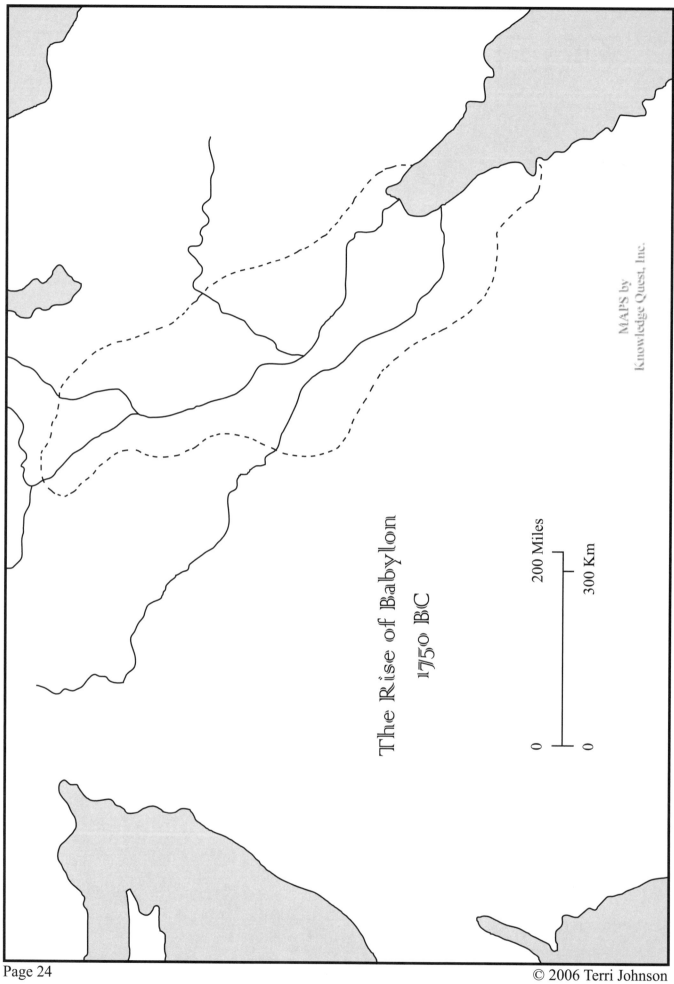

The Rise of Babylon
1750 BC

0   200 Miles

0   300 Km

MAPS by
Knowledge Quest, Inc.

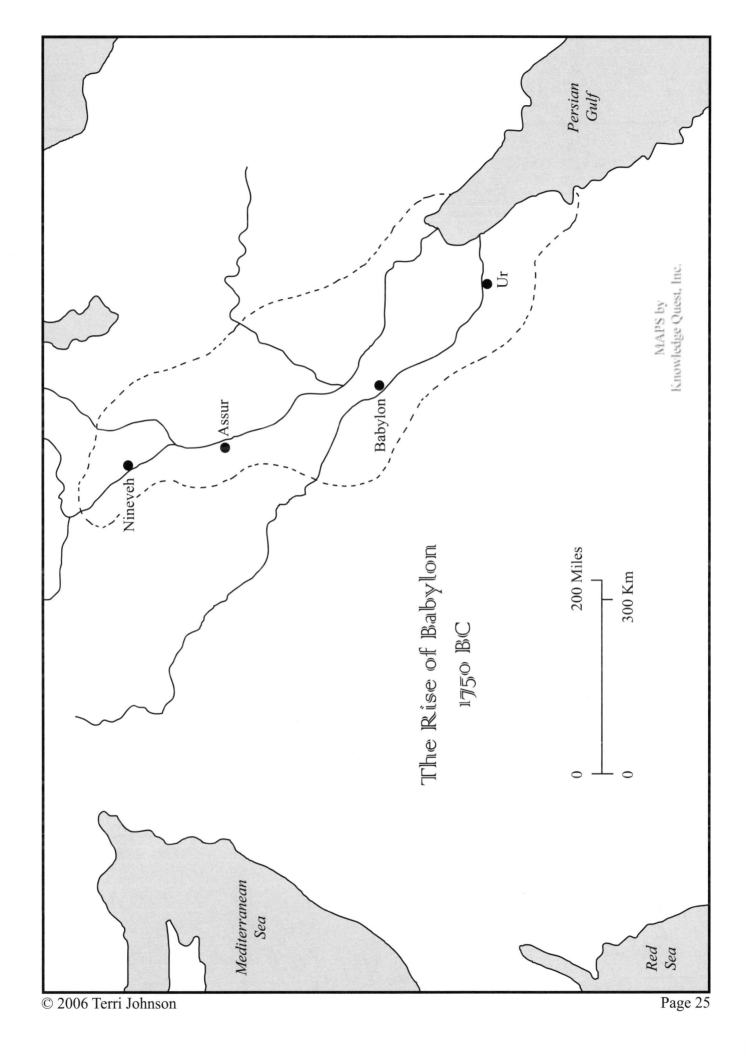

The Rise of Babylon

1750 BC

Persian Gulf

Ur

Assur

Babylon

Nineveh

Mediterranean Sea

Red Sea

MAPS by
Knowledge Quest, Inc.

0   200 Miles

0   300 Km

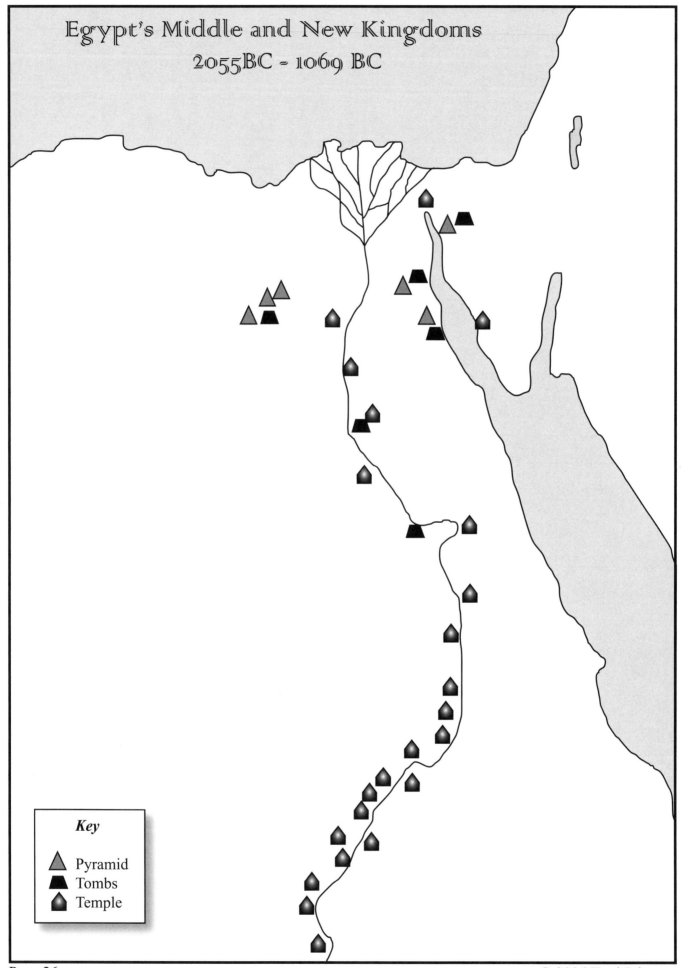

Egypt's Middle and New Kingdoms
2055BC - 1069 BC

Key

△ Pyramid
▲ Tombs
⬠ Temple

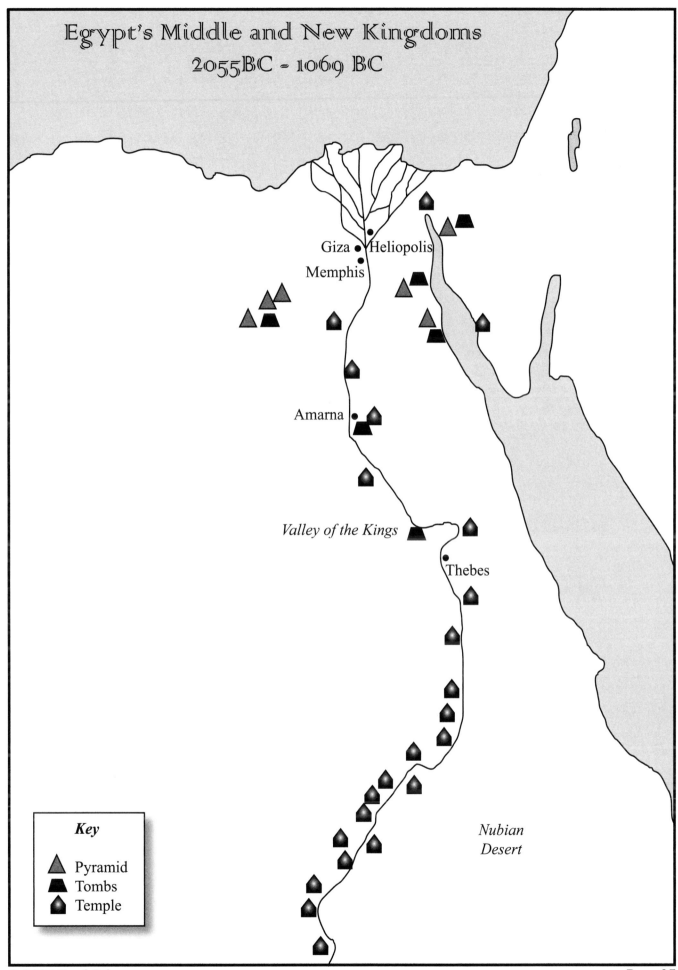

Egypt's Middle and New Kingdoms
2055BC – 1069 BC

Giza • Heliopolis

Memphis

Amarna •

Valley of the Kings

• Thebes

Nubian Desert

Key

▲ Pyramid
◼ Tombs
⬠ Temple

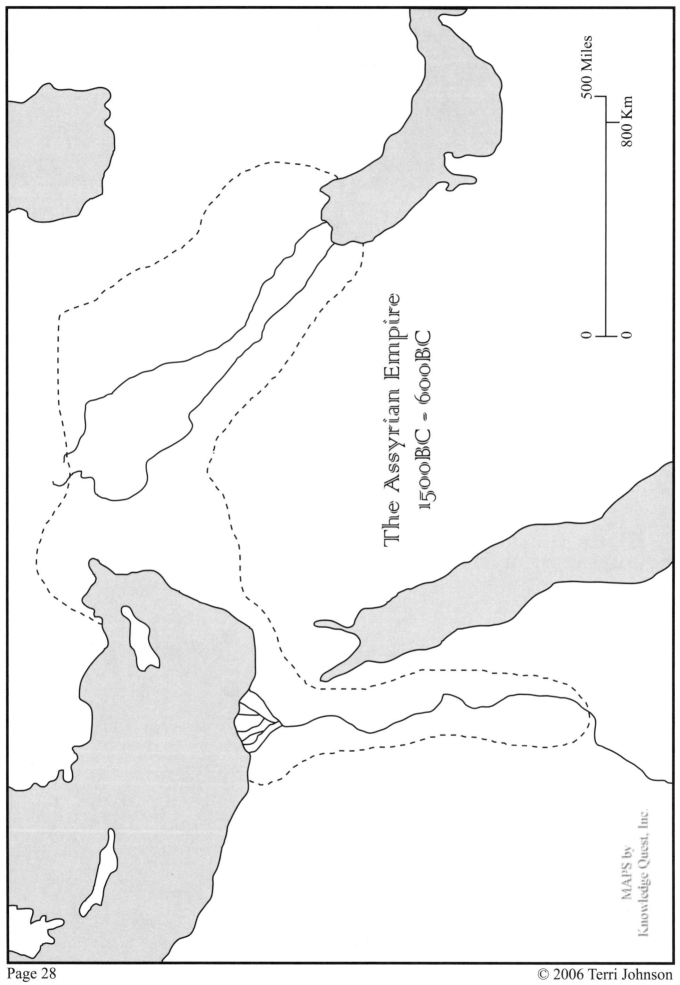

The Assyrian Empire
1500BC ~ 600BC

500 Miles

800 Km

0

0

MAPS by
Knowledge Quest, Inc.

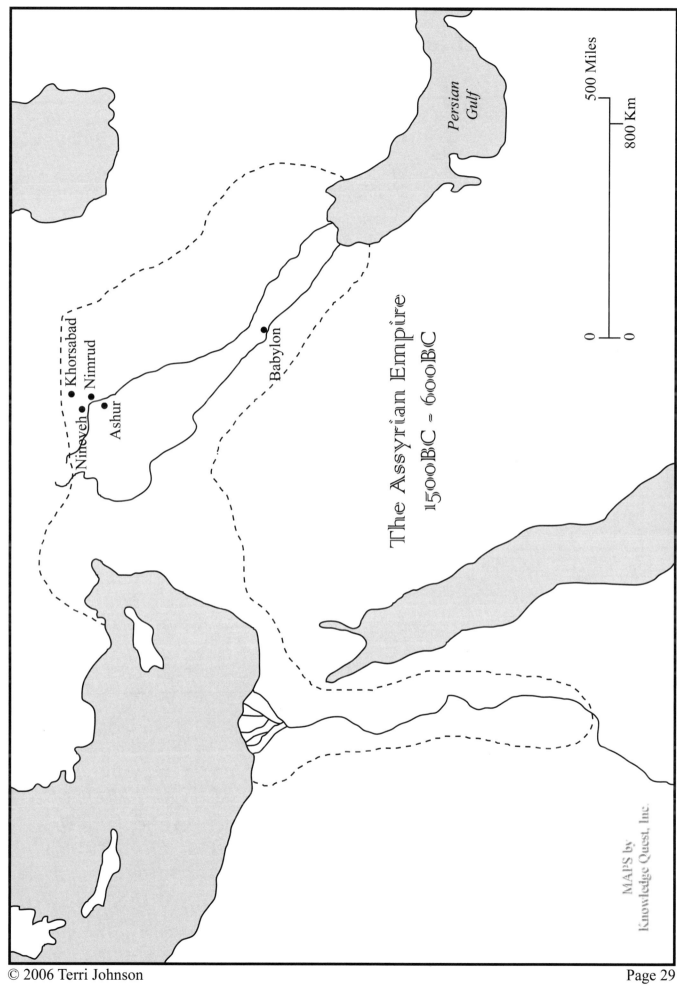

The Assyrian Empire
1500BC ~ 600BC

Persian
Gulf

Khorsabad
Nimrud
Nineveh
Ashur

Babylon

500 Miles

800 Km

0

0

MAPS by
Knowledge Quest, Inc.

China's Shang Kingdom
1750BC - 500BC

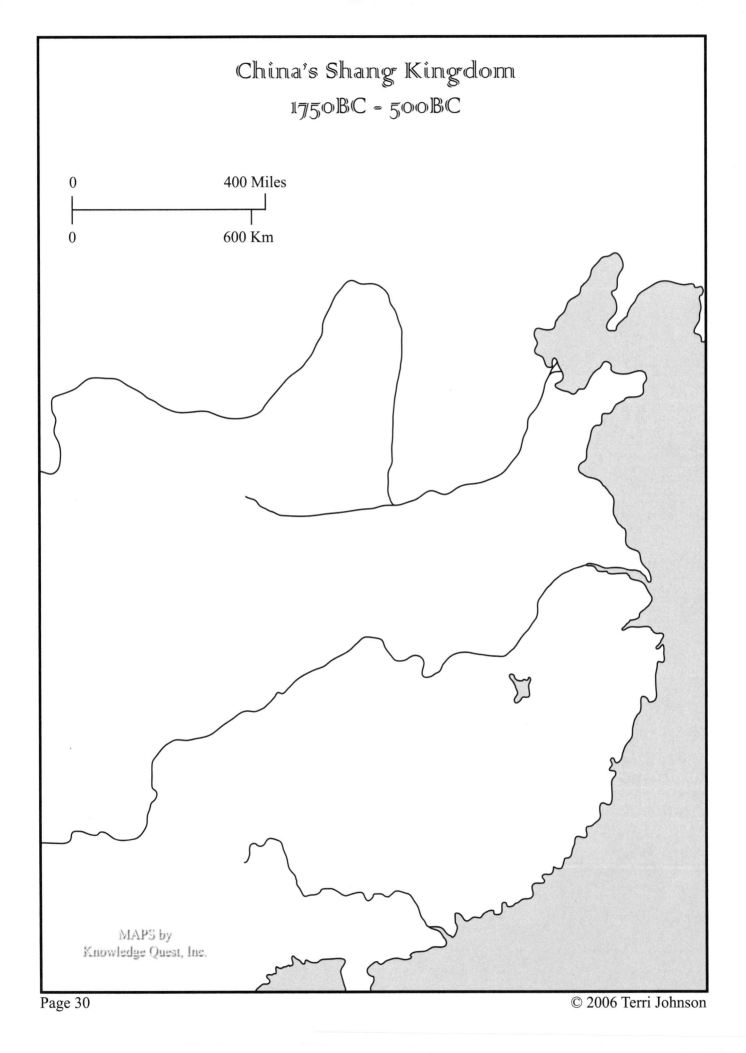

China's Shang Kingdom
1750BC - 500BC

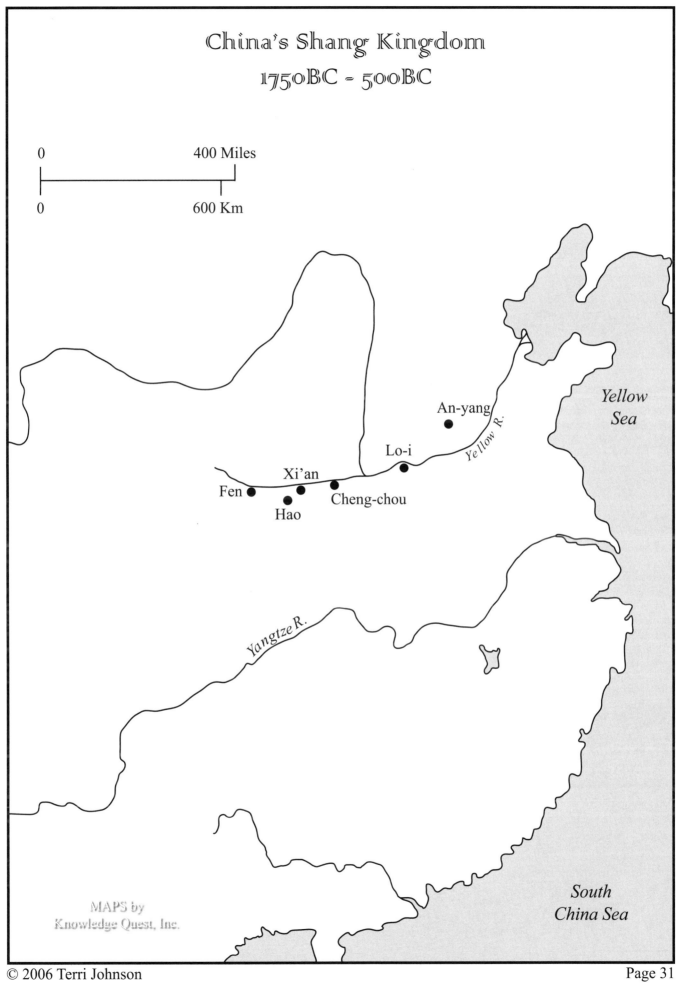

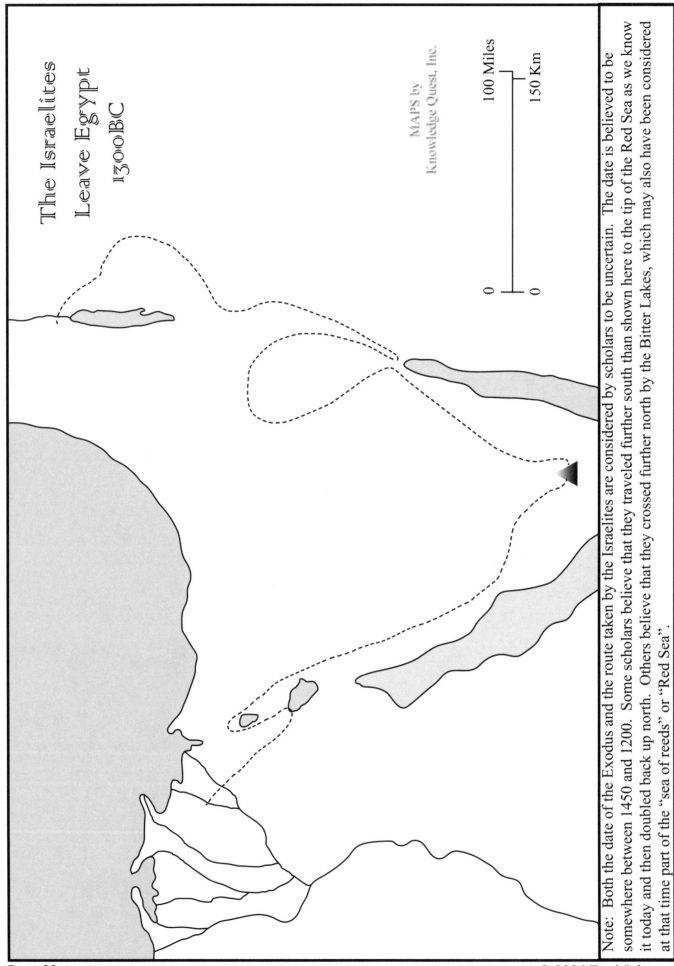

The Israelites Leave Egypt 1300BC

MAPS by
Knowledge Quest, Inc.

100 Miles

150 Km

0

0

Note: Both the date of the Exodus and the route taken by the Israelites are considered by scholars to be uncertain. The date is believed to be somewhere between 1450 and 1200. Some scholars believe that they traveled further south than shown here to the tip of the Red Sea as we know it today and then doubled back up north. Others believe that they crossed further north by the Bitter Lakes, which may also have been considered at that time part of the "sea of reeds" or "Red Sea".

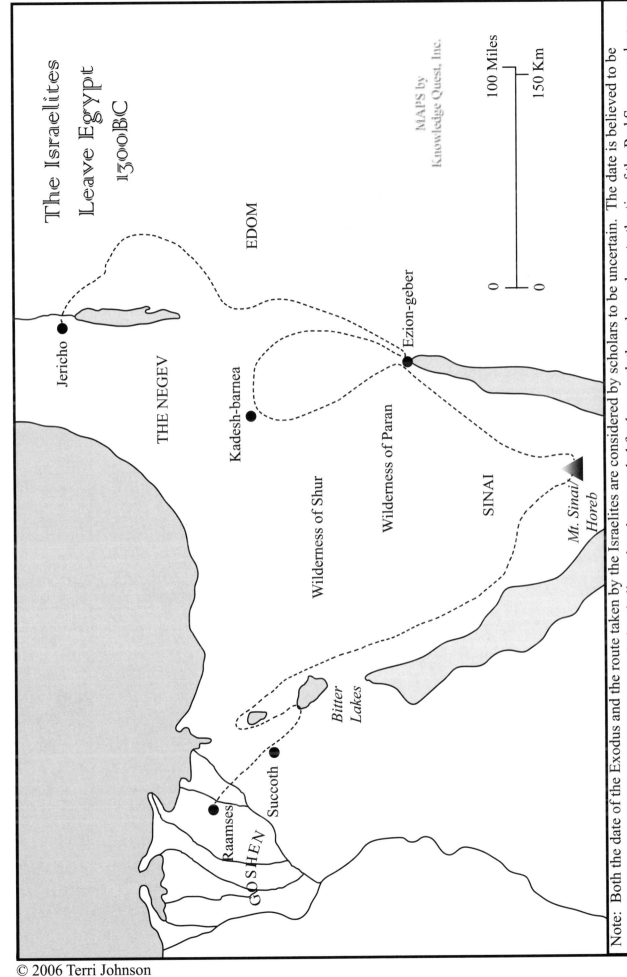

The Israelites Leave Egypt 1300BC

EDOM

Jericho

THE NEGEV

Kadesh-barnea

Wilderness of Shur

Wilderness of Paran

Ezion-geber

SINAI

Mt. Sinai/ Horeb

Bitter Lakes

Succoth

Raamses

GOSHEN

MAPS by
Knowledge Quest, Inc.

100 Miles

150 Km

0

0

Note: Both the date of the Exodus and the route taken by the Israelites are considered by scholars to be somewhere between 1450 and 1200. Some scholars believe that they traveled further south than shown here to the tip of the Red Sea as we know it today and then doubled back up north. Others believe that they crossed further north by the Bitter Lakes, which may also have been considered at that time part of the "sea of reeds" or "Red Sea".

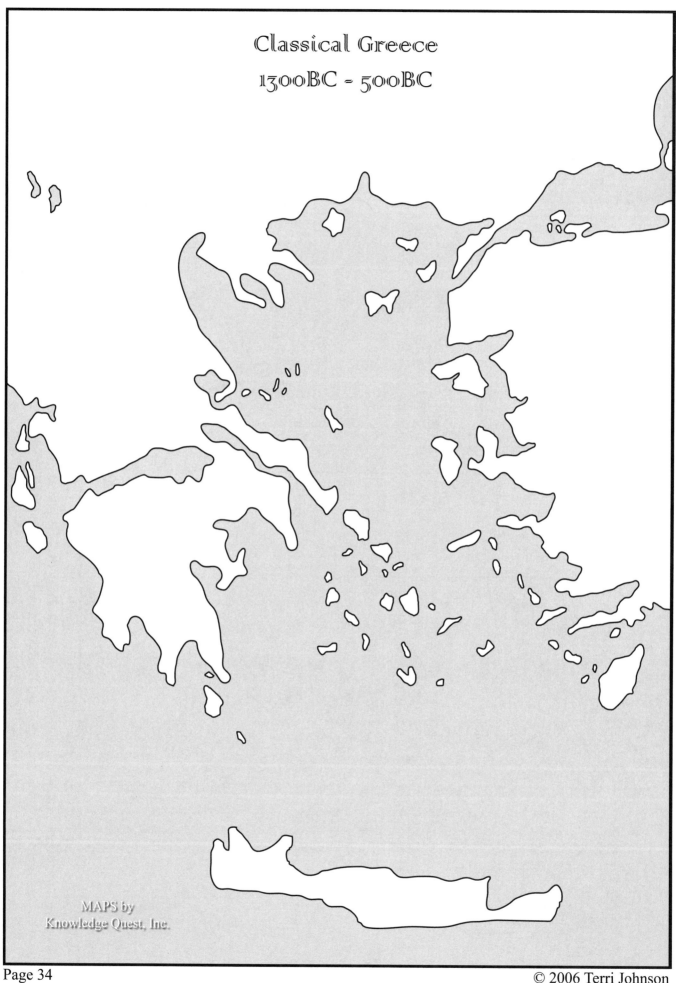

Classical Greece
1300BC ~ 500BC

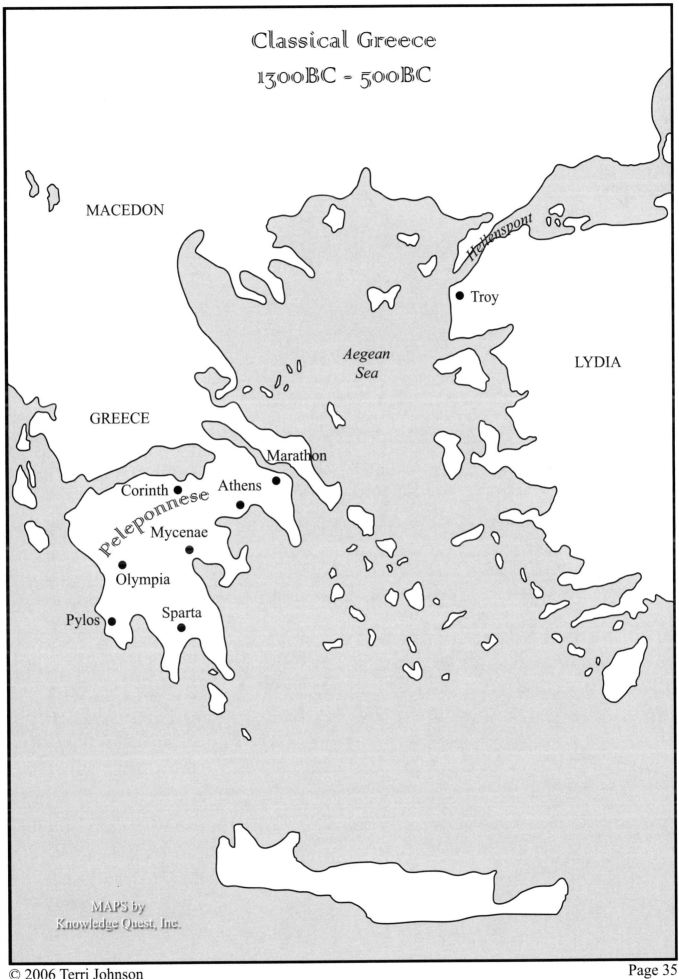

Classical Greece
1300BC - 500BC

MACEDON

Hellespont

● Troy

LYDIA

Aegean Sea

GREECE

Marathon

Corinth ●   Athens ●

Peleponnese

Mycenae ●

Olympia ●

Pylos ●   Sparta ●

MAPS by
Knowledge Quest, Inc.

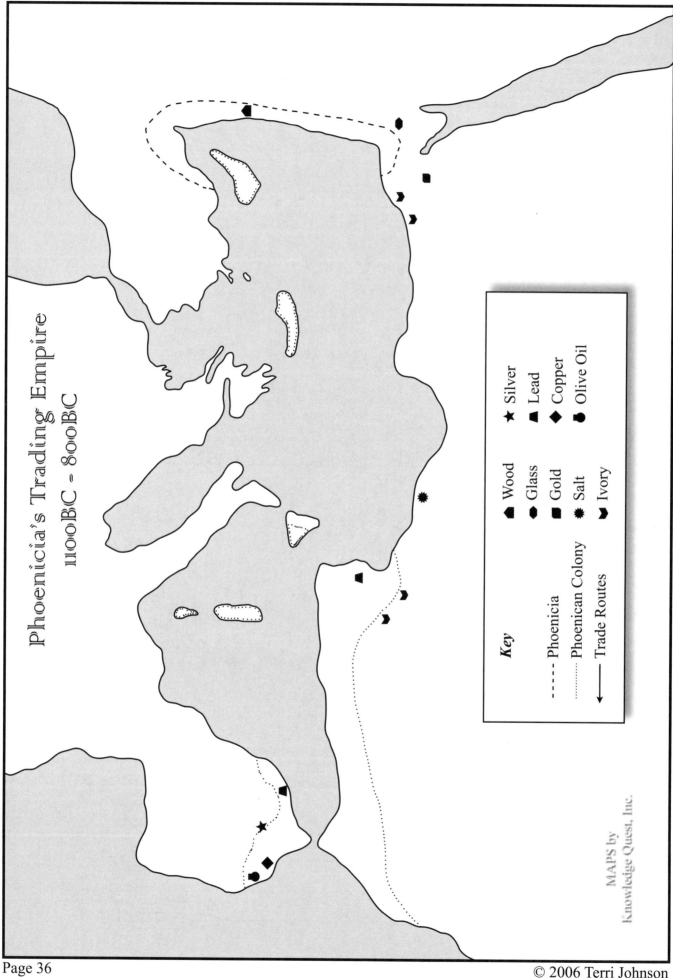

Phoenicia's Trading Empire
1100BC – 800BC

Key

⬟ Wood	★ Silver
⬡ Glass	◀ Lead
⬛ Gold	◆ Copper
⬛ Salt	⬟ Olive Oil
⬢ Ivory	

- - - - Phoenicia

.... Phoenican Colony

———→ Trade Routes

MAPS by
Knowledge Quest, Inc.

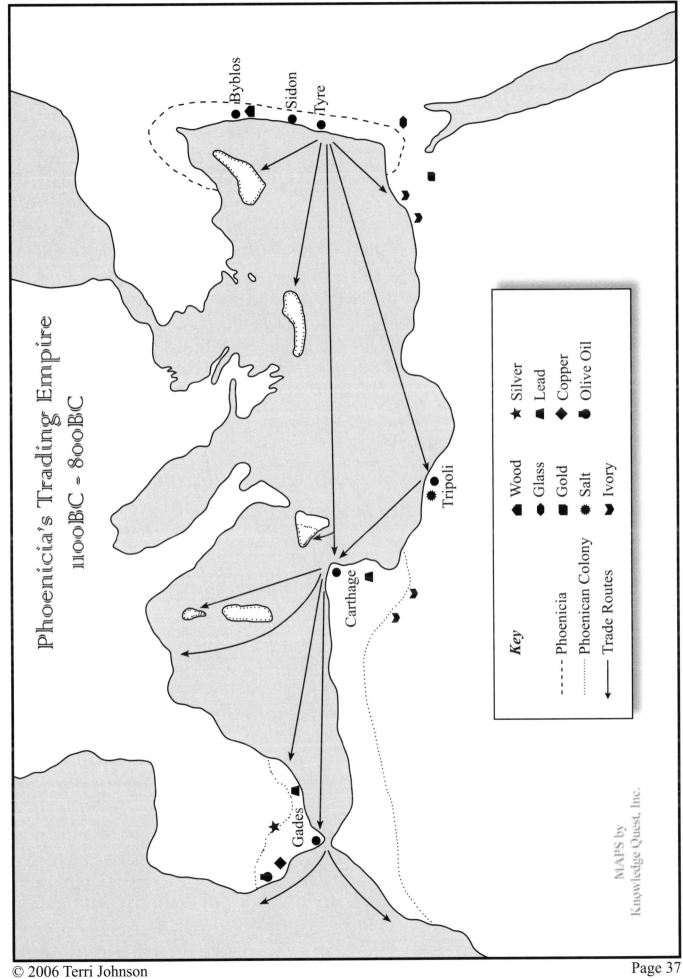

Phoenicia's Trading Empire 1100BC - 800BC

Byblos
Sidon
Tyre
Tripoli
Carthage
Gades

Key

★ Silver			
◣ Wood	★ Silver		
⬢ Glass	◣ Lead	◆ Copper	⬢ Olive Oil
■ Gold	■ Copper		
✱ Salt	⬢ Olive Oil		
▸ Ivory			

- - - - Phoenicia

· · · · · Phoenican Colony

→ Trade Routes

MAPS by
Knowledge Quest, Inc.

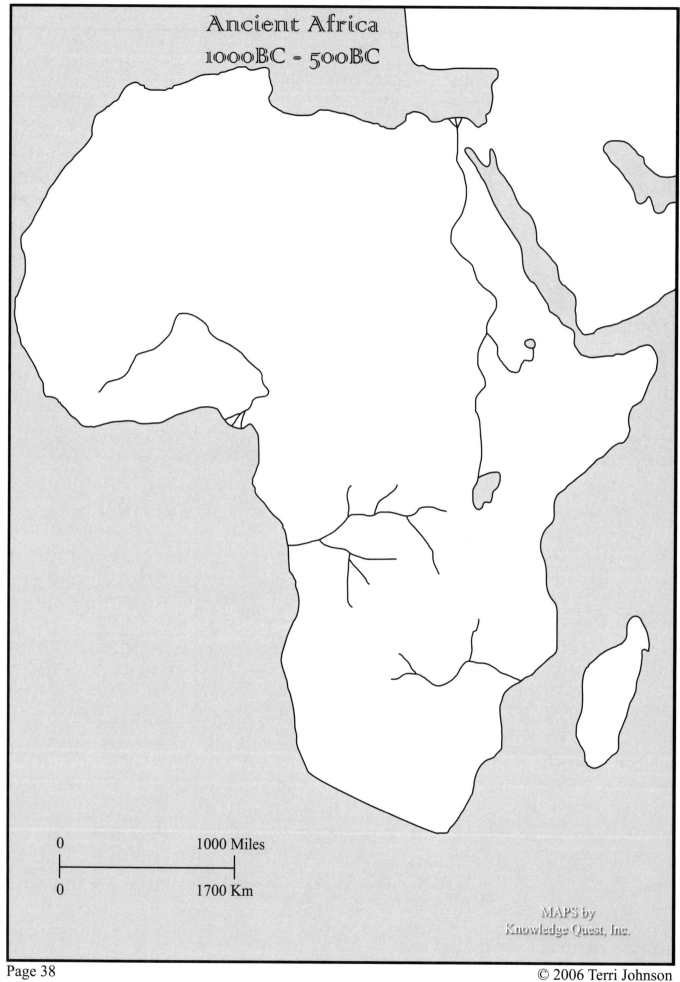

Ancient Africa
1000BC - 500BC

0   1000 Miles

0   1700 Km

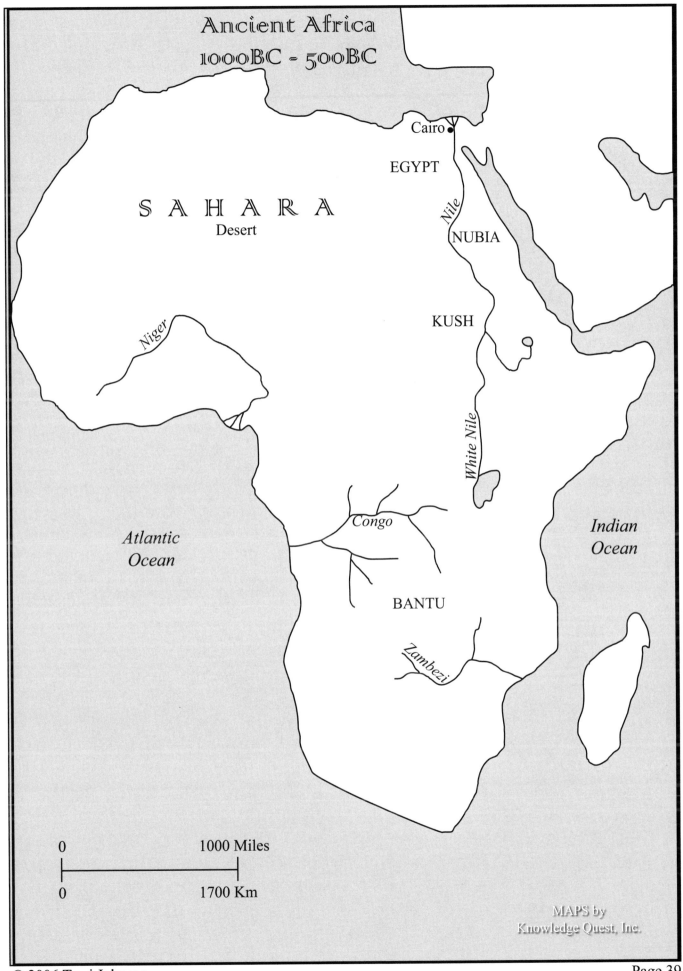

Ancient Africa
1000BC - 500BC

Cairo

EGYPT

SAHARA
Desert

Nile

NUBIA

Niger

KUSH

White Nile

*Atlantic
Ocean*

Congo

*Indian
Ocean*

BANTU

Zambezi

0	1000 Miles
0	1700 Km

MAPS by
Knowledge Quest, Inc.

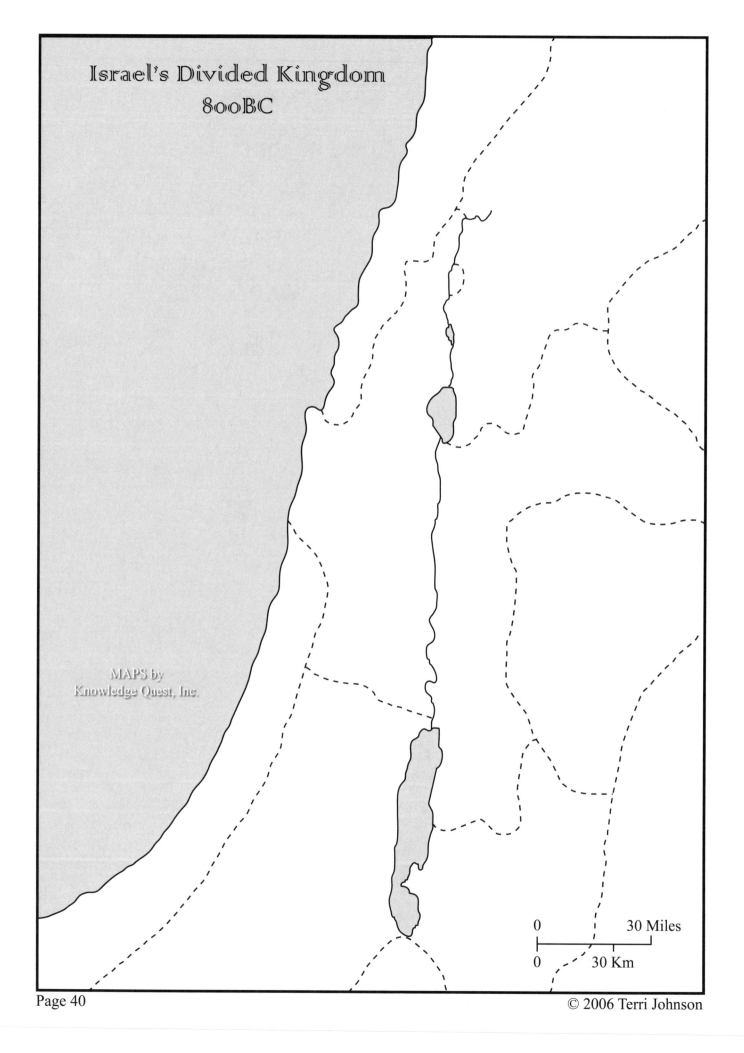

Israel's Divided Kingdom
800BC

MAPS by
Knowledge Quest, Inc.

0   30 Miles

0   30 Km

© 2006 Terri Johnson

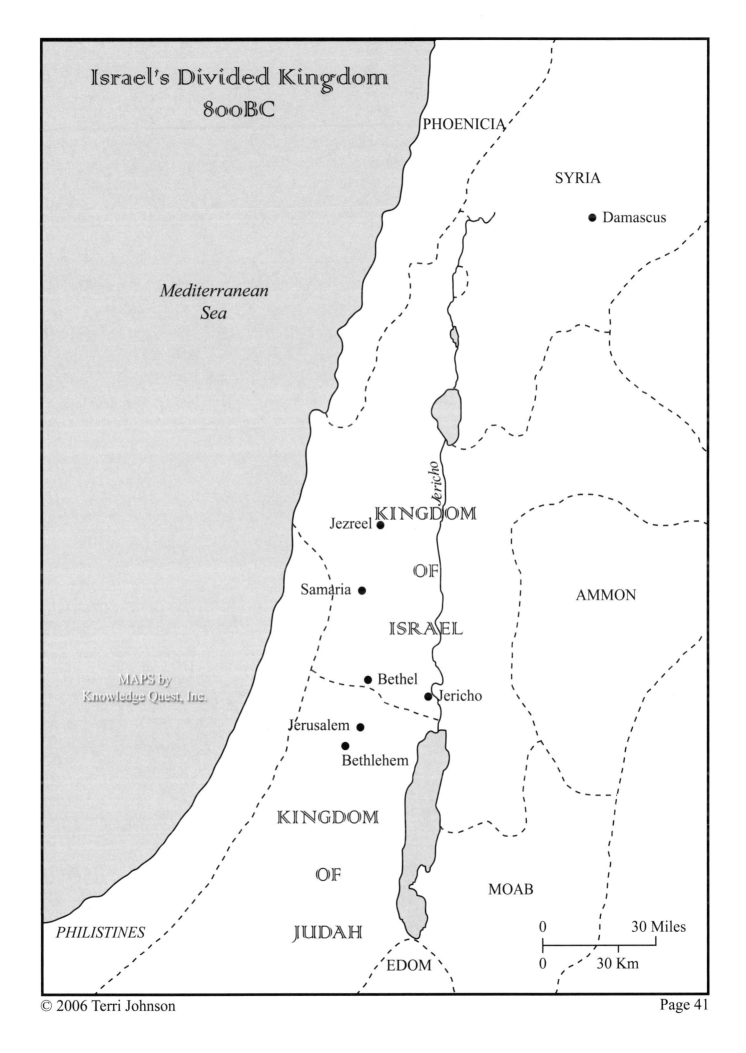

Israel's Divided Kingdom
800BC

PHOENICIA

SYRIA

● Damascus

*Mediterranean
Sea*

Jericho

KINGDOM

Jezreel ●

OF

Samaria ●

ISRAEL

AMMON

MAPS by
Knowledge Quest, Inc.

● Bethel

● Jericho

Jerusalem ●

● Bethlehem

KINGDOM

OF

MOAB

PHILISTINES

JUDAH

0   30 Miles

0   30 Km

EDOM

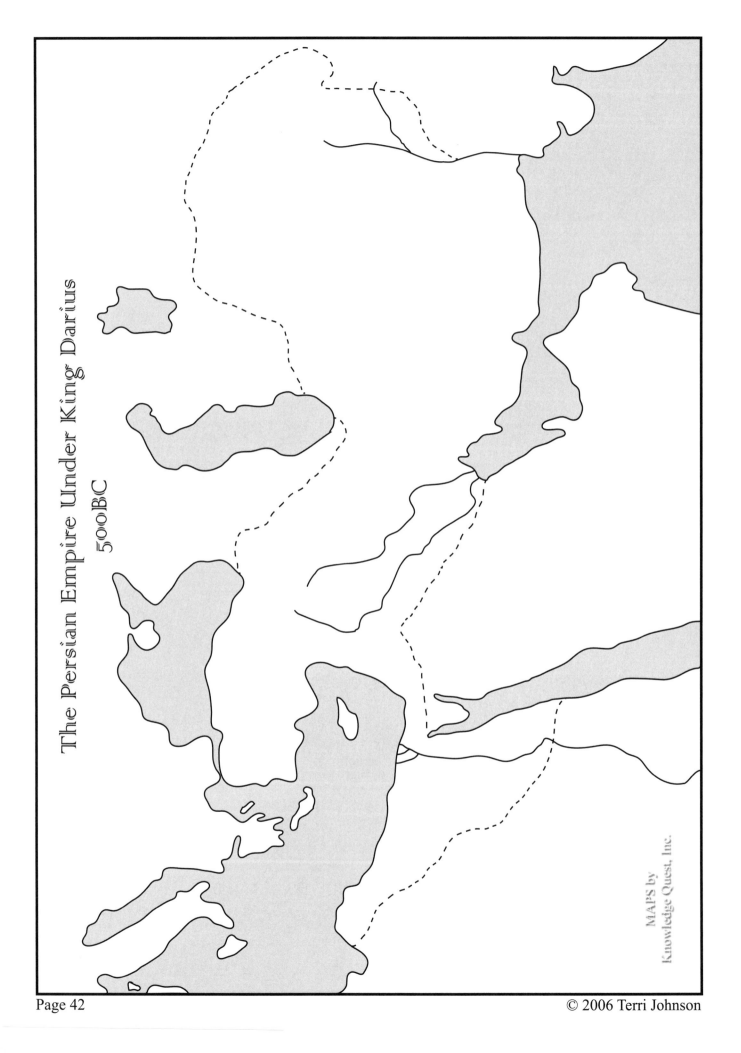

The Persian Empire Under King Darius

500BC

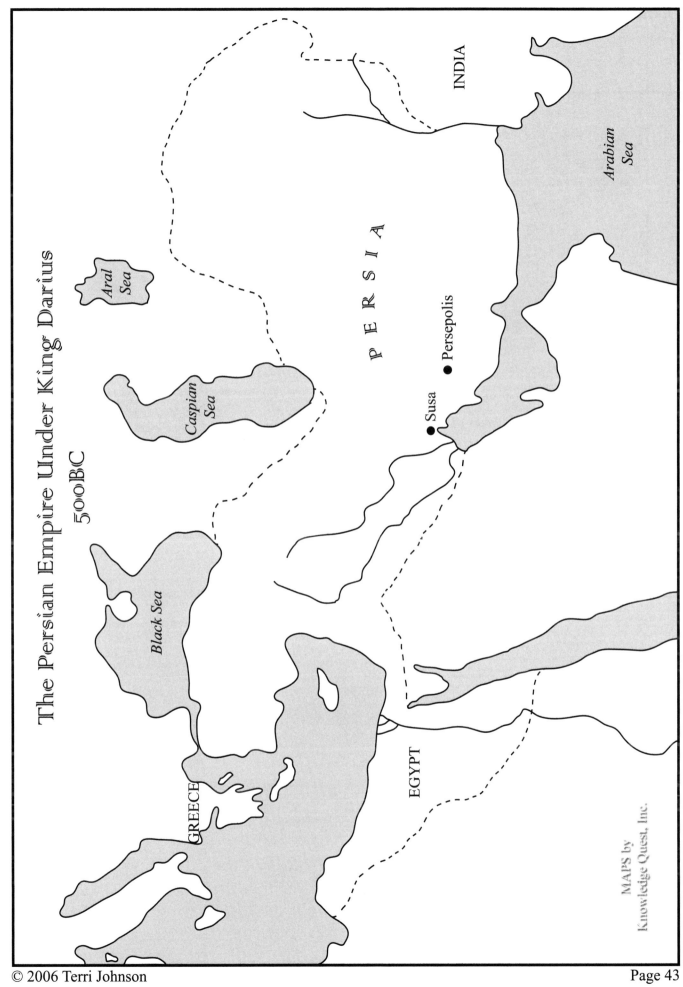

The Persian Empire Under King Darius

500BC

Aral Sea

Caspian Sea

Black Sea

Arabian Sea

GREECE

PERSIA

Persepolis

Susa

EGYPT

INDIA

MAPS by
Knowledge Quest, Inc.

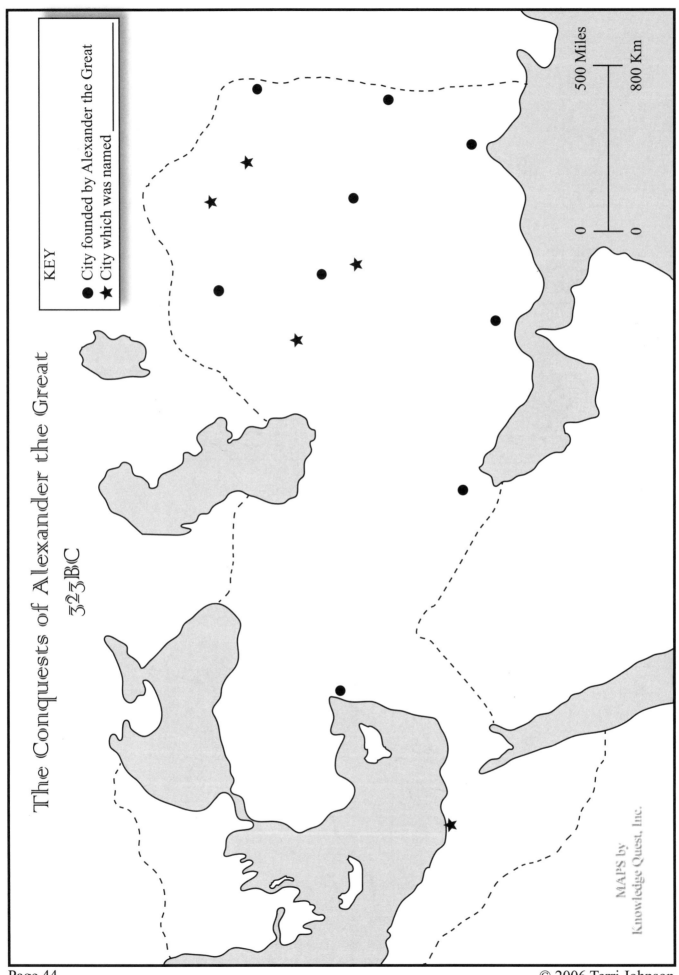

The Conquests of Alexander the Great

323BC

KEY

● City founded by Alexander the Great
★ City which was named _____

500 Miles

800 Km

MAPS by
Knowledge Quest, Inc.

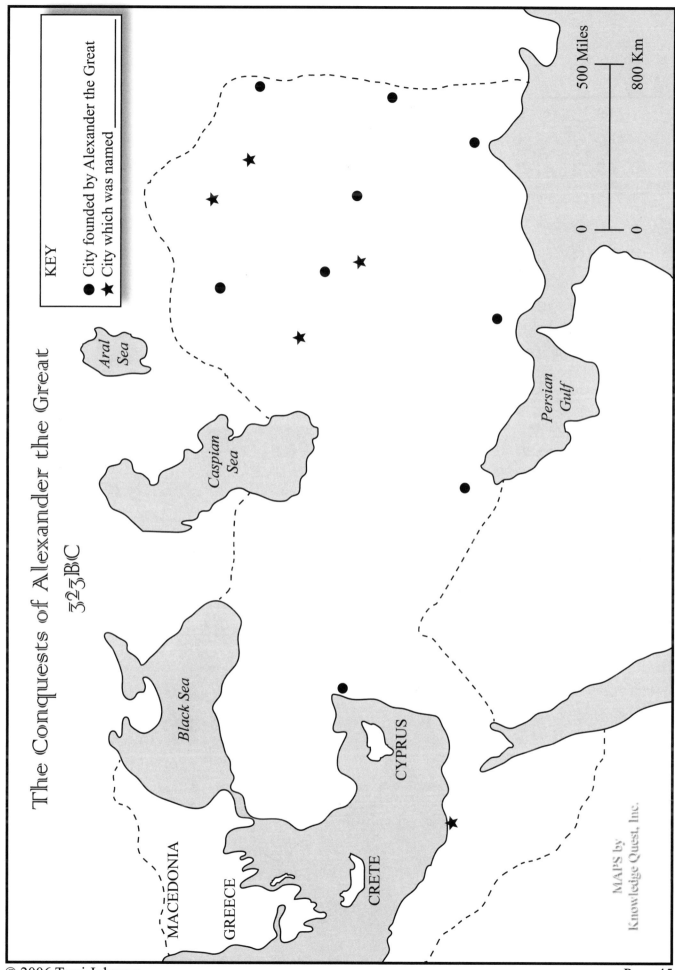

The Conquests of Alexander the Great

323BC

KEY

● City founded by Alexander the Great

★ City which was named _____

Aral Sea

Caspian Sea

Black Sea

Persian Gulf

MACEDONIA

GREECE

CRETE

CYPRUS

500 Miles

800 Km

0

0

MAPS by
Knowledge Quest, Inc.

India's Mauryan Empire
300BC

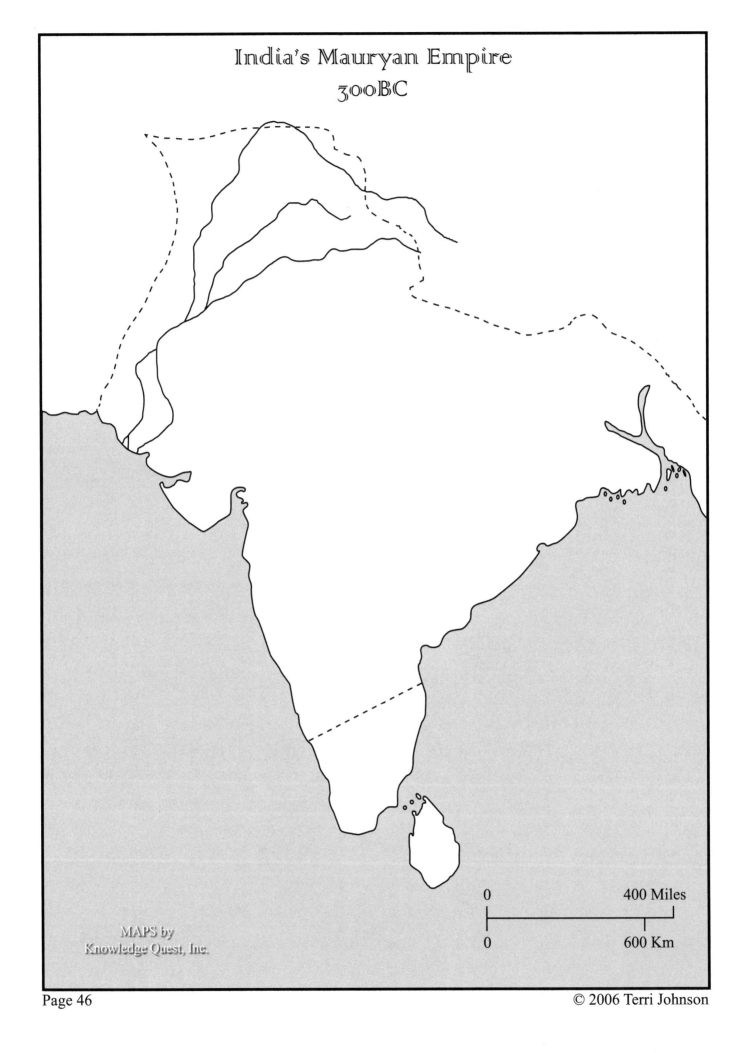

0   400 Miles

0   600 Km

MAPS by
Knowledge Quest, Inc.

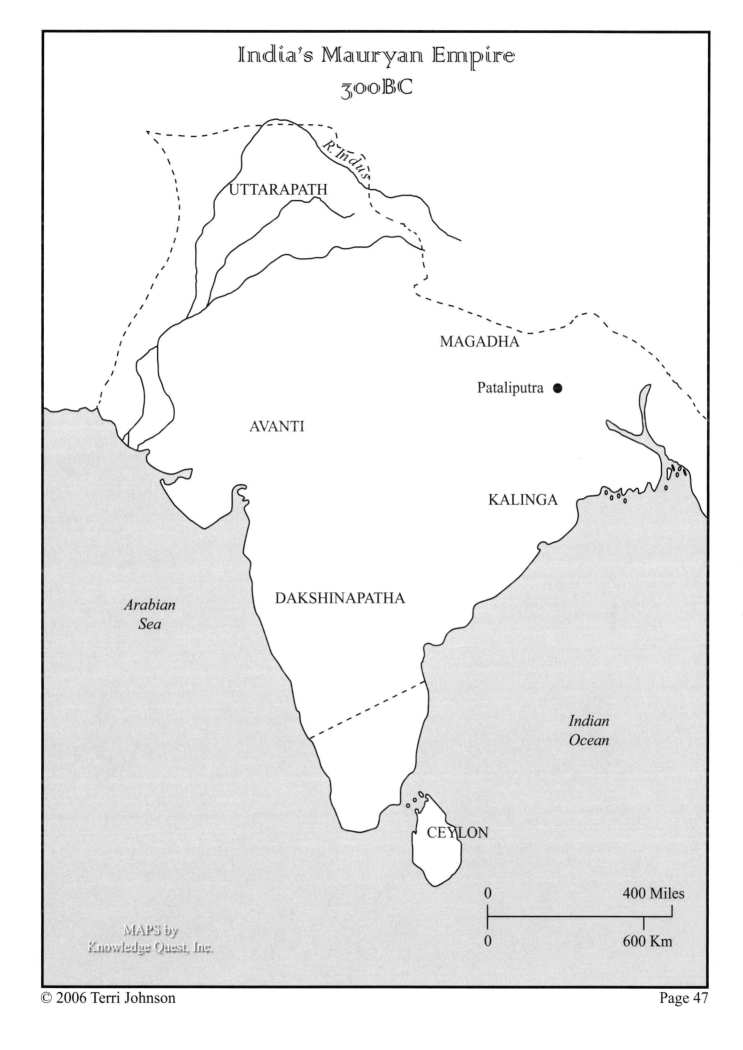

India's Mauryan Empire
300BC

UTTARAPATH

R. Indus

MAGADHA

Pataliputra ●

AVANTI

KALINGA

Arabian
Sea

DAKSHINAPATHA

Indian
Ocean

CEYLON

0   400 Miles

0   600 Km

MAPS by
Knowledge Quest, Inc.

Qin Empire of China
500BC - 200BC

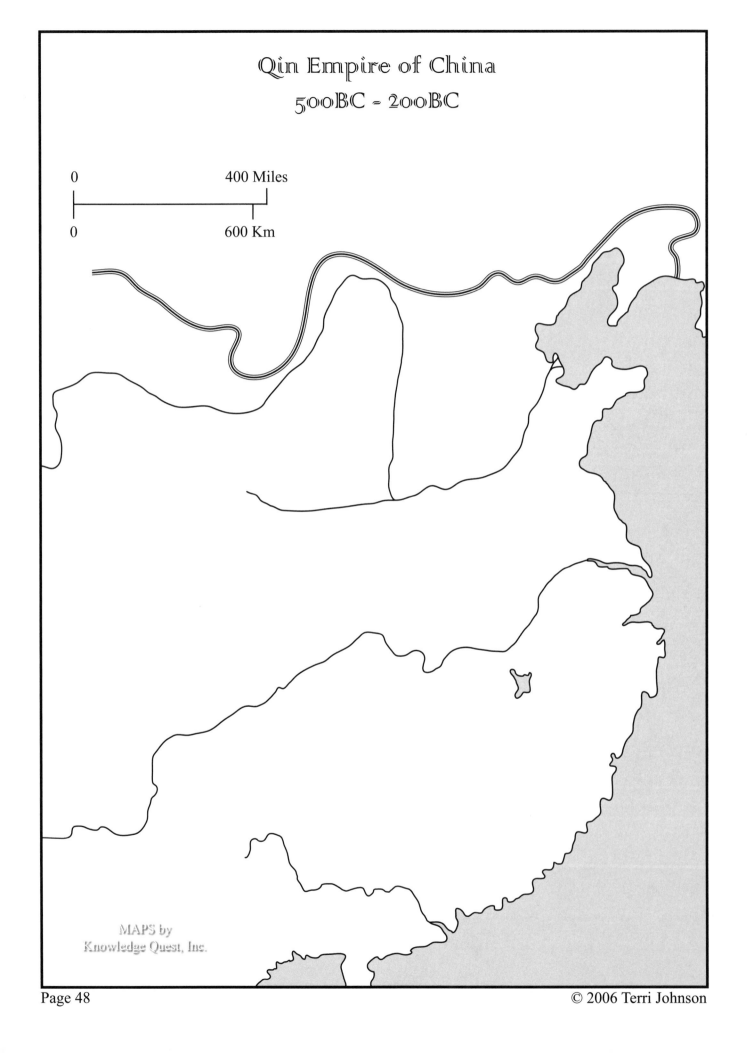

0   400 Miles

0   600 Km

MAPS by
Knowledge Quest, Inc.

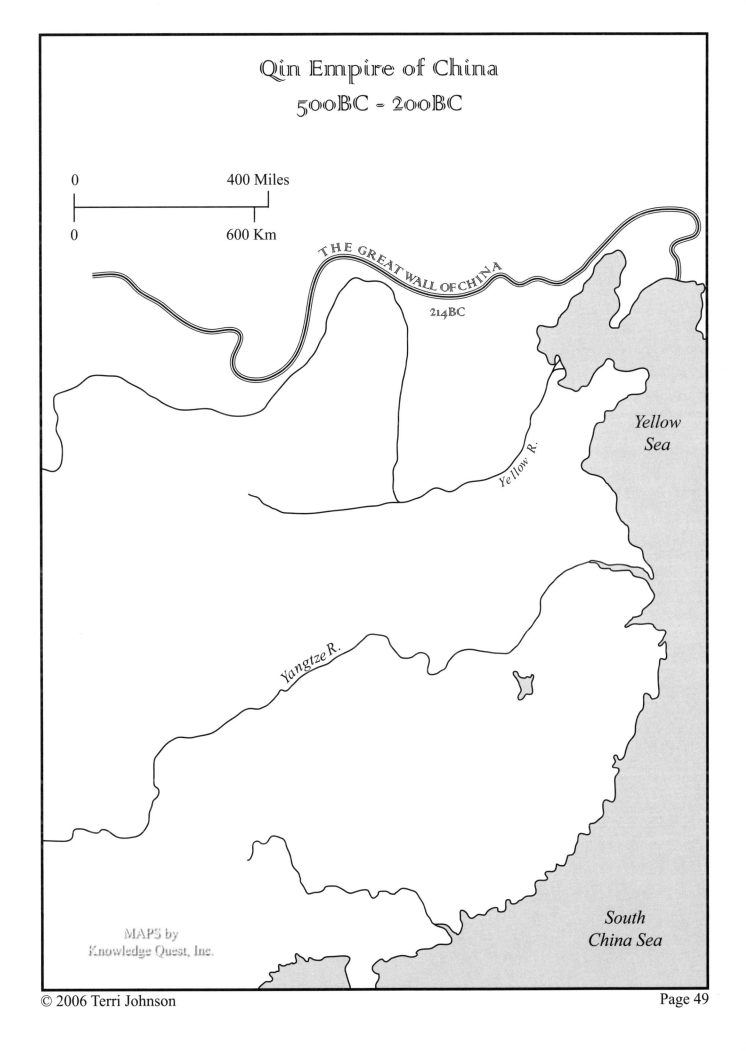

Qin Empire of China
500BC - 200BC

0

400 Miles

0

600 Km

THE GREAT WALL OF CHINA

214BC

Yellow R.

Yellow Sea

Yangtze R.

South China Sea

The Republic of Rome
300BC - 20BC

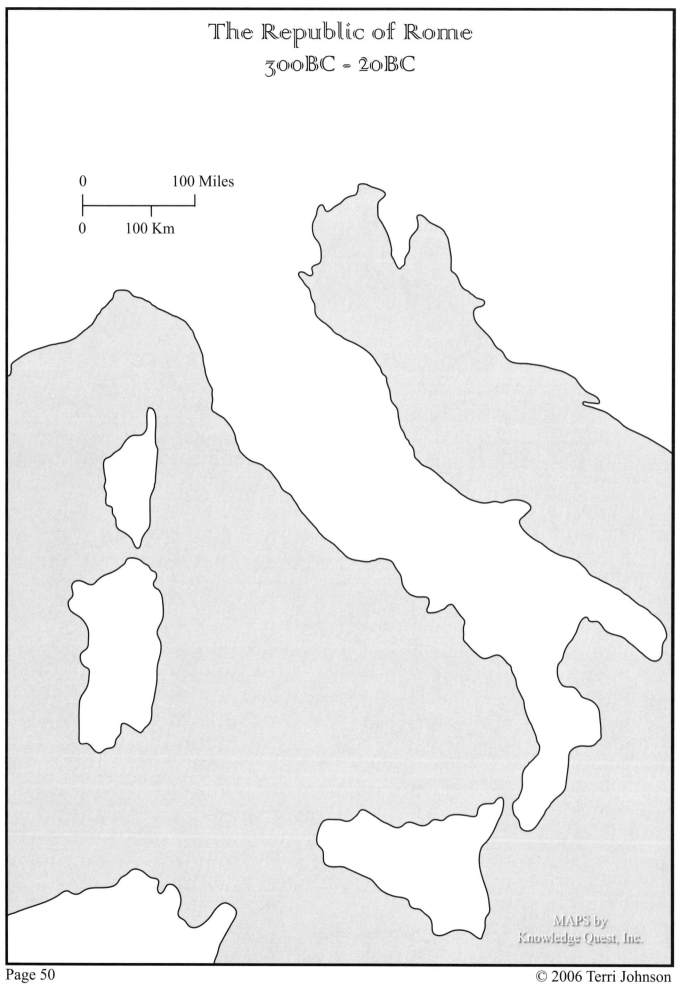

MAPS by
Knowledge Quest, Inc.

0   100 Miles

0   100 Km

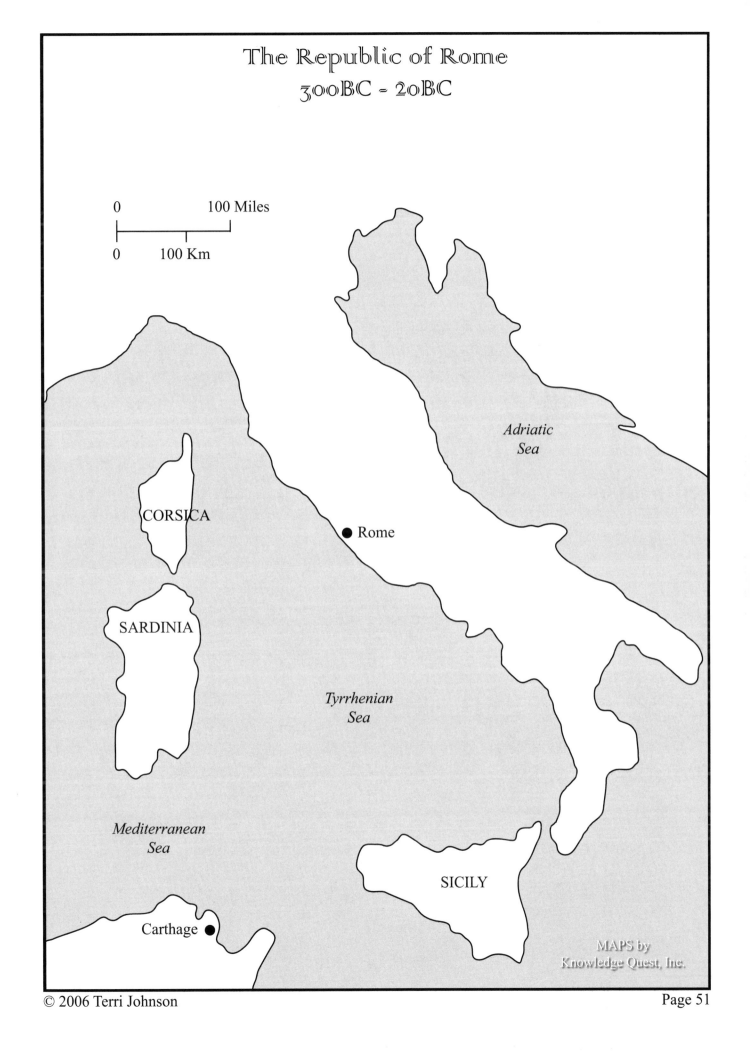

The Republic of Rome
300BC ~ 20BC

0   100 Miles

0   100 Km

CORSICA

● Rome

SARDINIA

Adriatic Sea

Tyrrhenian Sea

Mediterranean Sea

SICILY

Carthage ●

MAPS by
Knowledge Quest, Inc.

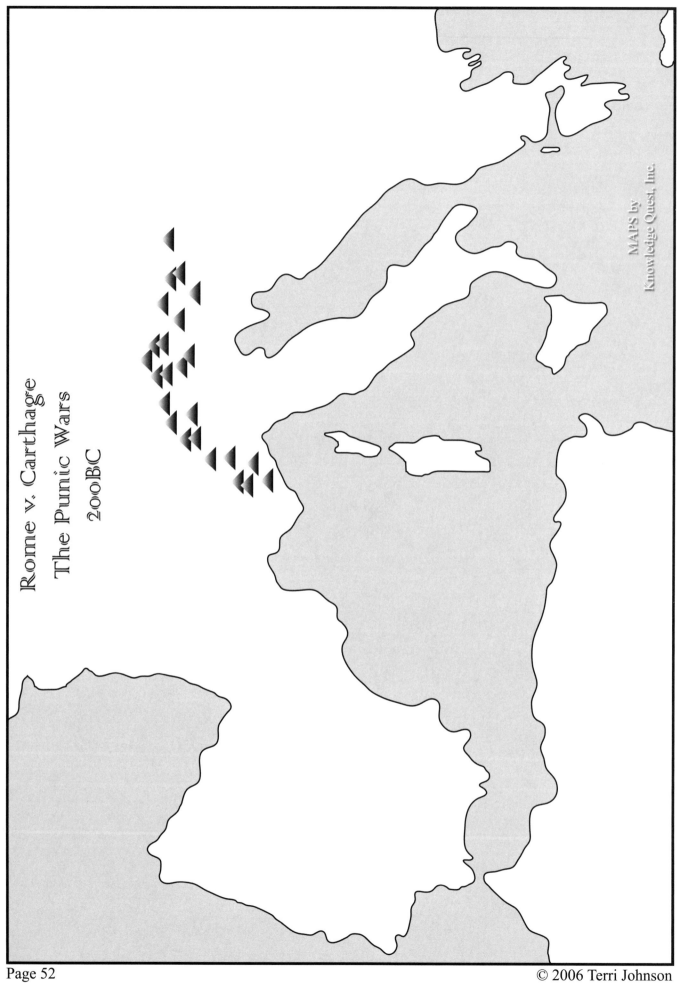

Rome v. Carthage
The Punic Wars
200BC

MAPS by
Knowledge Quest, Inc.

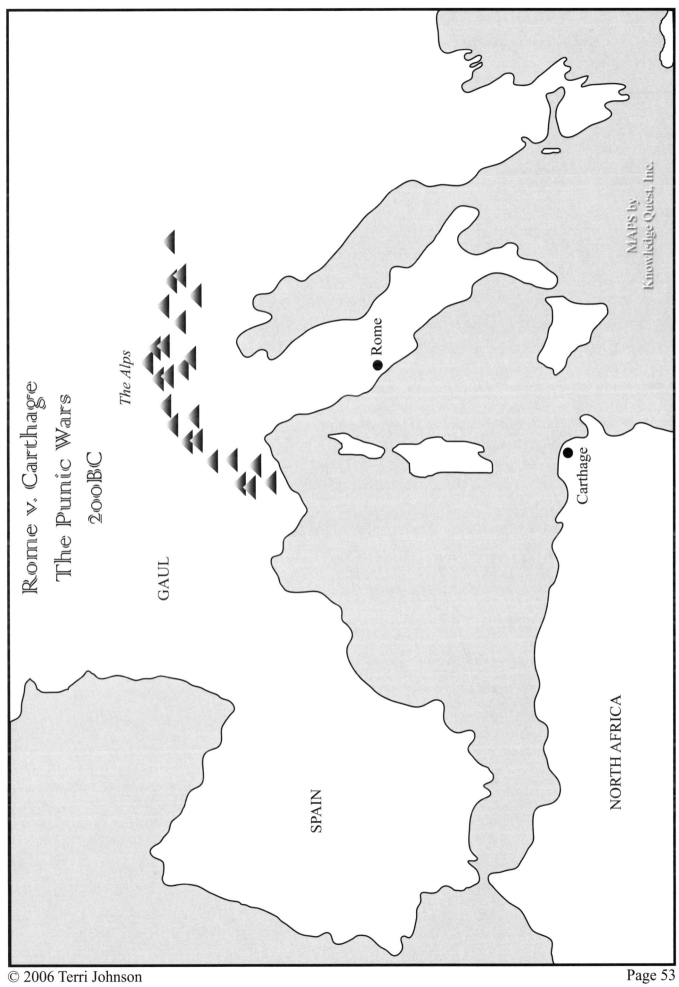

Rome v. Carthage
The Punic Wars
200BC

The Alps

GAUL

SPAIN

NORTH AFRICA

● Rome

● Carthage

MAPS by
Knowledge Quest, Inc.

Palestine During the
Time of Christ
30AD

0   30 Miles

0   30 Km

Palestine During the
Time of Christ
30AD

SYRIA

PHOENICIA

Caesarea
Philippi

Princedom
of Herod
Antipas

Princedom
of Philip

Capernum

Cana

Sea of
Galilee

GALILEE

Nazareth

DECAPOLIS

Caesarea

SAMARIA

Jericho

JUDAEA

Emmaus

Bethany

Jerusalem

Princedom
of Herod
Antipas

Bethlehem

Dead
Sea

0   30 Miles

0   30 Km

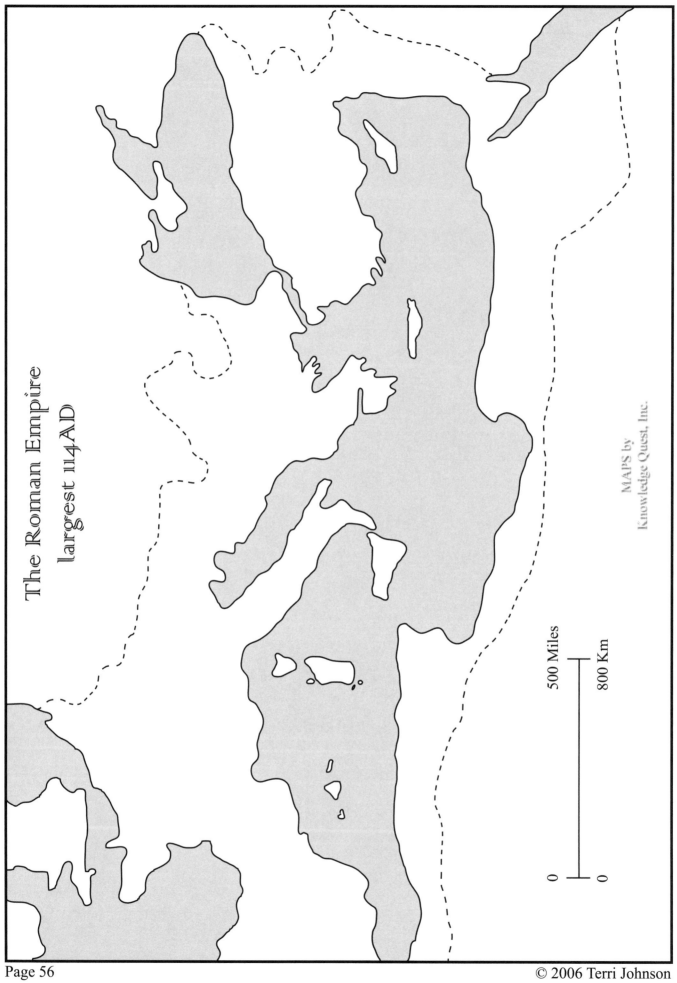

The Roman Empire
largest 114AD

MAPS by
Knowledge Quest, Inc.

500 Miles

800 Km

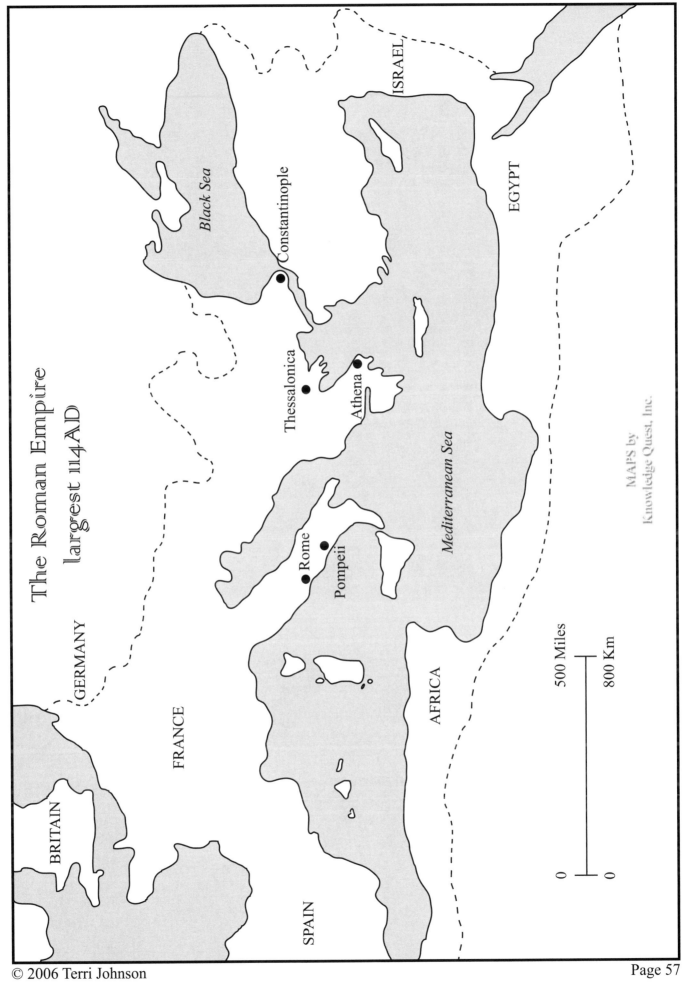

The Roman Empire
largest 114 AD

BRITAIN

GERMANY

FRANCE

SPAIN

Black Sea

Constantinople

ISRAEL

EGYPT

Thessalonica

Athena

Mediterranean Sea

Rome

Pompeii

AFRICA

500 Miles

800 Km

0

0

MAPS by
Knowledge Quest, Inc.

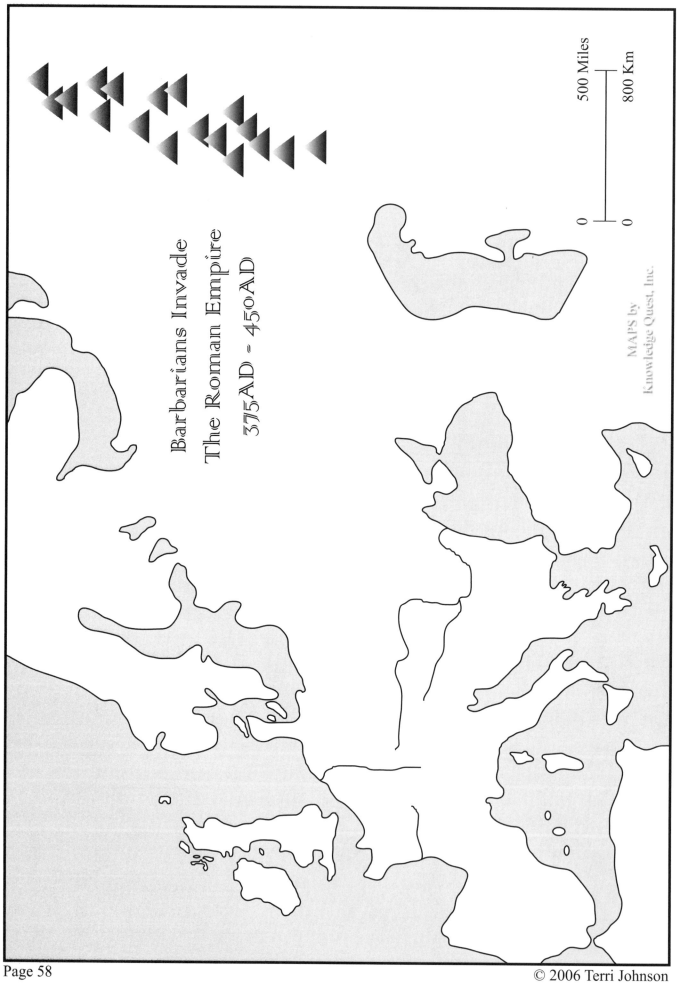

Barbarians Invade
The Roman Empire
375AD - 450AD

500 Miles

800 Km

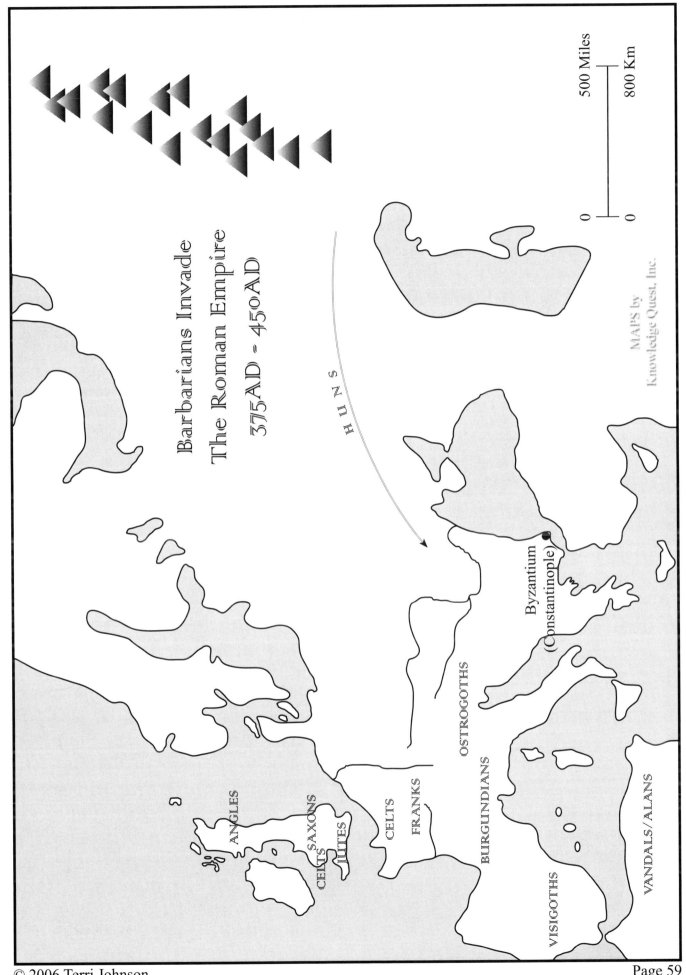

Barbarians Invade
The Roman Empire
375AD = 450AD

HUNS

ANGLES

CELTS
SAXONS
JUTES

CELTS

FRANKS

BURGUNDIANS

OSTROGOTHS

Byzantium
(Constantinople)

VISIGOTHS

VANDALS/ALANS

500 Miles

800 Km

0   0

"The kind of events that once took place will by reason of human nature take place again."

— Thucydides

"That is the supreme value of history. The study of it is the best guarantee against repeating it."

— John Buchan, Baron Tweedsmuir

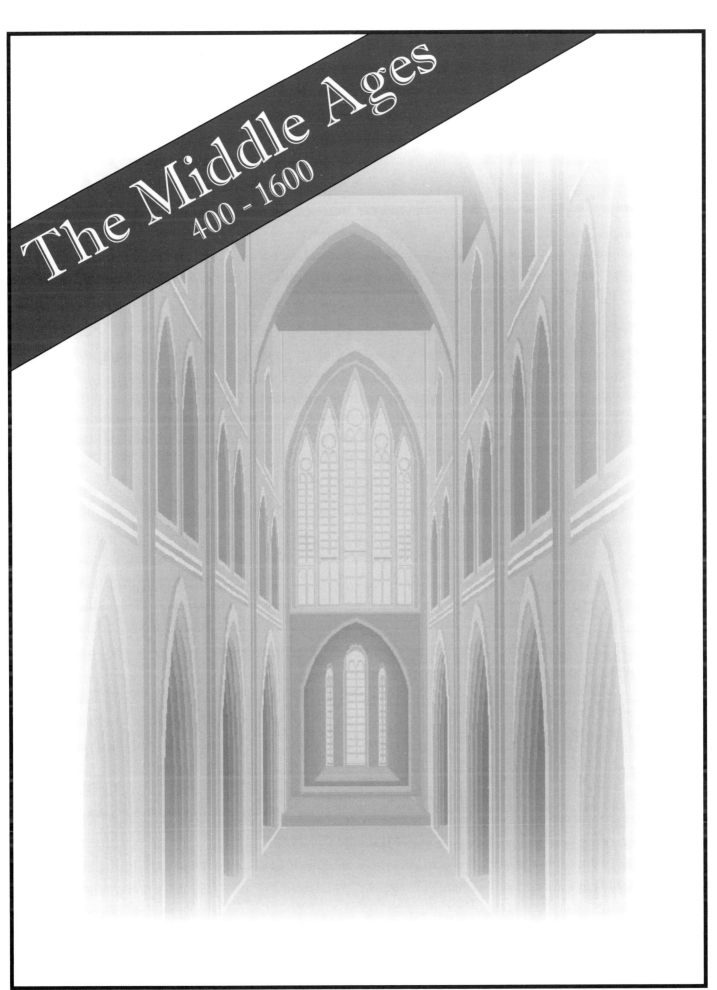

The Middle Ages
400 - 1600

Lesson Plans

Discussion Questions:

1. Barbarian Europe – Page 68
   - Point to the land areas and bodies of water that you recognize. Name them.
   - Are you familiar with the terms "island", "peninsula" and "bay"? Find and label an island *(ex: Crete, Sicily or England)*. Find and label a peninsula *(ex: Italy, Greece or Denmark)*. Find and label a bay *(ex: Bay of Biscay – left of the Kingdom of the Franks)*. Find a sea that you recognize *(ex: Mediterranean, Aegean or Black)*.
   - *Unlabeled map exercise: Label the rivers. Name the barbarian tribes and draw in the directions of their attacks upon Rome. Label the cities of Constantinople and Rome. Draw your own scale (hint: it is roughly 500 miles across the middle of the Black Sea - E to W).*

2. The Byzantine Empire – Page 70
   - Referring to your first map entitled "Barbarian Europe," find the Kingdom of the Franks. This land is now called France. Label *France* on this map (area northeast of Spain).
   - Label *Egypt* on your map. Is Egypt part of the Byzantine Empire? At what time in history, 565 or 1360?
   - Color the two sizes of the Byzantine Empire in different colors to show the distinction between the time periods. Color-code your key, if you choose.
   - *Unlabeled map exercise: Draw in the boundaries of the Byzantine Empire for each year in time – 565 and 1360. Use the key for type of line to use for each. Label all islands and bodies of water. Label major cities.*

3. Viking Expansion – Page 72
   - Choose a color and fill in the countries of Norway, Sweden, England, Ireland, Iceland, Greenland and Newfoundland. These are just some of the countries that the Vikings raided and settled in.
   - Label the ocean to the left of Europe. Label other familiar bodies of water.
   - What continent is Newfoundland on? Label it.
   - *Unlabeled map exercise: Draw in the major movements and the direction taken by the Vikings as they raided and explored new lands. Label all of the countries listed in point one of this section. Label the areas of the Ottoman and Byzantine Empires as well.*

4. The Empire of Charlemagne – Page 74
   - Draw a compass rose on your map which shows the four directions *(N, S, E & W)*.
   - Label the island country to the north of Brittany.
   - Label the sea to the east of England *(North Sea)*. Label the ocean to the west.
   - Label the continent on the southwest corner of your map.
   - *Unlabeled map exercise: Label all of the regions incorporated into the Empire of Charlemagne. Label all bodies of water. Label the continent of Africa and the region of the Byzantine Empire.*

5. The Holy Roman Empire – Page 76

- Label the sea to the south on your map. Can you name the three larger islands *(Corsica, Sardinia and Sicily)*? Label the capital city of the Roman Empire.
- Label the country to the west of the North Sea.
- What country is just north of and not a part of the Holy Roman Empire?
- *Unlabeled map exercise: Label the countries and cities incorporated into the Holy Roman Empire. Label the surrounding bodies of water and the islands they contain. Find out the name of the small chain of islands off the eastern coast of Spain.*

6. African Kingdoms – Page 78

- Name the island to the east of the continent of Africa *(Madagascar)*.
- Label the Red Sea and the Persian Gulf.
- Using the scale as your reference, approximately how long is the Congo River? The Zambezi River?
- *Unlabeled map exercise: Draw in the boundary of the Islamic Empire. Label all rivers, regions, and cities from companion map.*

7. The Norman Conquests – Page 80

- Using the scale as your reference, what is the approximate distance across the English Channel from the northeast tip of Normandy to the town of Hastings?
- Using the key as your reference, what does the symbol next to the town of Hastings and York represent?
- Label the island country to the west of Wales and Scotland *(Ireland)*.
- *Unlabeled map exercise: Label the regions of England and France. Draw in significant battle sites. Label the English Channel and other bodies of water.*

8. The First Crusade – Page 82

- Through which sea did the Crusaders journey?
- Label as many seas as you can? Can you name five *(Black, Red, Aegean, Adriatic and Mediterranean)*?
- *Unlabeled map exercise: Draw in the routes and destinations of the crusaders. Label the countries through which they journeyed.*

9. Medieval Europe – Page 84

- The Papal States and Naples are part of which country?
- Which empire now includes Greece?
- The Baltic Sea is between Sweden and Estonia. Label four seas and an ocean.
- *Unlabeled map exercise: Label the countries of Medieval Europe. Draw in the boundaries of the Holy Roman Empire and label it. Label the Ottoman Empire. Draw a scale using the information from your first map, entitled "Barbarian Europe".*

10. The Third Crusade – Page 86

- Using the key as your reference, trace over the route of Richard the First with a blue pencil or marker. Trace the route taken by Frederick I in green. Finally, trace in red the route taken by Philip Augustus. Now color-code your key.

- Label the islands on which Philip Augustus's army stopped or journeyed across *(Crete, Cyprus)*.
- From the information given on your map, did Frederick I arrive in Israel?
- *Unlabeled map exercise: Draw in the routes and destination of the crusaders. Use the key for types of lines to use and then complete the key.*

11. Medieval China – Page 88

- Find the canals on your map and trace over them with a blue pencil or marker. Do the same with the Great Wall of China, only use brown or gray.
- Label the sea to the east *(Yellow Sea)* and the sea to the south *(South China Sea)*.
- Make sure to color each kingdom with a different color.
- *Unlabeled map exercise: Label the rivers and other bodies of water. Draw in the Great Wall of China and the canal waterways. Draw and label the kingdoms of Medieval China.*

12. Mongol Expansion – Page 90

- Do you recognize the Song Empire? To which country does it belong?
- Label the island country to the east of the Mongol Empire *(Japan)*.
- Is Egypt included in the Mongol Expansion? India? Greece? Persia?
- Label at least four bodies of water.
- *Unlabeled map exercise: Label the Khanate regions of the Mongol kingdom. Label all bodies of water and the Song Empire of China.* **Extra challenge:** *Draw in the route taken by Marco Polo in 1271 when he traveled to China from Italy and then back again in 1295.*

13. Islamic Empire – Page 92

- The Arabian Sea is to the east of Arabia. Label it.
- Find and label the Caspian Sea.
- Where is Constantinople, the capital city of the Byzantine Empire? Label it.
- *Unlabeled map exercise: Draw in the boundaries of the Islamic Empire. Label the countries and major cities that were incorporated into it. Label all bodies of water.*

14. The Ottoman Empire – Page 94

- The Ottoman Empire surrounds which sea?
- Label the two islands to the south.
- Transylvania is north of Wallachia, but outside the Ottoman border. Label it.
- *Unlabeled map exercise: Draw in the boundaries of the Ottoman Empire. Label the countries that were included in it and the dates they were over-taken. Label the surrounding countries and bodies of water.*

15. The Hundred Years' War – Page 96

- Look up Plantagenet in Webster's Dictionary. During which years in France and England's history did this royal dynasty reign?
- Of the battles shown here, which one occurred first? Which one was fought last?
- Which bay is to the west of Poitou and Gascony? *(The Bay of Biscay)*
- *Unlabeled map exercise: Draw in the territory being fought over by the French and English. Mark the significant battle sites and label them. Label the surrounding countries. Label the English Channel.*

16. The Black Death – Page 98

- Label the sea to the north, between England and Denmark. Label the sea to the south.
- Choose six different colors and using the dates listed, color this map by number *(for example, all areas with 1348 might be green)*. Then color-code the boxes in your key.
- *Unlabeled map exercise: Draw in the areas unaffected by the Black Death. Label the areas with the date they were infected by the plague. **Extra challenge:** Using a previous map, such as "Medieval Europe", label the European countries on this map.*

17. The Voyage of Christopher Columbus – Page 100

- Find and label the sea town which Columbus called home *(Genoa, Italy)*.
- Draw in the islands which the Niña, the Pinta and the Santa Maria anchored off of the coast of Africa before heading due west into uncharted seas. *(Canary Islands)*
- Label the ocean though which they sailed.
- Draw a scale for your map. It is approximately 600 miles or 1000 kilometers across Spain's widest distance. Use this information to draw your own scale.
- *Unlabeled map exercise: Draw the route taken by Christopher Columbus when he set sail for the New World (which he believed to be the Indies). Label all continents, islands and bodies of water shown on this map.*

18. European Expansion – Page 102

- Trace the routes taken by the three explorers in three different colors.
- From which countries did these explorers set sail? Label them.
- Label the continents shown on this map.
- *Unlabeled map exercise: Draw in the routes of the explorers – use the key as your guide for type of line to use. Label all continents and oceans.*

19. Renaissance Italy – Page 104

- Using an atlas or globe, locate and draw in these cities: Rome, Napes, Genoa, Venice and Milan.
- Label the two islands to the west and the seas surrounding Italy.
- Three regions on your map have the same name *(Republic of Venice)*. Color all three of these areas the same color to show they belong together.
- *Unlabeled map exercise: Label the Duchies and Republics of Italy. Label the surrounding seas and islands.*

20. The Safavid Persian Empire – Page 106

- Using an atlas or a globe, label at least five bodies of water.
- Draw a compass rose – the symbol that shows the directions for north, south, east and west. Which continent is to the west of the Red Sea? Which continent is to the northwest of Persia? Which continent is to the northeast?
- *Unlabeled map exercise: Draw in the boundary of the Safavid Persian Empire. Label the surrounding empires (Ottoman, Mughal) and bodies of water.*

21. The Powerful Habsburgs – Page 108

- Label the largest country on the Iberian Peninsula *(Spain)*. To which Habsburg dynasty does it belong? Does Portugal belong to this dynasty as well?
- From memory, or using an atlas or globe, name the islands on this map.
- Color the two Habsburg land holdings differently. Color-code your key.
- *Unlabeled map exercise: Trace the boundary lines of each dynasty with a different color. Label the countries included and surrounding the two Habsburg Dynasties. Label all bodies of water.*

22. The New Ottoman Empire – Page 110

- Using a globe or atlas, find the modern day country in which Smyrna is located.
- Label the bodies of water shown on this map.
- Which country is located to the west of Hungary and Albania? Is it part of the Ottoman Empire? Referring to the previous map *(Powerful Habsburgs – Page 50)*, which ruling family owns at least half of Italy?
- The entire portion of Africa which can be seen on your map is part of the Ottoman Empire. Color it accordingly.
- *Unlabeled map exercise: Label the major cities and countries included in the New Ottoman Empire. Consult your previous Ottoman Empire map (Pages 36 and 37) and notice any changes in area. Is the empire larger now or smaller?*

23. The Expansion of Russia – Page 112

- Label the country south of eastern Russia.
- Label the two countries located on the peninsula northwest of Russia. *(Sweden and Norway)*
- Color the Russian Empire by number *(date)* and then color-code your map key.
- *Unlabeled map exercise: Use your companion map to fill in the dates of expansion on this map. Label the countries surrounding Russia both to the northwest and southeast.*

24. The Spanish and Portuguese Empires – Page 114

- The Spanish Empire and its colonies are enclosed by dashes. Color all of these areas with the same color.
- The Portuguese Empire and its colonies are enclosed by dots. Color all of these areas with the same color.
- Color-code your key.
- What is the name of the line dividing South America? *(Line of Treaty of Tordesillas – this line was the agreed-upon separation between the colonies of the Spanish and Portuguese Empires in South America)*
- Using an atlas or globe if needed, label the large island continent in the lower right hand corner of your map. Amazingly, this large piece of land had not yet been discovered at this time in history.
- *Unlabeled map exercise: Draw in the boundary lines of the Spanish and Portuguese Empires. Draw in the Line of Treaty of Tordesillas. Label all continents and oceans.*

Glossary of Terms Used

Atlas – a book containing a collection of maps.

Bay – a wide inlet of the sea.

Canal – a man-made waterway used for irrigation or traveling purposes.

Capital City – the city in which the ruling government is located.

Channel – a narrow stretch of water connecting two larger bodies of water.

Compass Rose – a directional symbol on a chart used for navigation.

Continent – one of the seven great land masses of the world – *Europe, Asia, Africa, North America, South America, Australia and Antarctica.*

Empire – a kingdom which has been extended by military might to include countries which were originally independent.

Globe – a spherical model of the earth or heavens.

Island – a piece of land, smaller than a continent, entirely surrounded by water.

Key – something to help you decipher a code.

Kilometer – a unit of distance measurement equaling 1,000 meters.

Mile – a unit of distance measurement equaling 1,760 yards.

Ocean – the large bodies of salt water which comprise the majority (over ⅔) of the earth's surface.

Peninsula – a finger of land surrounded by sea on three sides.

Route – a course of travel, especially between two distant points.

Sea – a body of water smaller than an ocean, partially or completely enclosed by land.

Scale – a line on a map with marks dividing it to show proportional distance.

Geographical Regions Covered

Africa	Russia	Australia	Austria
Congo River	Zambezi River	Normandy	Wales
Crete	Sicily	England	Italy
Greece	Denmark	Bay of Biscay	Black Sea
Iberian Peninsula	Portugal	Hungary	Albania
Mediterranean	Aegean Sea	France	Egypt
Newfoundland	Brittany	North Sea	Corsica
Norway	Ireland	Iceland	Greenland
Persia	Arabia	Caspian Sea	Wallachia
Sardinia	Madagascar	Red Sea	Persian Gulf
Scotland	Adriatic Sea	English Channel	Baltic Sea
Sweden	Estonia	Cyprus	Great Wall
Transylvania	Constantinople	Canary Islands	Spain
Yellow Sea	S. China Sea	Japan	India

Teacher or parent, you may choose to use these terms and geographical regions listed to put together an end of the year quiz. However, if you follow the lesson plans throughout the year, you may not feel that this is necessary.

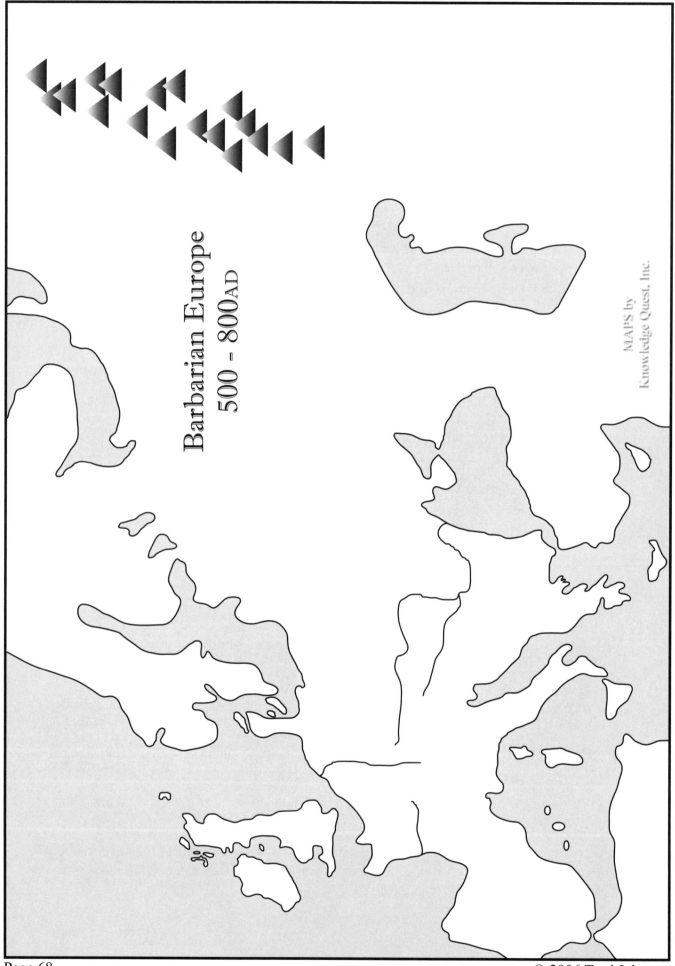

Barbarian Europe
500 – 800AD

MAPS by
Knowledge Quest, Inc.

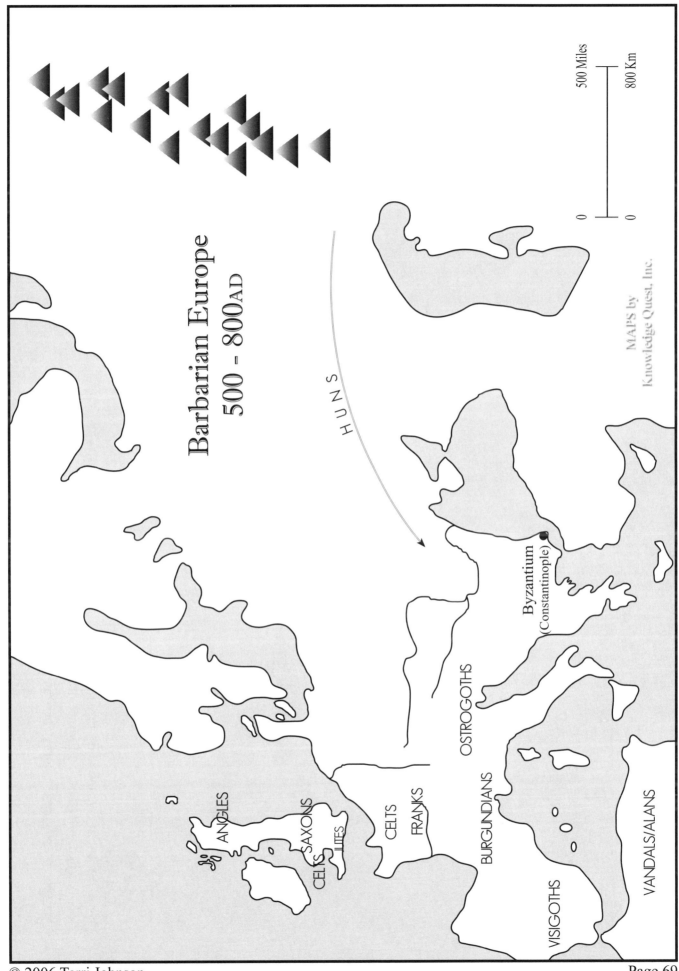

Barbarian Europe
500 - 800AD

HUNS

Byzantium
(Constantinople)

ANGLES

SAXONS
CELTS
JUTES

CELTS
FRANKS

OSTROGOTHS

BURGUNDIANS

VISIGOTHS

VANDALS/ALANS

500 Miles

800 Km

0

0

MAPS by
Knowledge Quest, Inc.

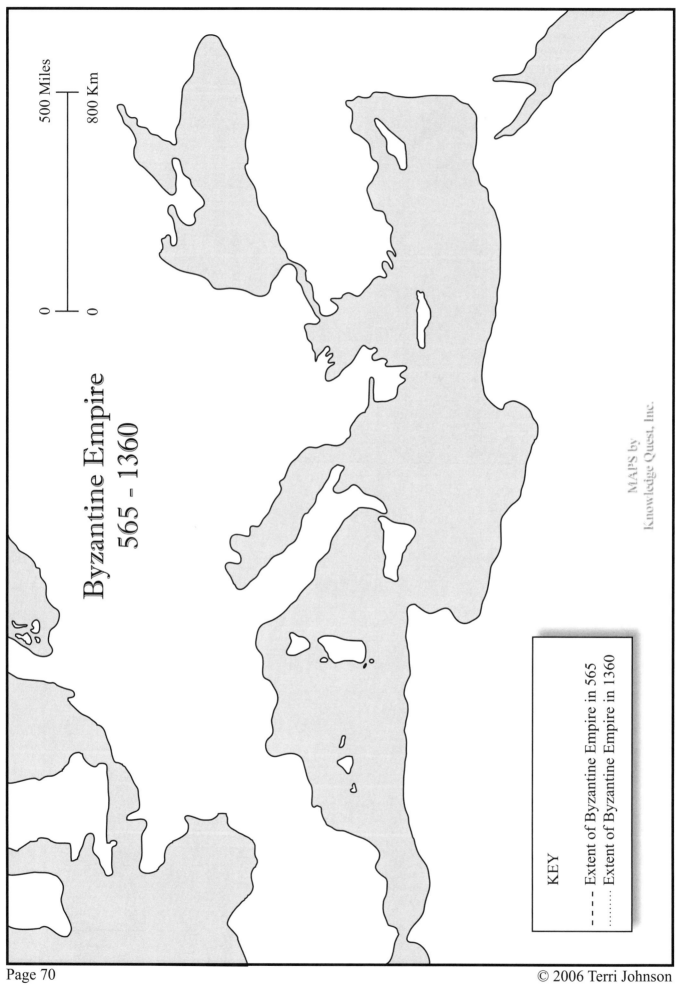

Byzantine Empire
565 - 1360

500 Miles

800 Km

MAPS by
Knowledge Quest, Inc.

KEY

- - - Extent of Byzantine Empire in 565

.... Extent of Byzantine Empire in 1360

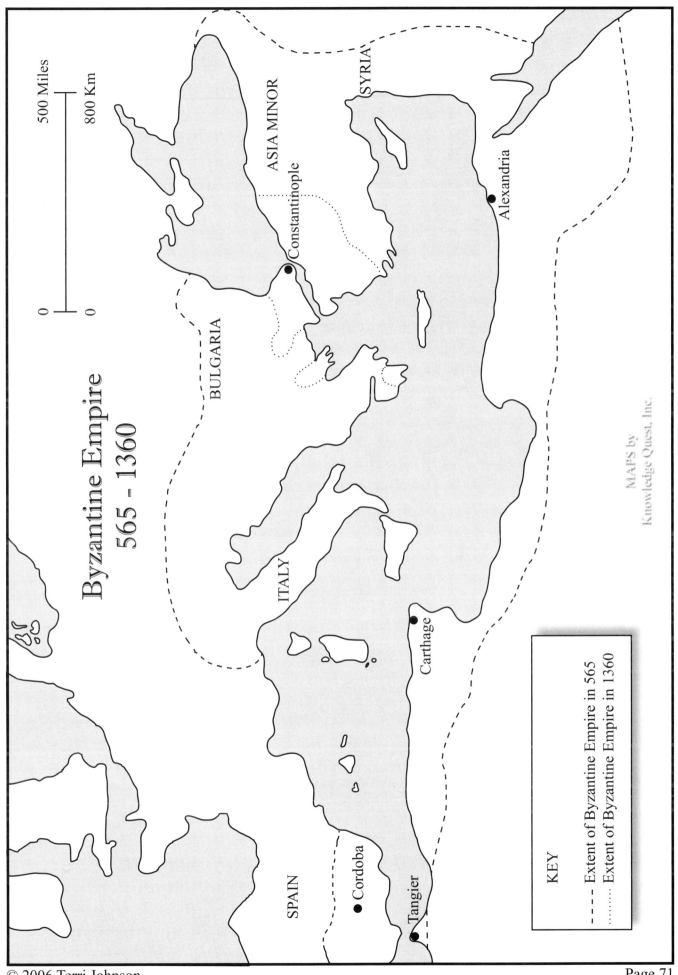

Byzantine Empire
565 - 1360

500 Miles

800 Km

0

0

SYRIA

ASIA MINOR

Constantinople

Alexandria

BULGARIA

ITALY

Carthage

SPAIN

Cordoba

Tangier

KEY

- - - Extent of Byzantine Empire in 565

.... Extent of Byzantine Empire in 1360

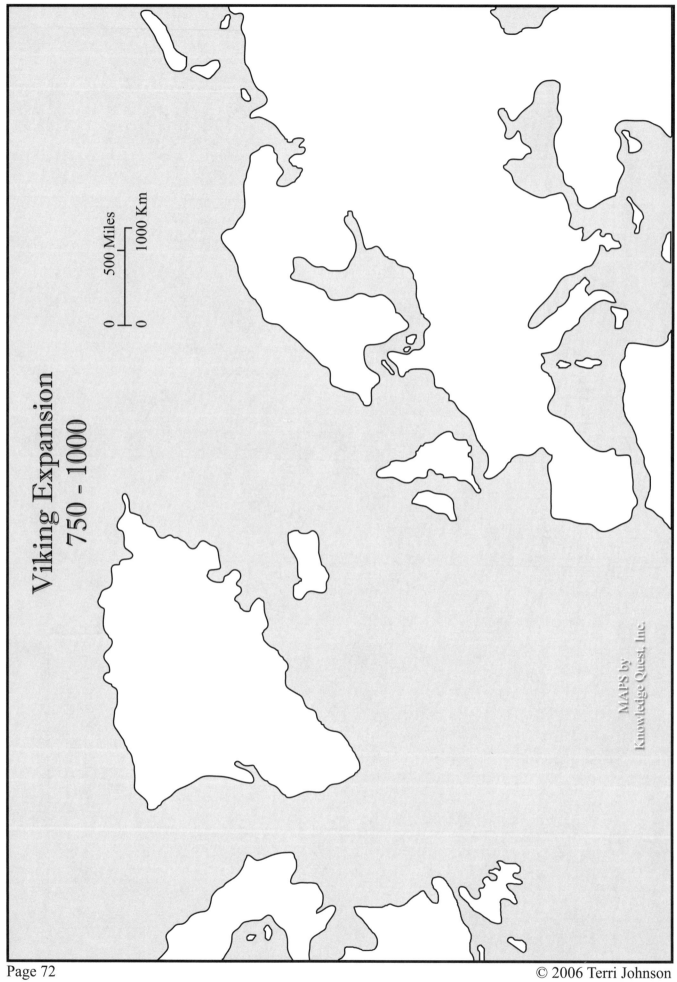

Viking Expansion
750 - 1000

500 Miles
1000 Km

MAPS by
Knowledge Quest, Inc.

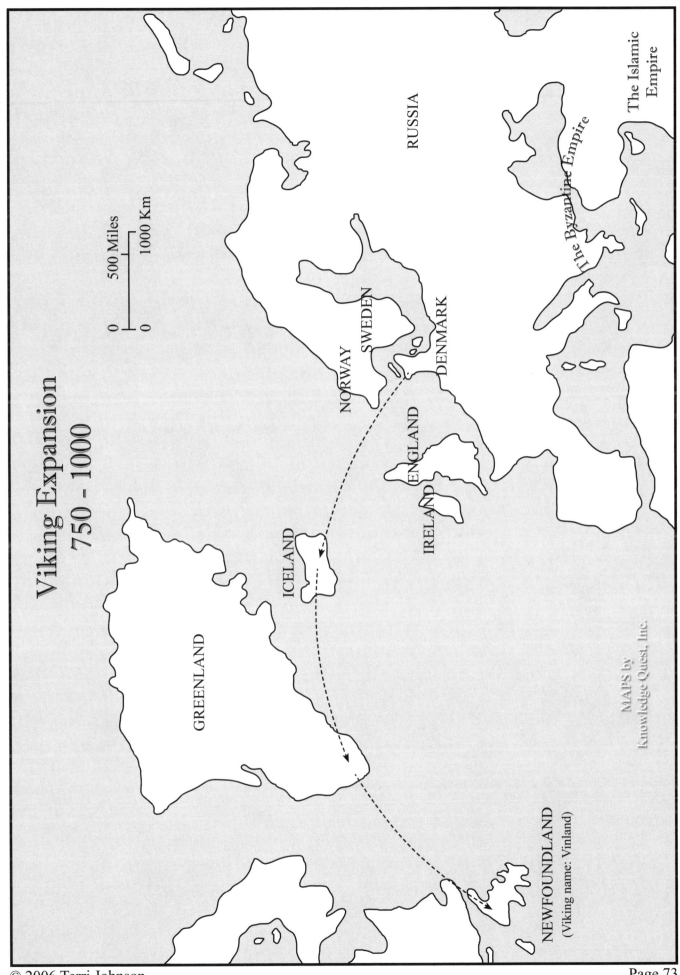

Viking Expansion
750 - 1000

500 Miles
1000 Km

GREENLAND

ICELAND

NORWAY

SWEDEN

DENMARK

ENGLAND

IRELAND

RUSSIA

The Byzantine Empire

The Islamic Empire

NEWFOUNDLAND
(Viking name: Vinland)

MAPS by
Knowledge Quest, Inc.

© 2006 Terri Johnson

Page 73

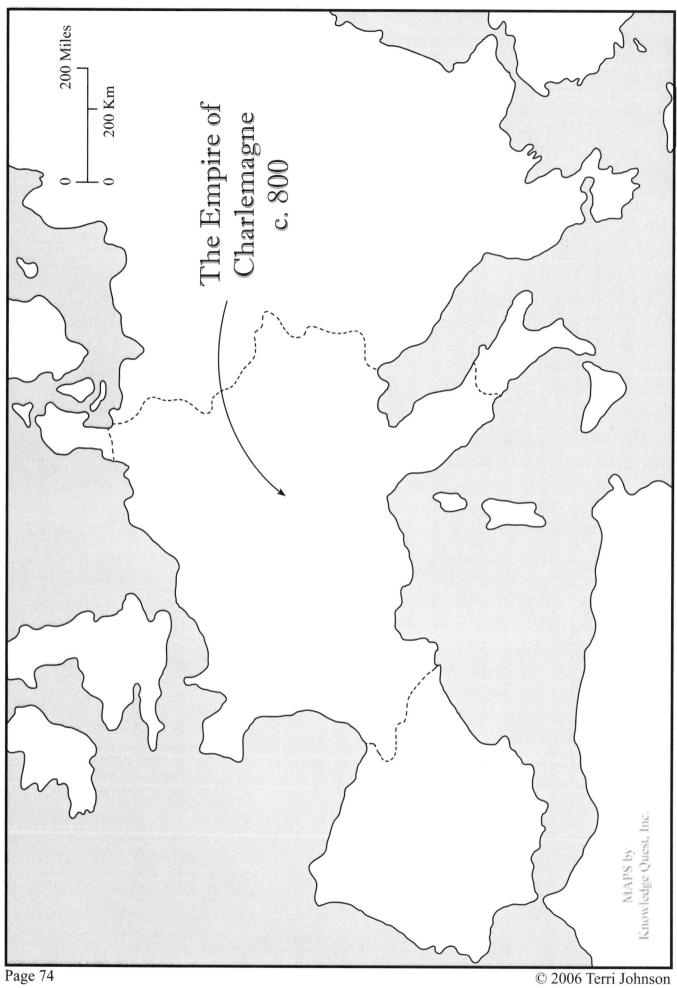

The Empire of Charlemagne
c. 800

200 Miles
200 Km
0
0

MAPS by
Knowledge Quest, Inc.

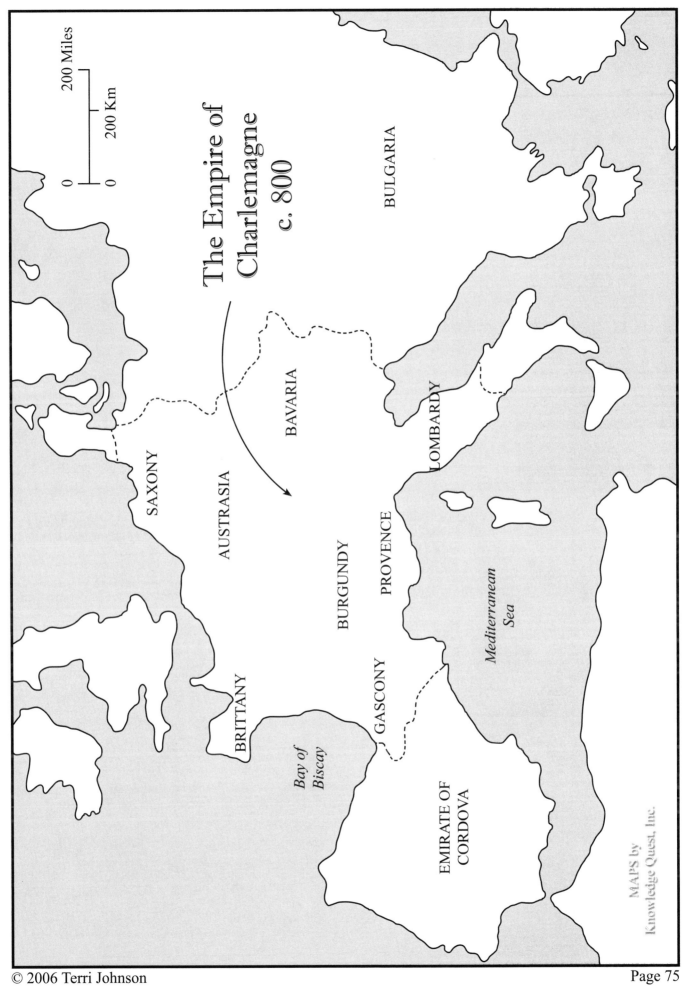

The Empire of Charlemagne c. 800

SAXONY

AUSTRASIA

BAVARIA

BULGARIA

BRITTANY

BURGUNDY

PROVENCE

LOMBARDY

GASCONY

Bay of Biscay

EMIRATE OF CORDOVA

Mediterranean Sea

200 Miles

200 Km

0

0

MAPS by Knowledge Quest, Inc.

The Holy
Roman Empire
950 - 1300

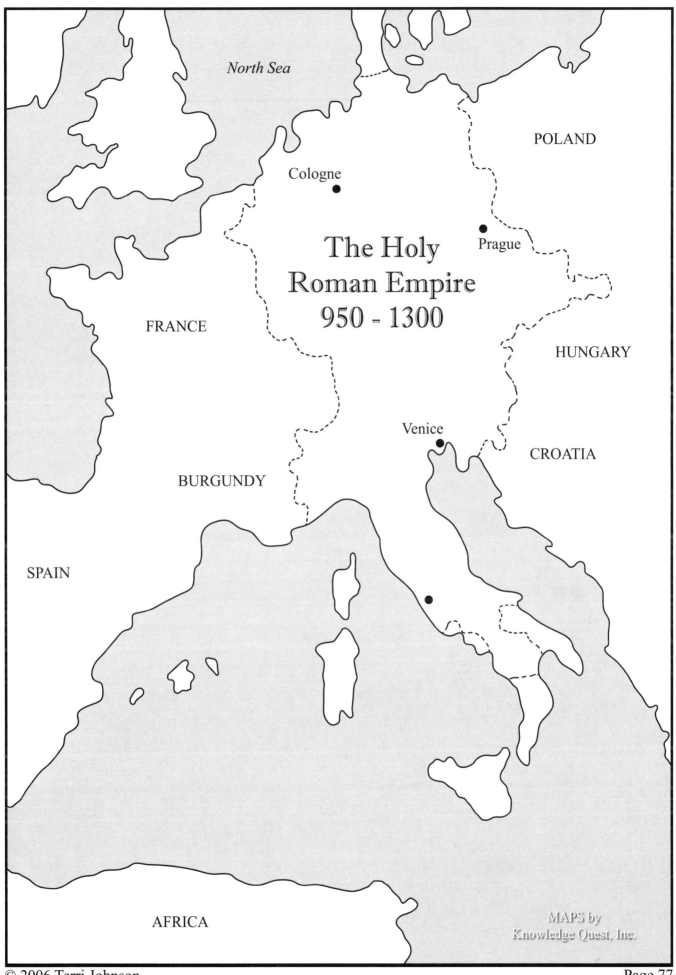

The Holy
Roman Empire
950 - 1300

North Sea

POLAND

Cologne

Prague

FRANCE

HUNGARY

Venice

CROATIA

BURGUNDY

SPAIN

AFRICA

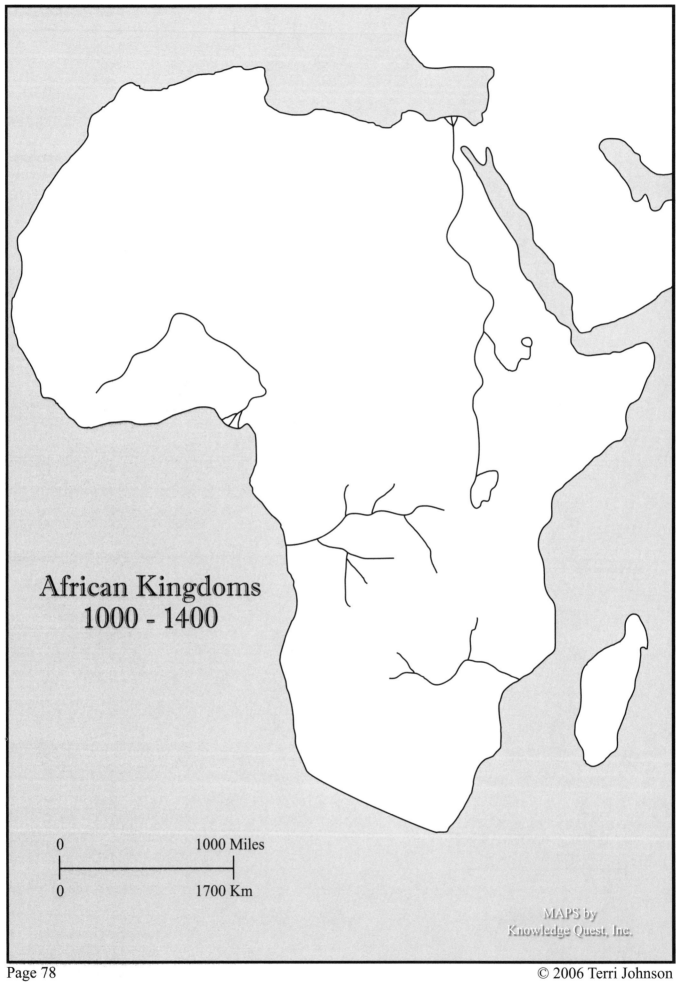

African Kingdoms
1000 - 1400

0   1000 Miles

0   1700 Km

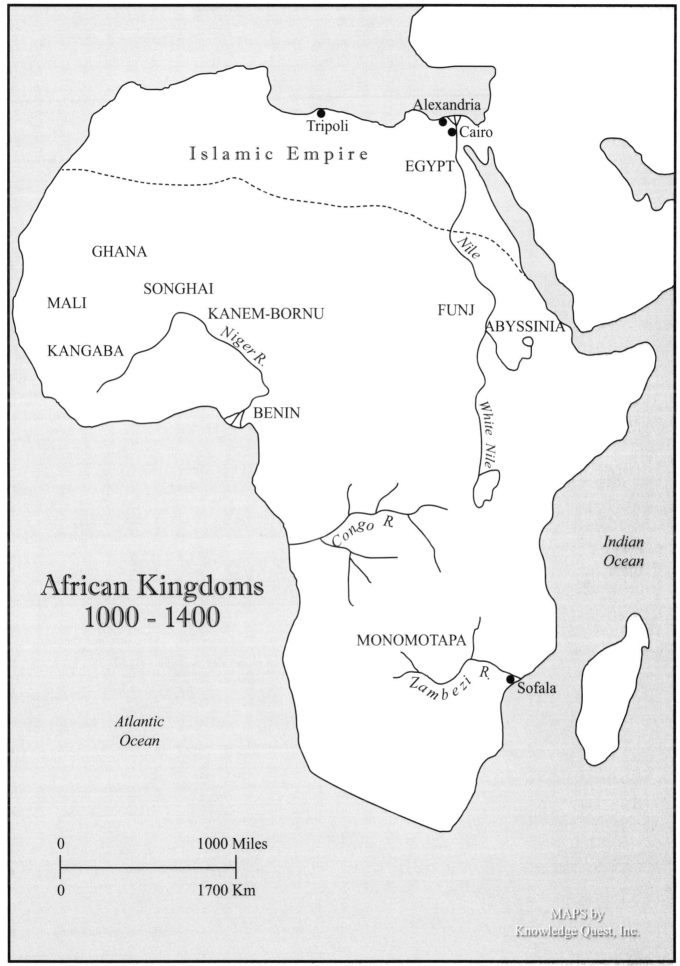

African Kingdoms
1000 - 1400

Islamic Empire

Tripoli

Alexandria

Cairo

EGYPT

GHANA

SONGHAI

MALI

KANEM-BORNU

KANGABA

Niger R.

BENIN

FUNJ

ABYSSINIA

Nile

White Nile

Congo R.

MONOMOTAPA

Zambezi R.

Sofala

Indian
Ocean

Atlantic
Ocean

0   1000 Miles

0   1700 Km

MAPS by
Knowledge Quest, Inc.

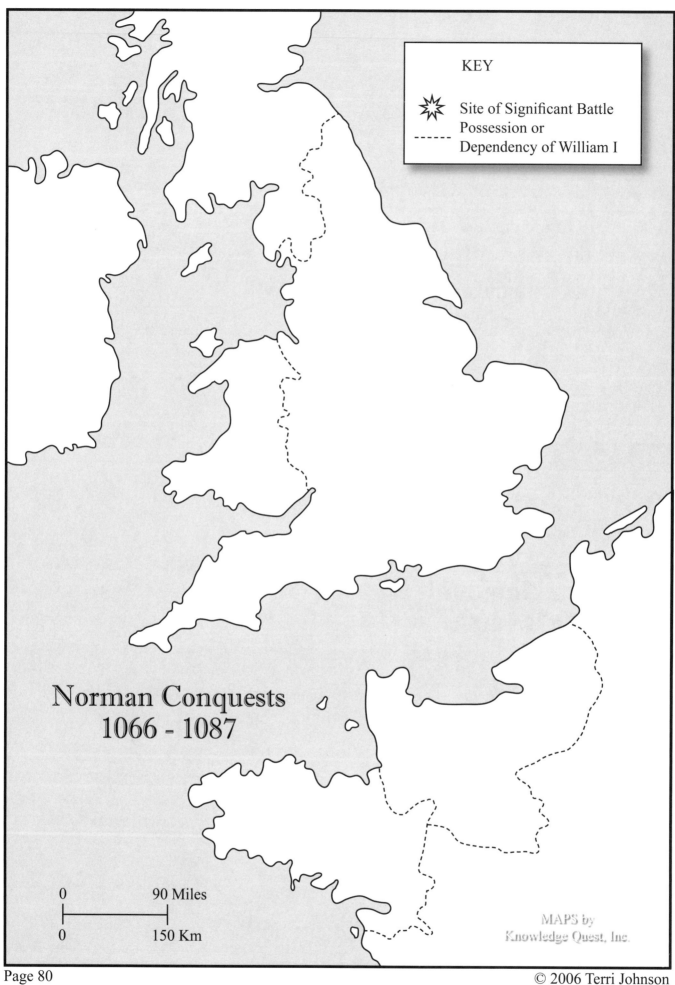

KEY

✸ Site of Significant Battle

- - - - Possession or Dependency of William I

Norman Conquests
1066 - 1087

0   90 Miles

0   150 Km

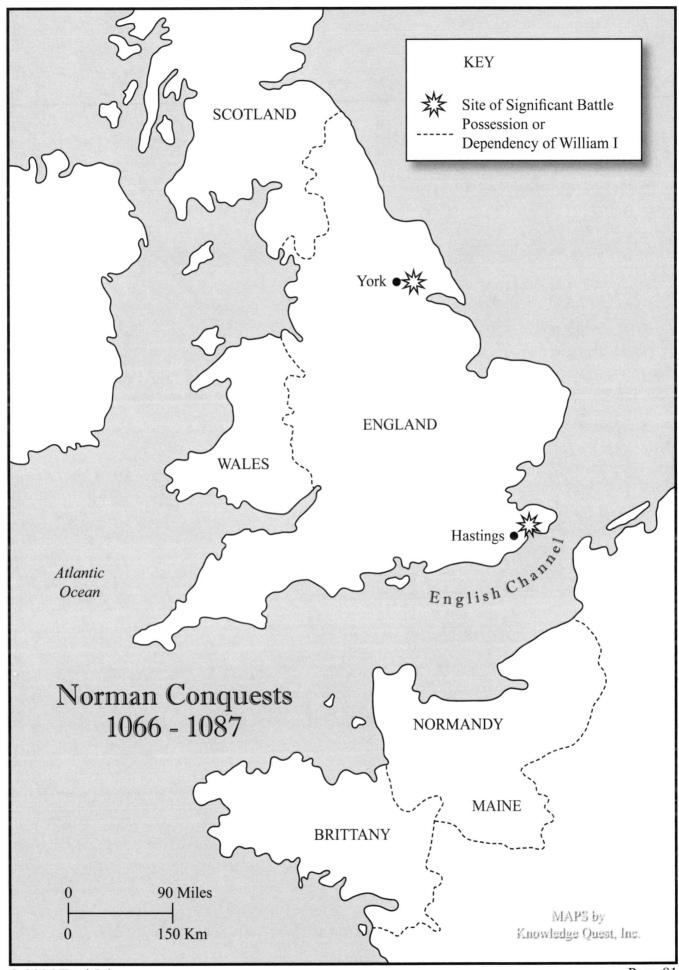

KEY

✺ Site of Significant Battle

- - - - Possession or Dependency of William I

SCOTLAND

York •✺

ENGLAND

WALES

Hastings •✺

English Channel

Atlantic Ocean

Norman Conquests
1066 - 1087

NORMANDY

MAINE

BRITTANY

0	90 Miles
0	150 Km

MAPS by
Knowledge Quest, Inc.

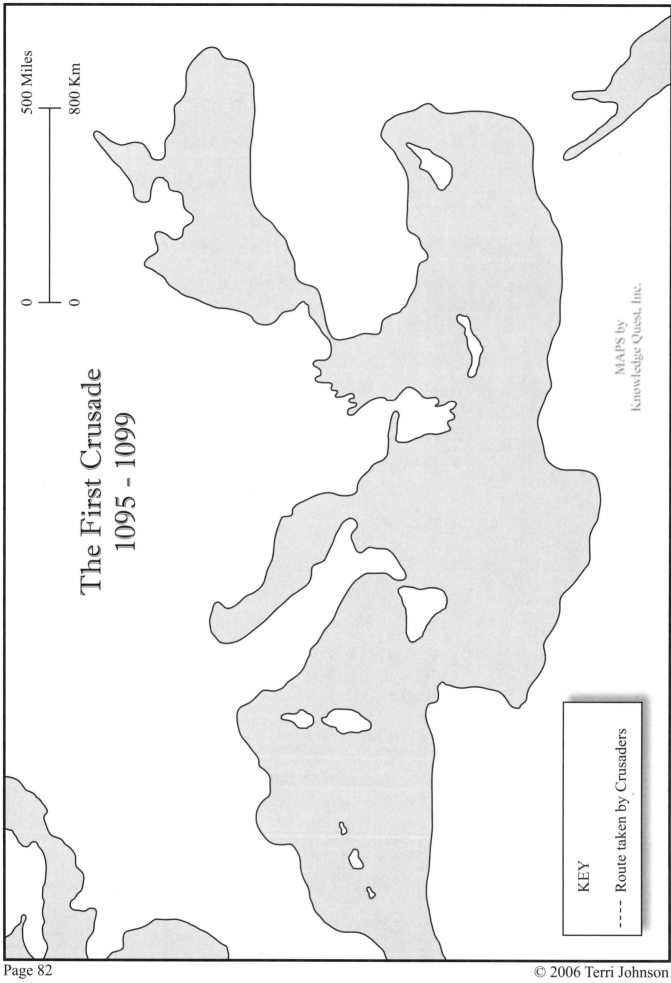

The First Crusade
1095 - 1099

500 Miles
800 Km

0
0

MAPS by
Knowledge Quest, Inc.

KEY
---- Route taken by Crusaders

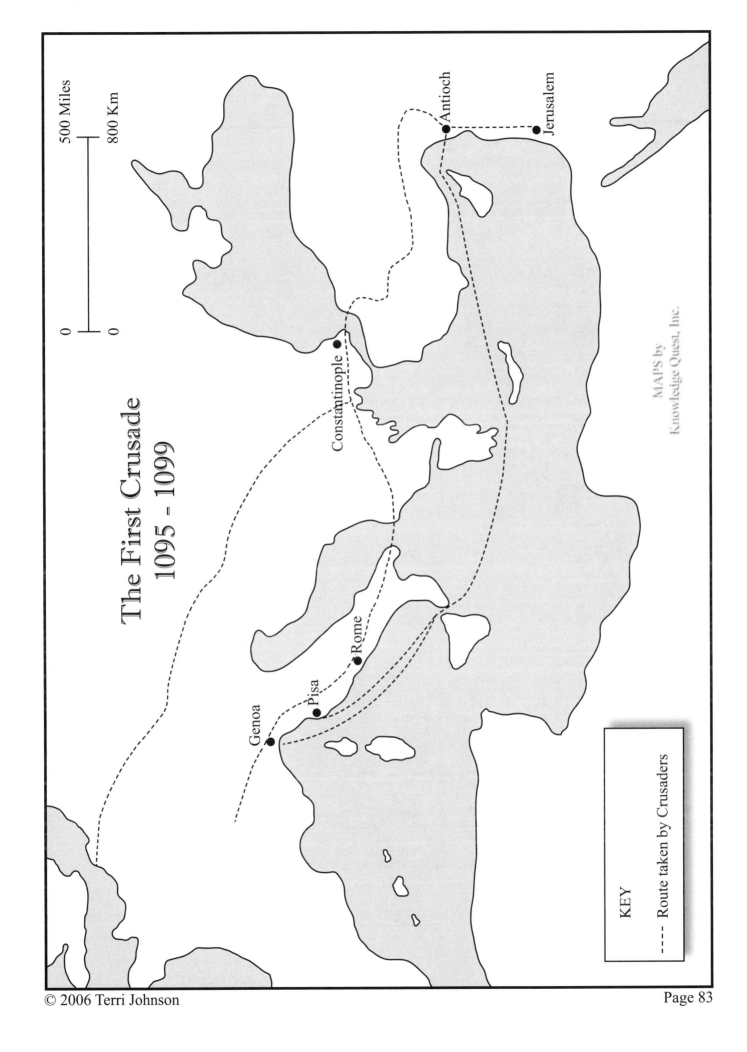

The First Crusade
1095 - 1099

500 Miles

800 Km

0

0

Antioch

Jerusalem

Constantinople

Rome

Pisa

Genoa

MAPS by
Knowledge Quest, Inc.

KEY

- - - Route taken by Crusaders

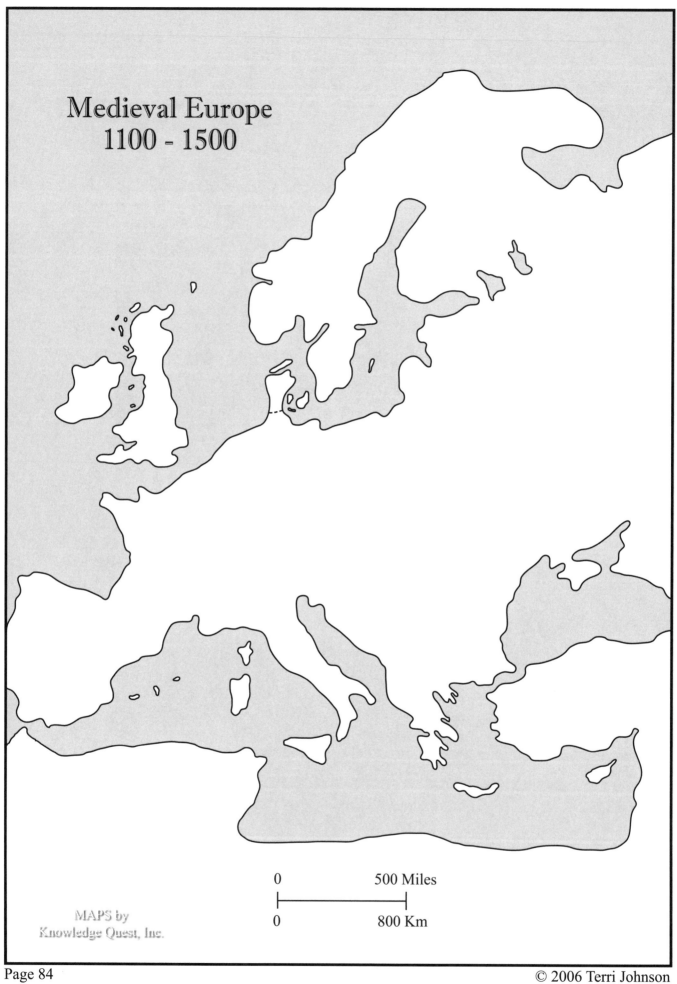

Medieval Europe
1100 - 1500

0   500 Miles

0   800 Km

MAPS by
Knowledge Quest, Inc.

© 2006 Terri Johnson

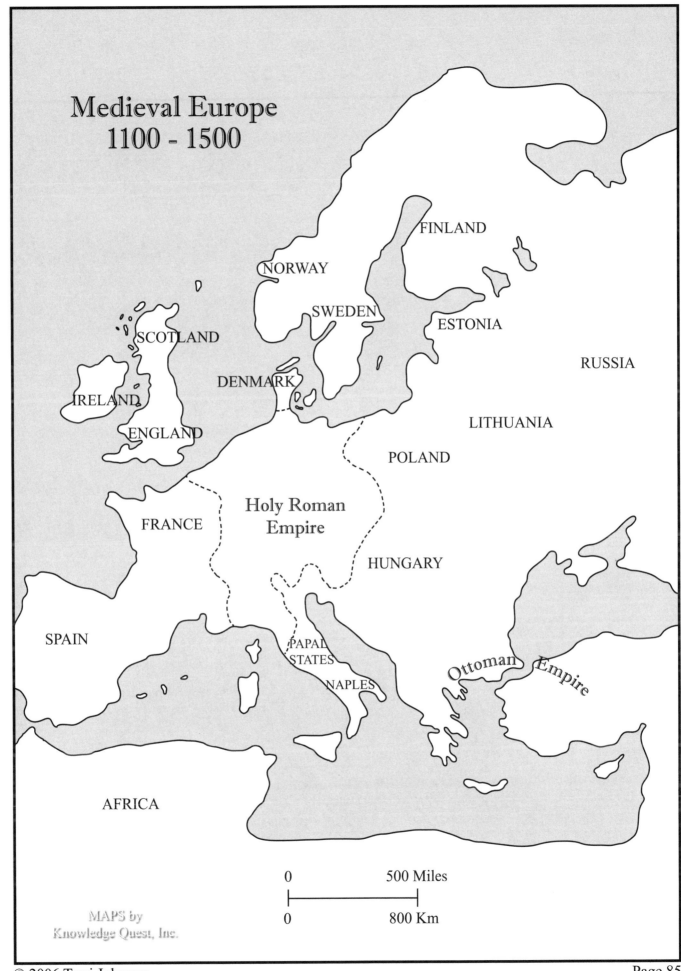

Medieval Europe
1100 - 1500

FINLAND

NORWAY

SWEDEN

ESTONIA

RUSSIA

SCOTLAND

DENMARK

LITHUANIA

IRELAND

POLAND

ENGLAND

Holy Roman
Empire

FRANCE

HUNGARY

SPAIN

PAPAL
STATES

NAPLES

Ottoman Empire

AFRICA

0	500 Miles
0	800 Km

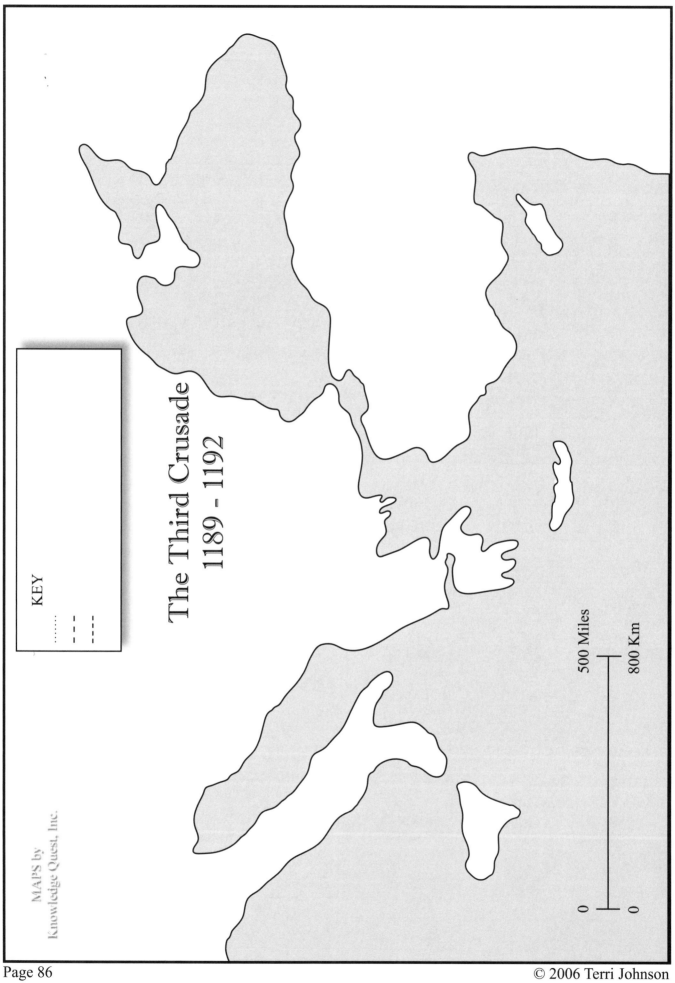

KEY

The Third Crusade
1189 - 1192

500 Miles
800 Km

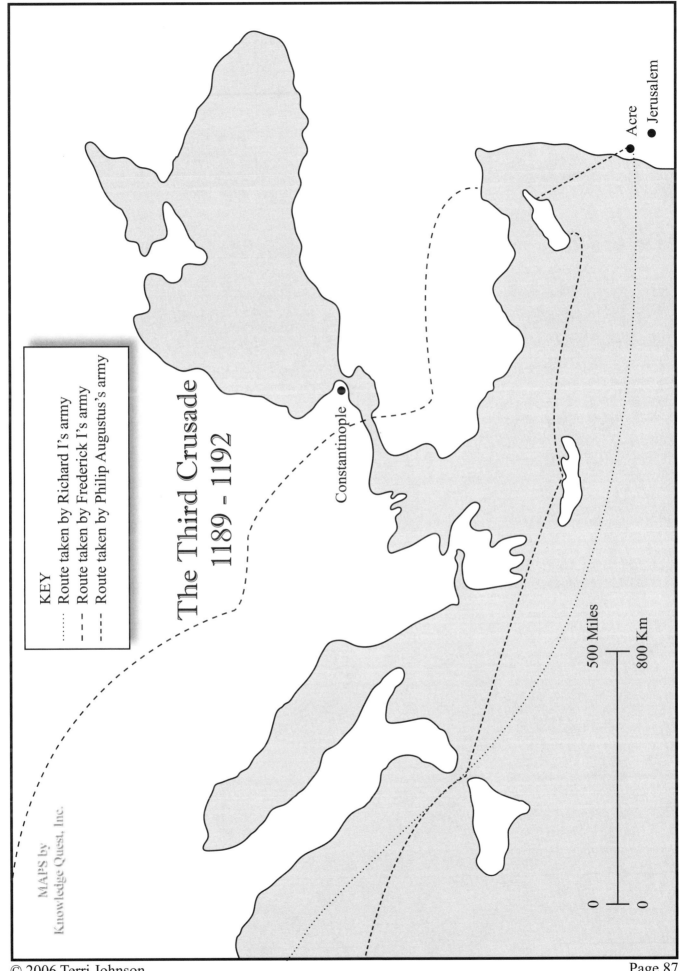

The Third Crusade
1189 – 1192

KEY
.... Route taken by Richard I's army
– – – Route taken by Frederick I's army
– – – – Route taken by Philip Augustus's army

Constantinople

Acre

Jerusalem

500 Miles

800 Km

Medieval China
c. 1200

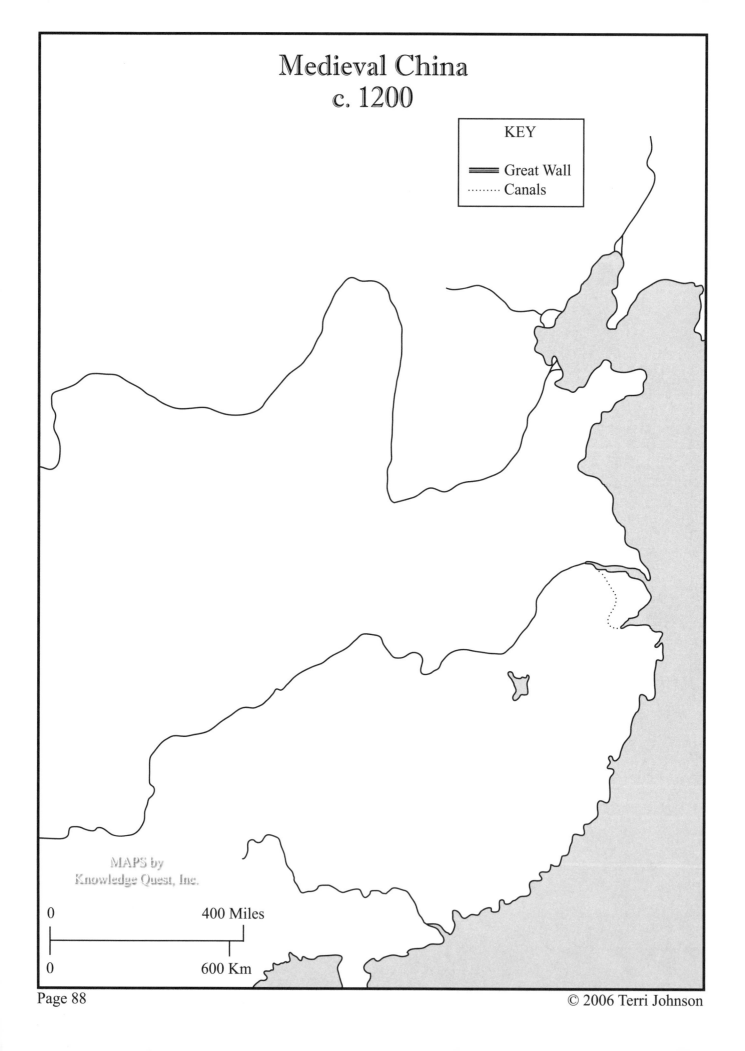

KEY

━━━ Great Wall

······ Canals

0   400 Miles

0   600 Km

MAPS by
Knowledge Quest, Inc.

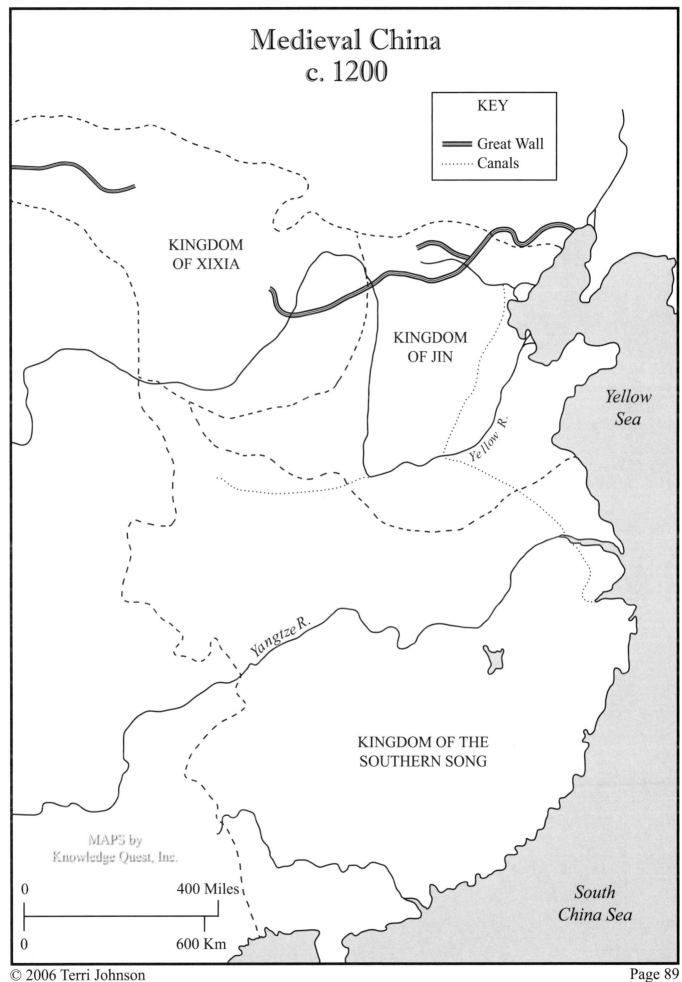

Medieval China
c. 1200

KEY

Great Wall

Canals

KINGDOM
OF XIXIA

KINGDOM
OF JIN

Yellow R.

*Yellow
Sea*

KINGDOM OF THE
SOUTHERN SONG

Yangtze R.

MAPS by
Knowledge Quest, Inc.

0		400 Miles

0		600 Km

*South
China Sea*

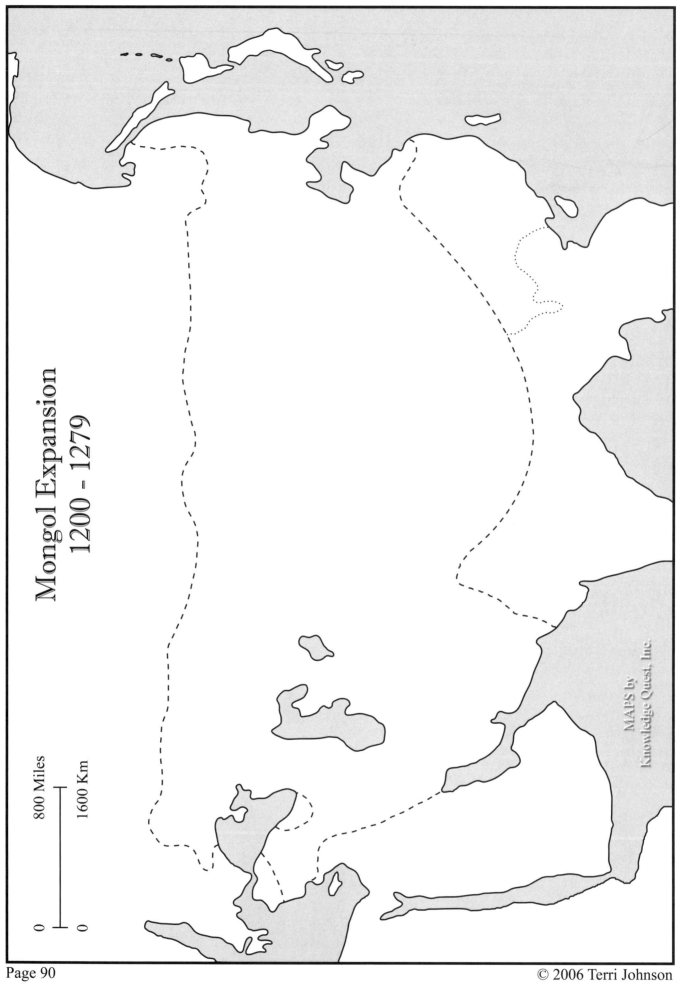

Mongol Expansion
1200 - 1279

800 Miles

1600 Km

0

0

MAPS by
Knowledge Quest, Inc.

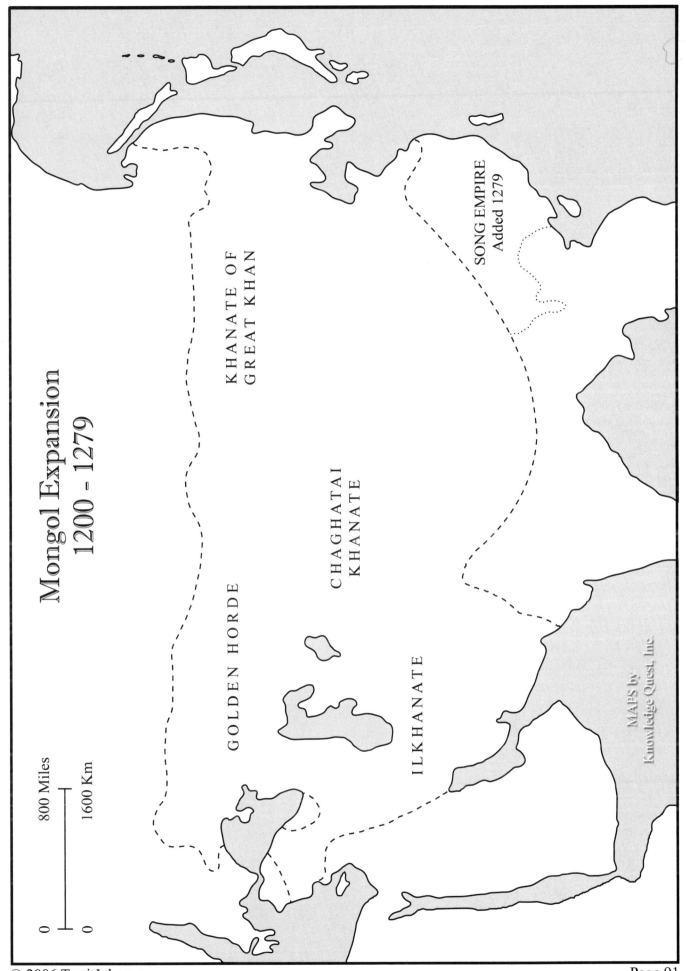

Mongol Expansion
1200 - 1279

KHANATE OF
GREAT KHAN

SONG EMPIRE
Added 1279

GOLDEN HORDE

CHAGHATAI
KHANATE

ILKHANATE

800 Miles

1600 Km

0

0

MAPS by
Knowledge Quest, Inc.

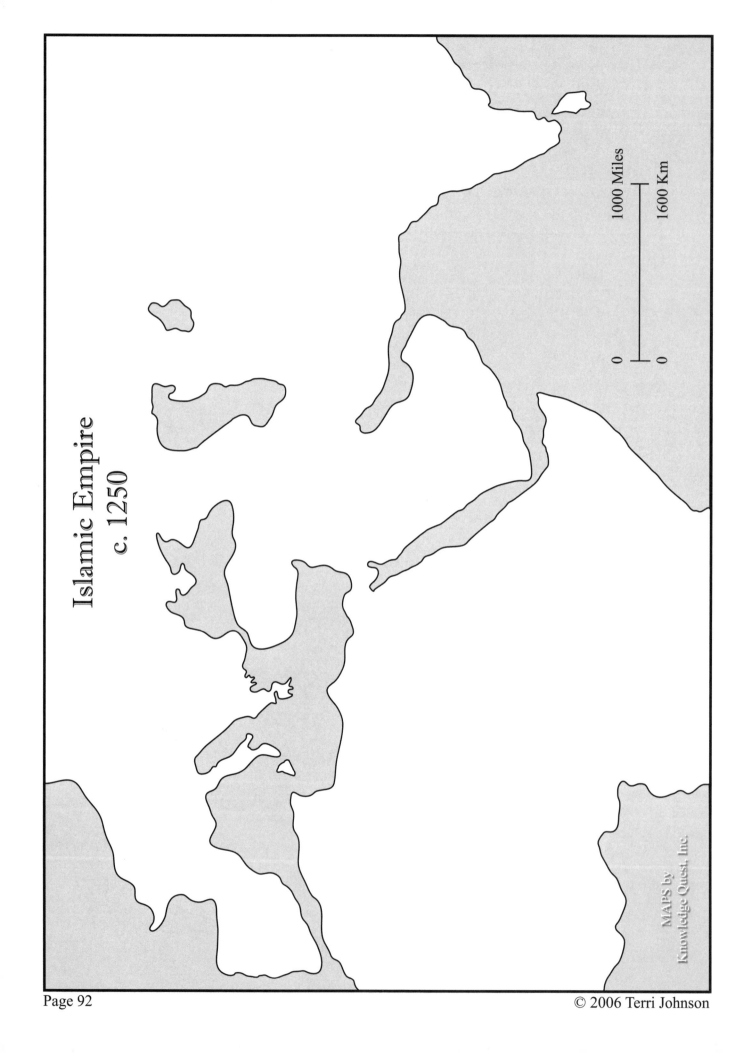

Islamic Empire
c. 1250

1000 Miles

1600 Km

0

0

MAPS by
Knowledge Quest, Inc.

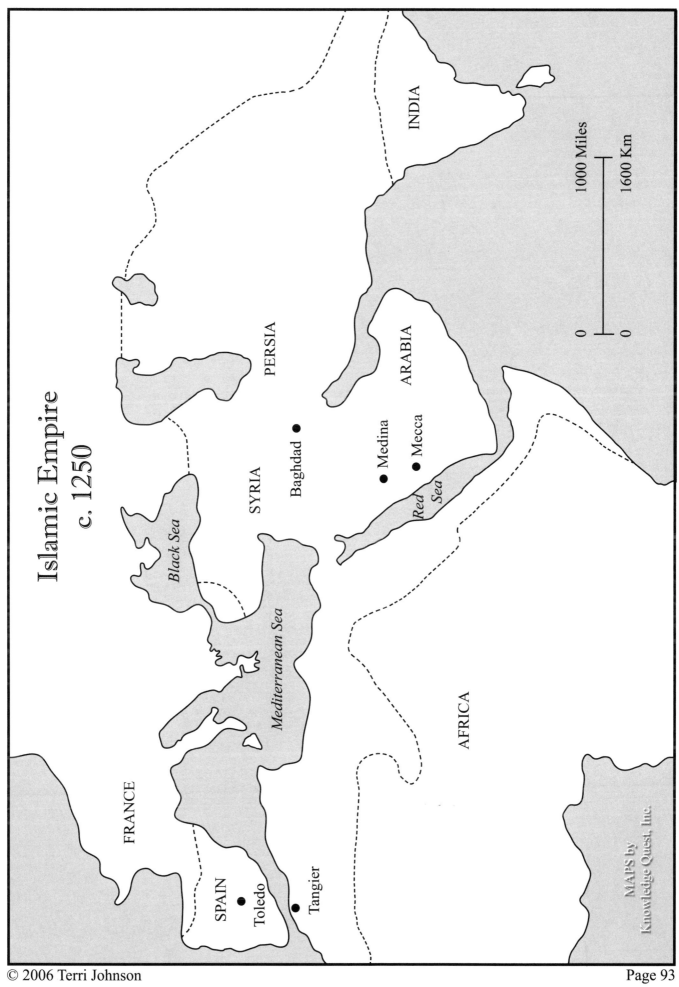

Islamic Empire
c. 1250

FRANCE

SPAIN

Toledo ●

Tangier ●

Black Sea

Mediterranean Sea

SYRIA

PERSIA

Baghdad ●

Medina ●

Mecca ●

Red Sea

ARABIA

INDIA

AFRICA

1000 Miles

1600 Km

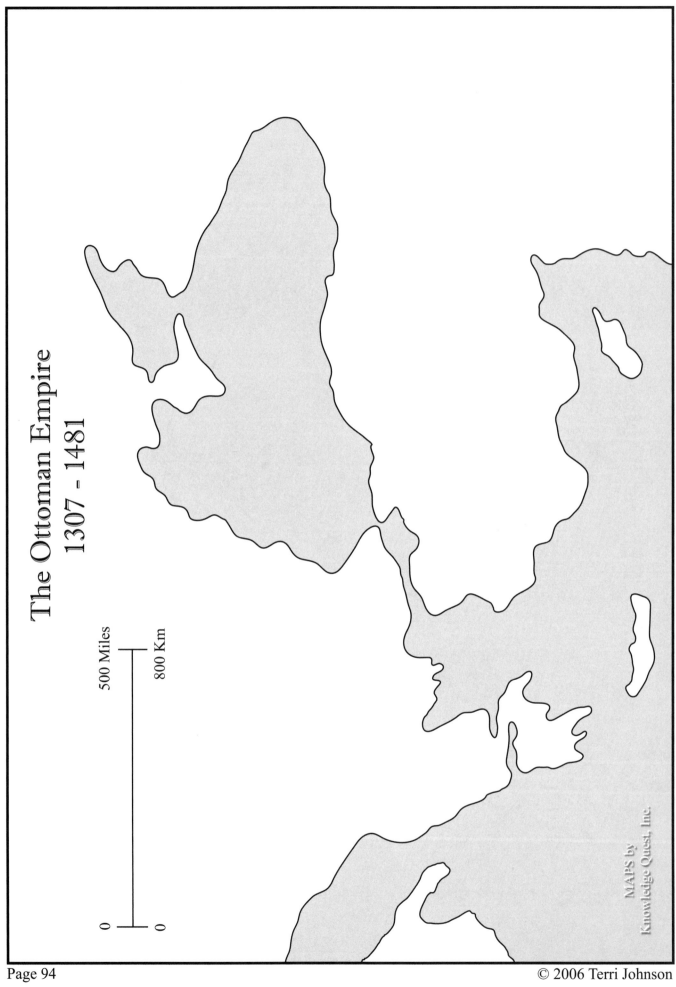

The Ottoman Empire
1307 – 1481

500 Miles

800 Km

MAPS by
Knowledge Quest, Inc.

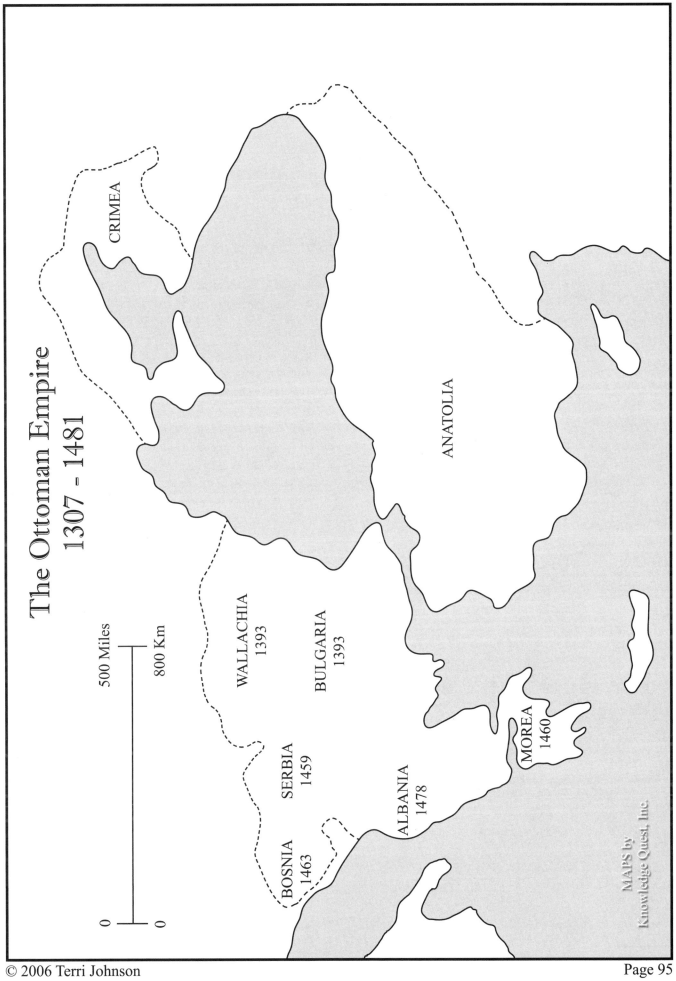

The Ottoman Empire
1307 - 1481

500 Miles

800 Km

CRIMEA

ANATOLIA

WALLACHIA
1393

BULGARIA
1393

SERBIA
1459

BOSNIA
1463

ALBANIA
1478

MOREA
1460

MAPS by
Knowledge Quest, Inc.

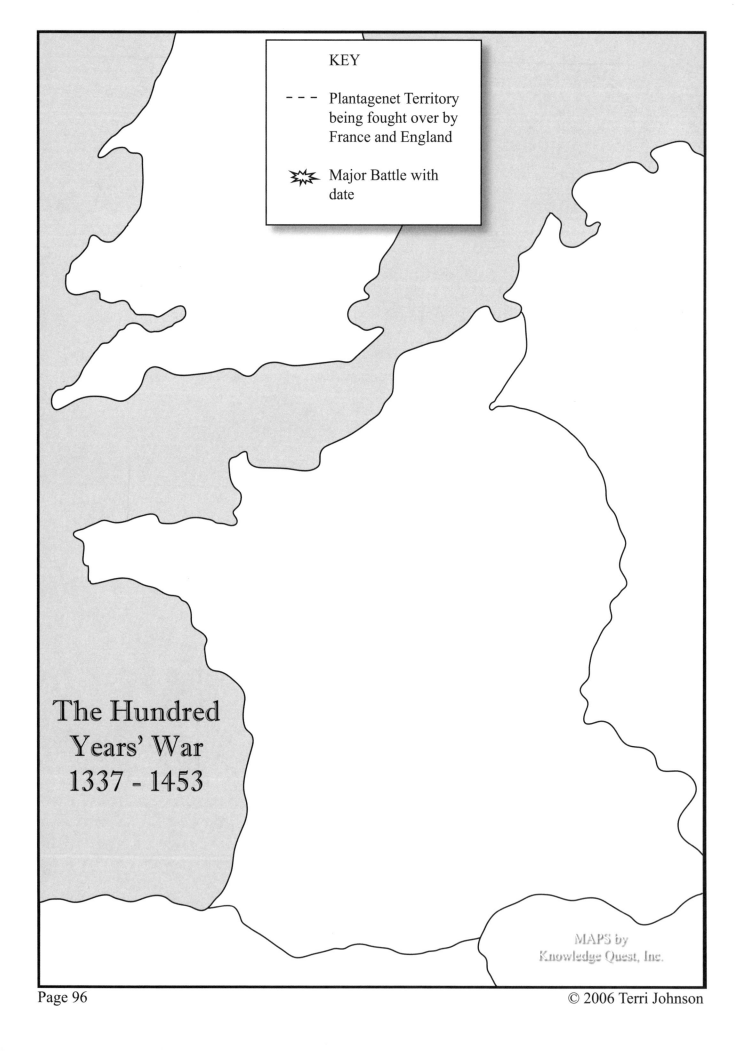

KEY

‐ ‐ ‐ Plantagenet Territory
being fought over by
France and England

Major Battle with
date

The Hundred
Years' War
1337 - 1453

MAPS by
Knowledge Quest, Inc.

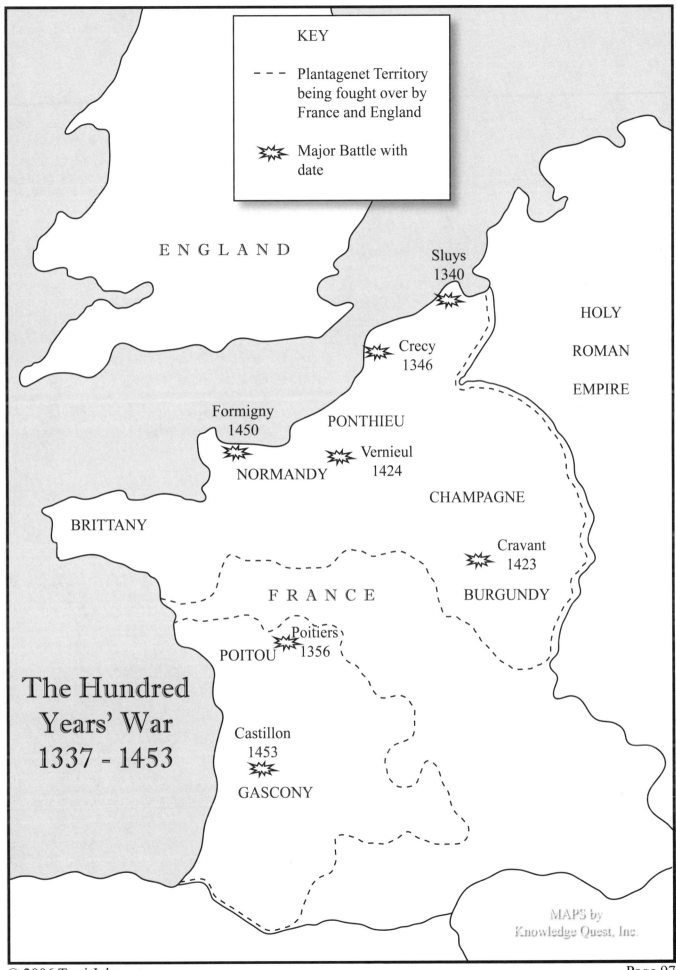

KEY

- - - Plantagenet Territory being fought over by France and England

Major Battle with date

ENGLAND

Sluys
1340

HOLY

ROMAN

EMPIRE

Crecy
1346

Formigny
1450

PONTHIEU

NORMANDY

Vernieul
1424

CHAMPAGNE

BRITTANY

Cravant
1423

FRANCE

BURGUNDY

Poitiers
1356

POITOU

The Hundred
Years' War
1337 - 1453

Castillon
1453

GASCONY

MAPS by
Knowledge Quest, Inc.

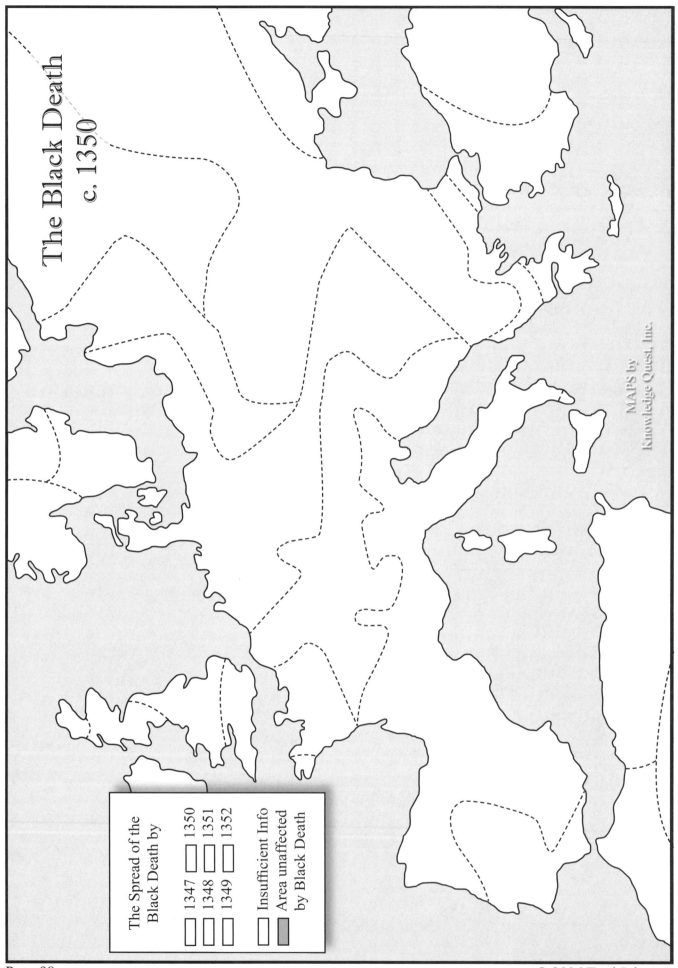

The Black Death
c. 1350

MAPS by
Knowledge Quest, Inc.

The Spread of the
Black Death by

☐ 1347   ☐ 1350
☐ 1348   ☐ 1351
☐ 1349   ☐ 1352

☐ Insufficient Info
▨ Area unaffected
   by Black Death

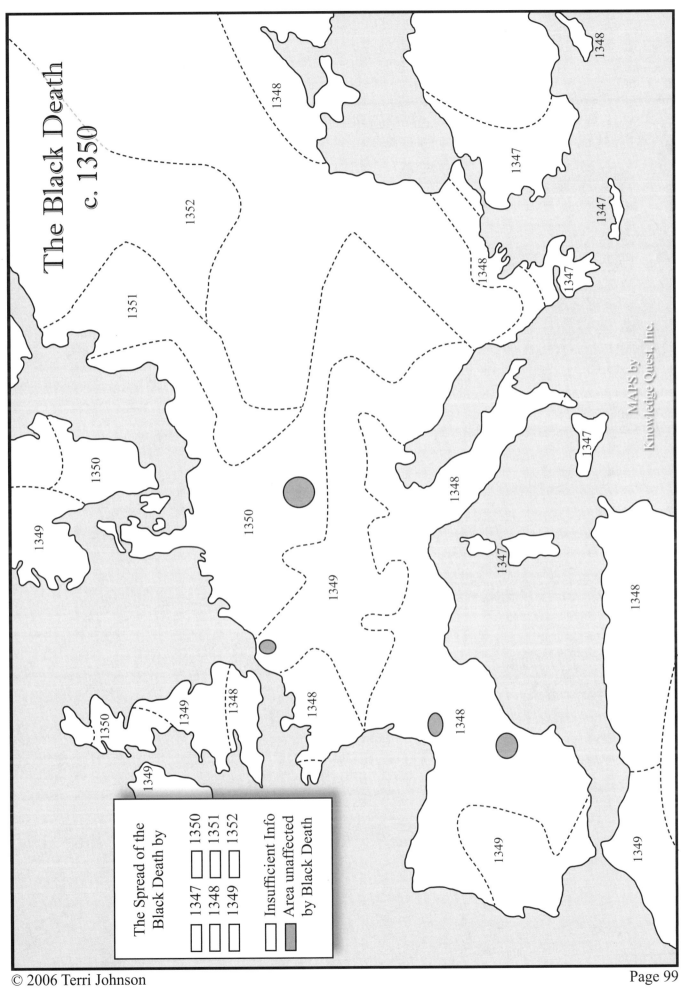

The Black Death c. 1350

The Spread of the Black Death by
1347 1350
1348 1351
1349 1352

Insufficient Info

Area unaffected by Black Death

MAPS by Knowledge Quest, Inc.

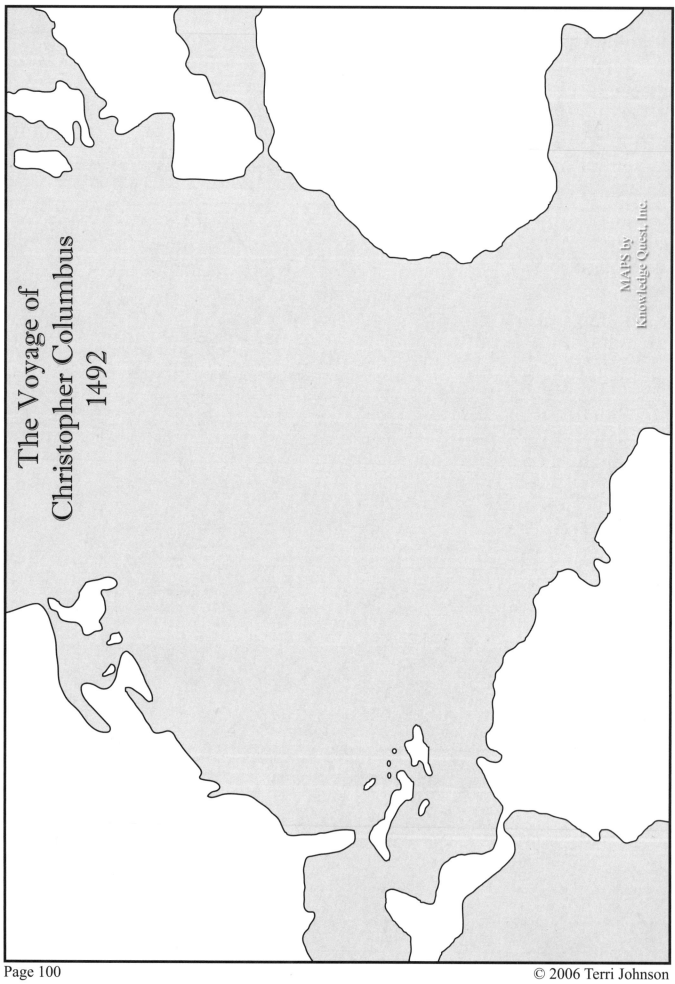

The Voyage of
Christopher Columbus
1492

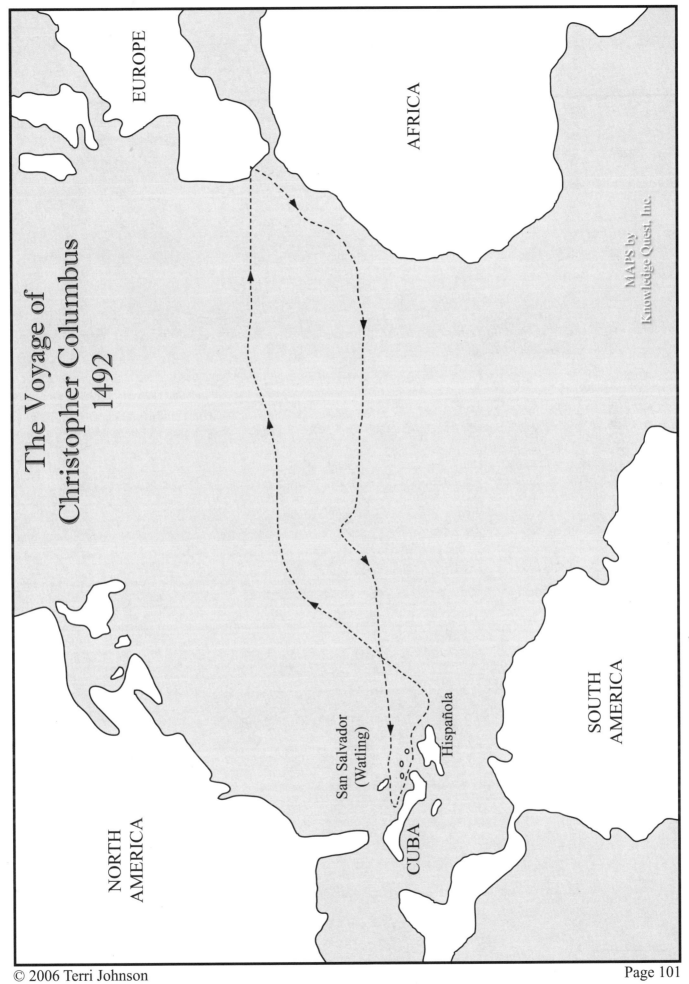

The Voyage of
Christopher Columbus
1492

EUROPE

AFRICA

NORTH
AMERICA

SOUTH
AMERICA

San Salvador
(Watling)

Hispañola

CUBA

MAPS by
Knowledge Quest, Inc.

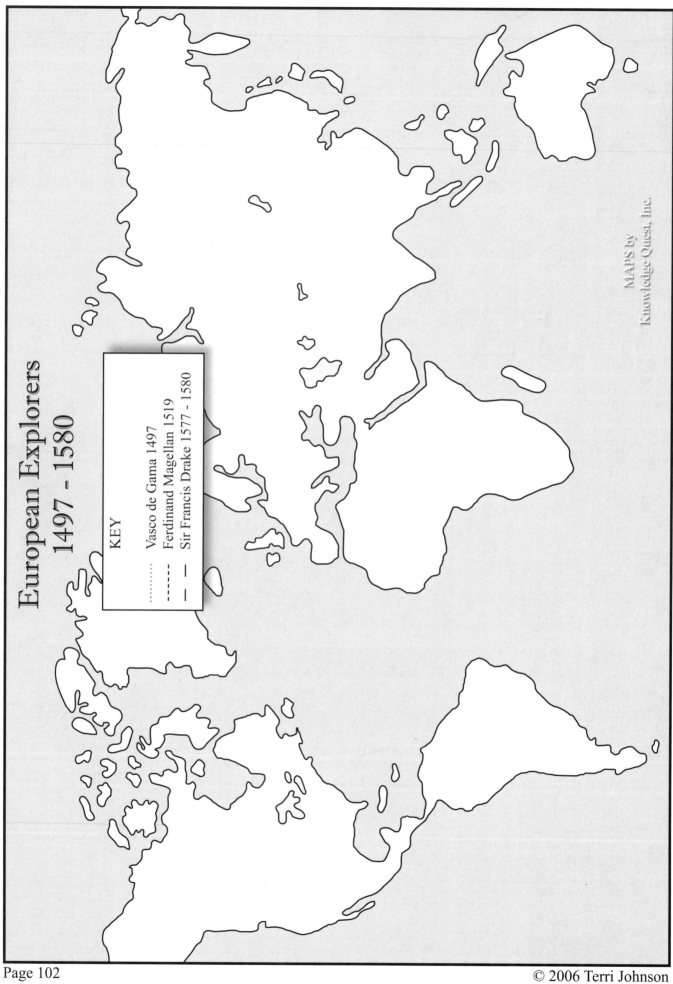

European Explorers
1497 - 1580

KEY

Vasco de Gama 1497
Ferdinand Magellan 1519
Sir Francis Drake 1577 - 1580

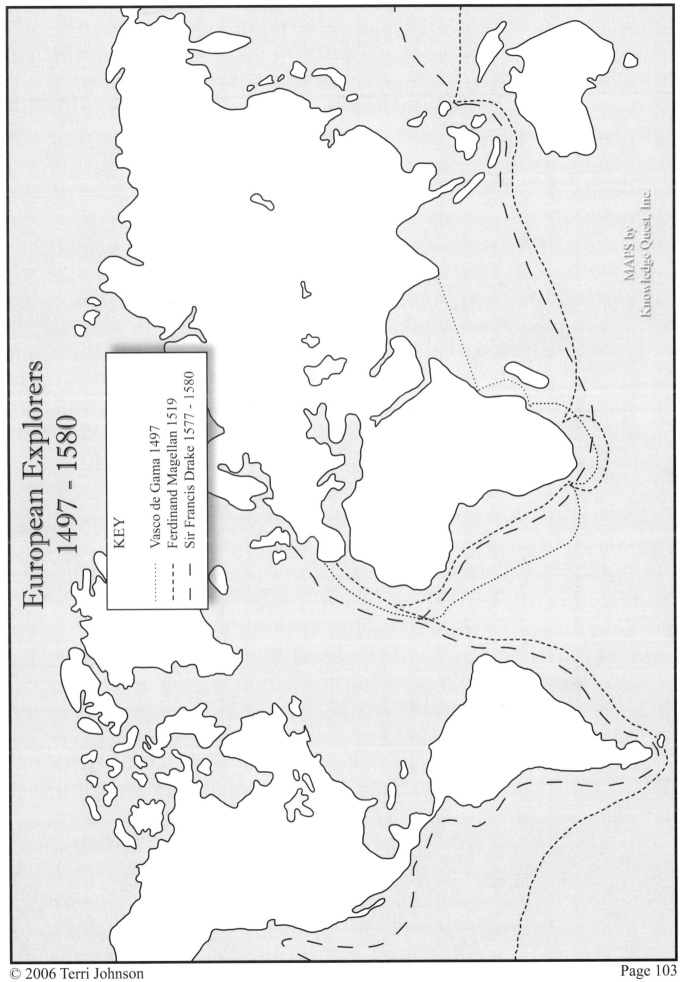

European Explorers
1497 - 1580

KEY

Vasco de Gama 1497
Ferdinand Magellan 1519
Sir Francis Drake 1577 - 1580

MAPS by
Knowledge Quest, Inc.

Renaissance Italy
c. 1500

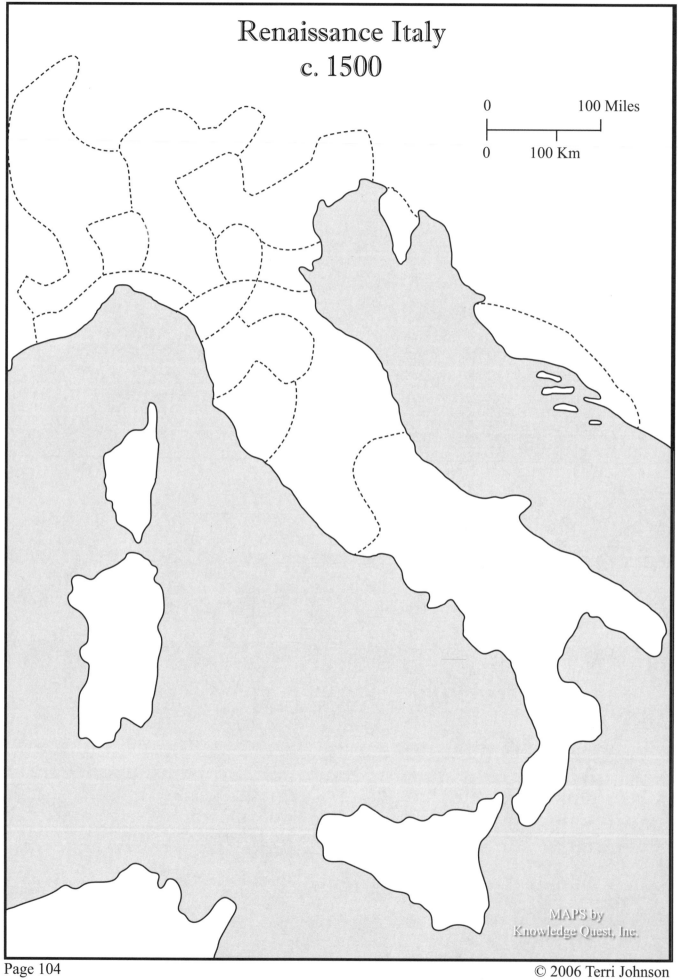

0   100 Miles

0   100 Km

MAPS by
Knowledge Quest, Inc.

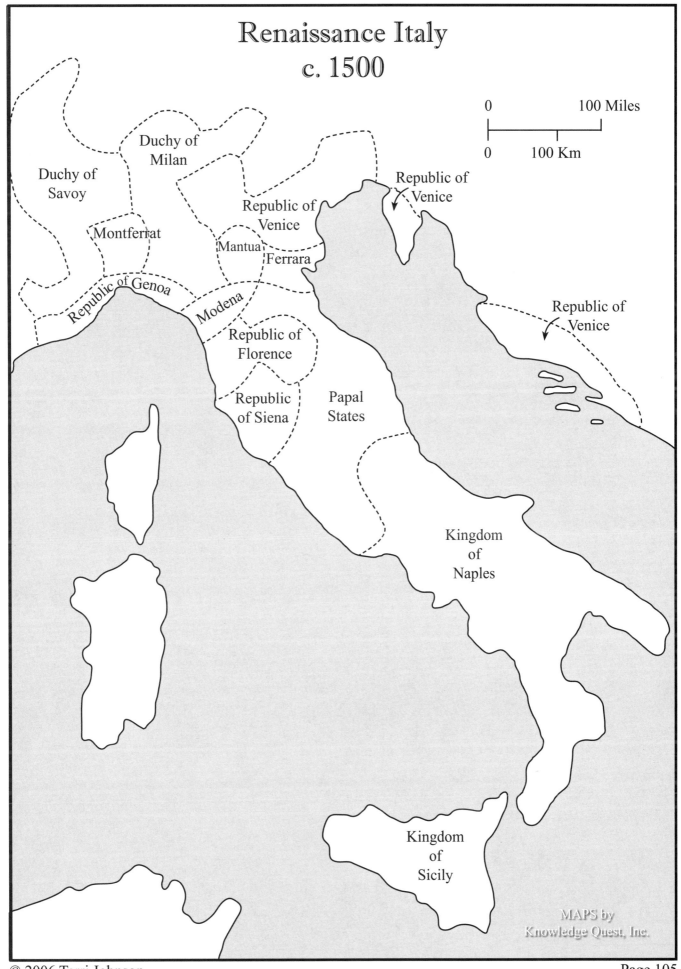

Renaissance Italy
c. 1500

0   100 Miles

0   100 Km

Duchy of
Milan

Duchy of
Savoy

Republic of
Venice

Montferrat

Republic of
Venice

Mantua

Ferrara

Republic of Genoa

Modena

Republic of
Florence

Republic of
Venice

Republic
of Siena

Papal
States

Kingdom
of
Naples

Kingdom
of
Sicily

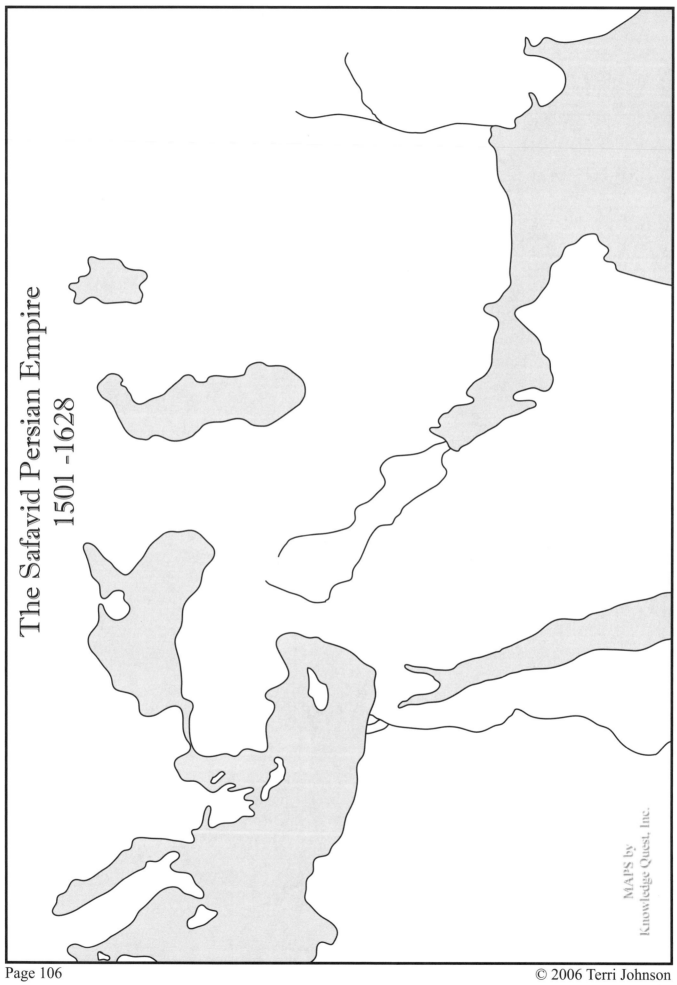

The Safavid Persian Empire
1501 -1628

MAPS by
Knowledge Quest, Inc.

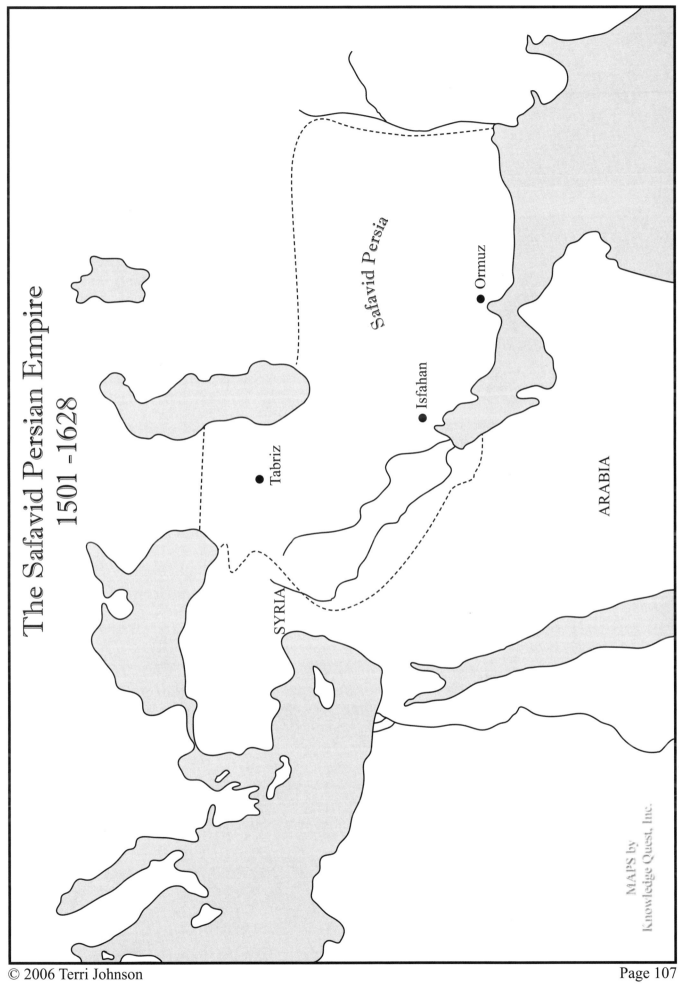

The Safavid Persian Empire 1501 -1628

Safavid Persia

Ormuz

Isfahan

Tabriz

SYRIA

ARABIA

The Powerful Habsburg
c. 1560

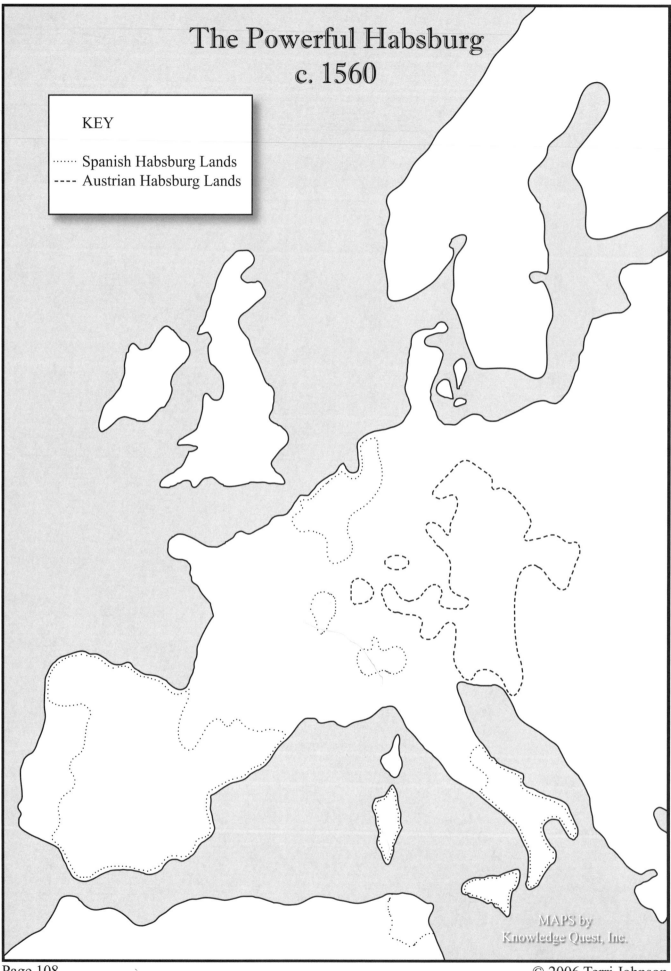

KEY

.... Spanish Habsburg Lands

‐‐‐‐ Austrian Habsburg Lands

MAPS by
Knowledge Quest, Inc.

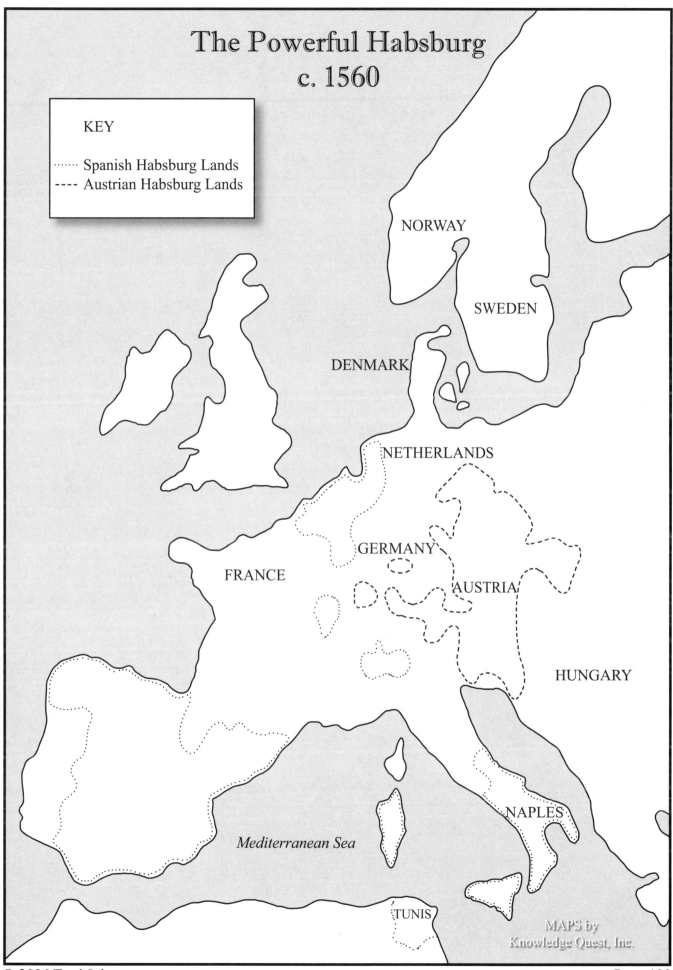

The Powerful Habsburg
c. 1560

KEY

.... Spanish Habsburg Lands

- - - - Austrian Habsburg Lands

NORWAY

SWEDEN

DENMARK

NETHERLANDS

GERMANY

FRANCE

AUSTRIA

HUNGARY

NAPLES

Mediterranean Sea

TUNIS

MAPS by
Knowledge Quest, Inc.

The New Ottoman Empire
c. 1566

500 Miles

800 Km

0

0

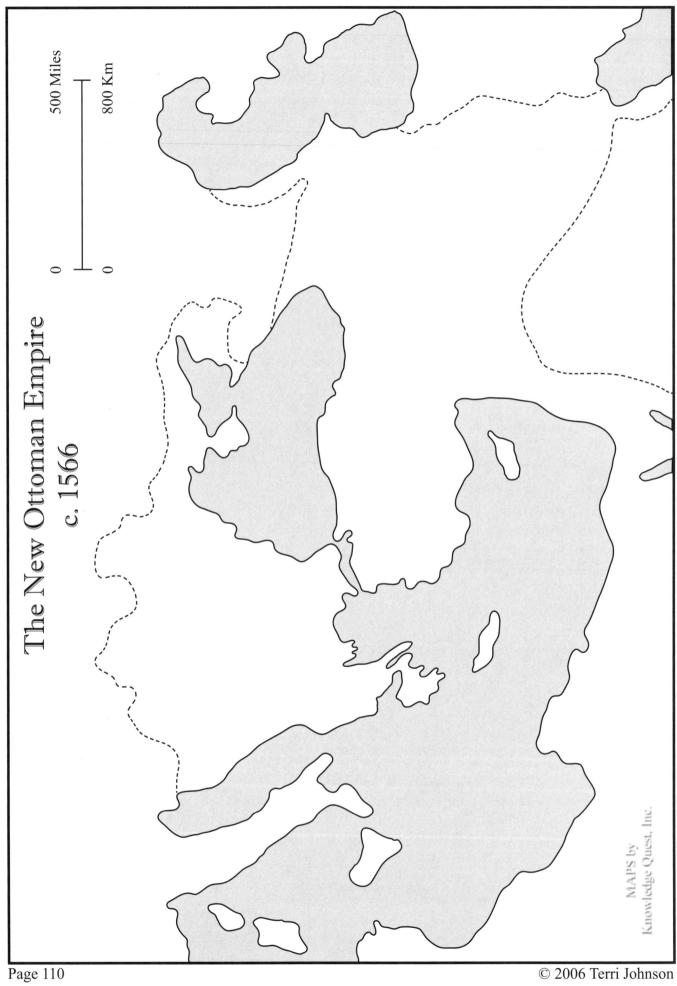

MAPS by
Knowledge Quest, Inc.

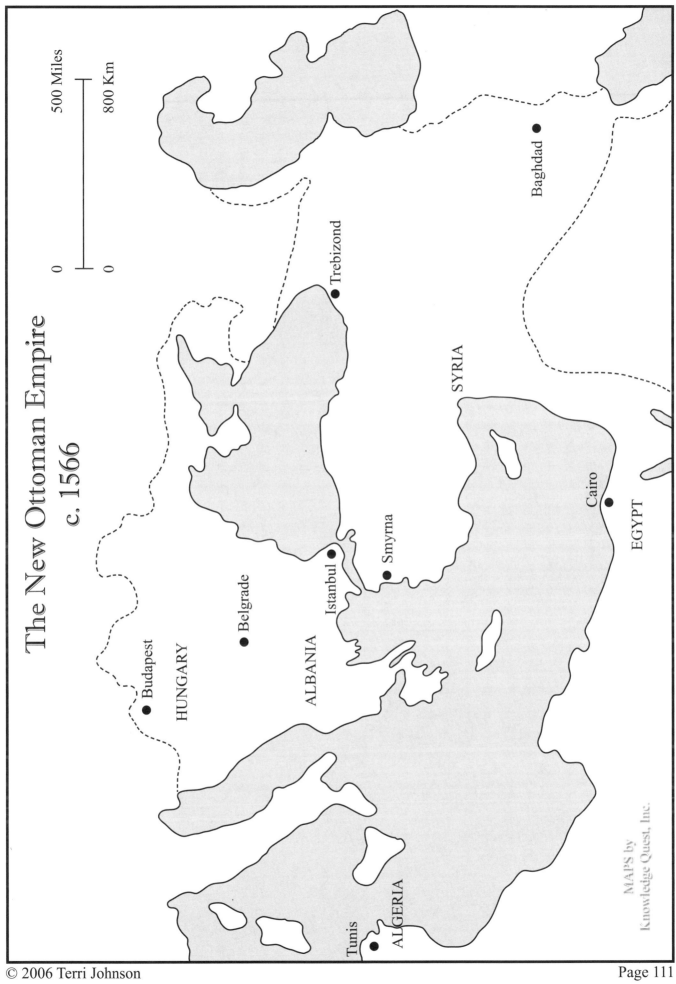

The New Ottoman Empire
c. 1566

500 Miles

800 Km

0

0

Baghdad

Trebizond

SYRIA

Smyrna

Istanbul

Belgrade

Budapest

HUNGARY

ALBANIA

Cairo

EGYPT

Tunis

ALGERIA

MAPS by
Knowledge Quest, Inc.

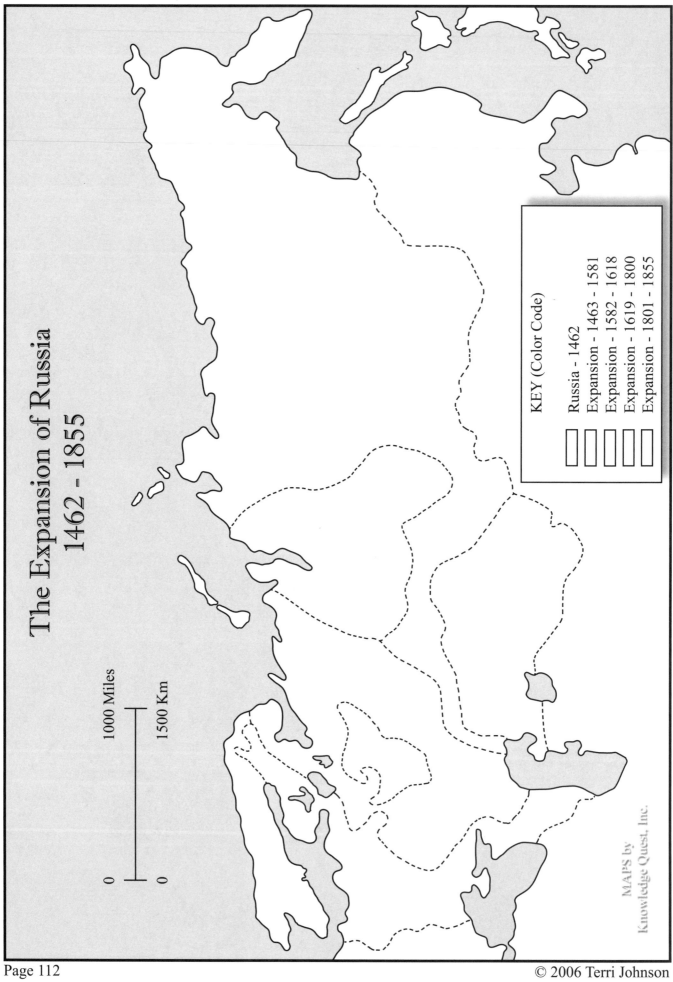

The Expansion of Russia
1462 - 1855

1000 Miles

1500 Km

0

0

KEY (Color Code)

Russia - 1462
Expansion - 1463 - 1581
Expansion - 1582 - 1618
Expansion - 1619 - 1800
Expansion - 1801 - 1855

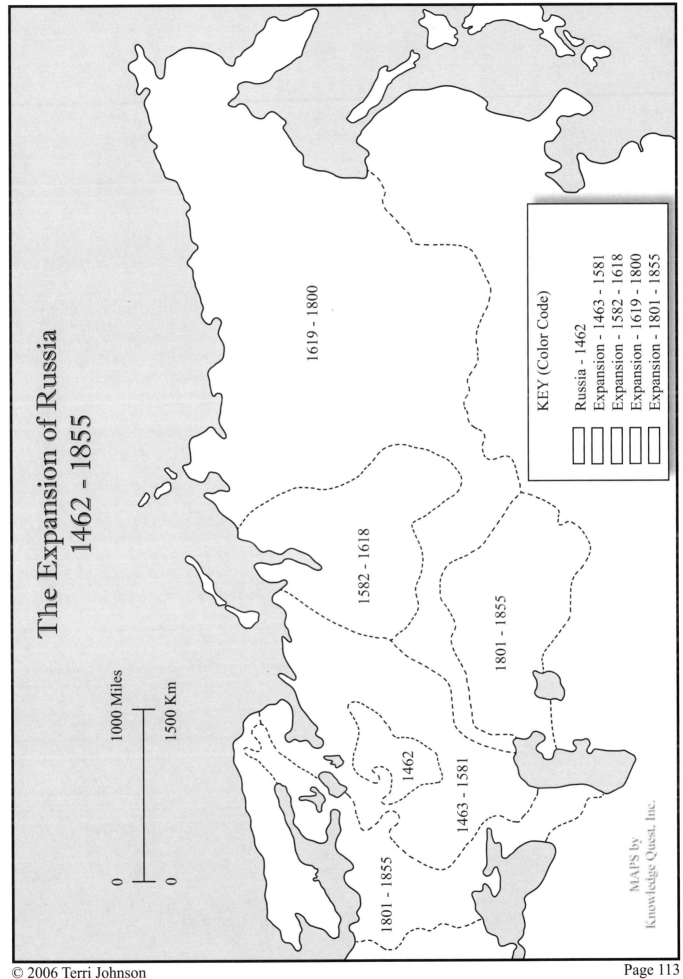

The Expansion of Russia
1462 - 1855

1000 Miles

1500 Km

1619 - 1800

1582 - 1618

1801 - 1855

1462

1463 - 1581

1801 - 1855

KEY (Color Code)

Russia - 1462
Expansion - 1463 - 1581
Expansion - 1582 - 1618
Expansion - 1619 - 1800
Expansion - 1801 - 1855

MAPS by
Knowledge Quest, Inc.

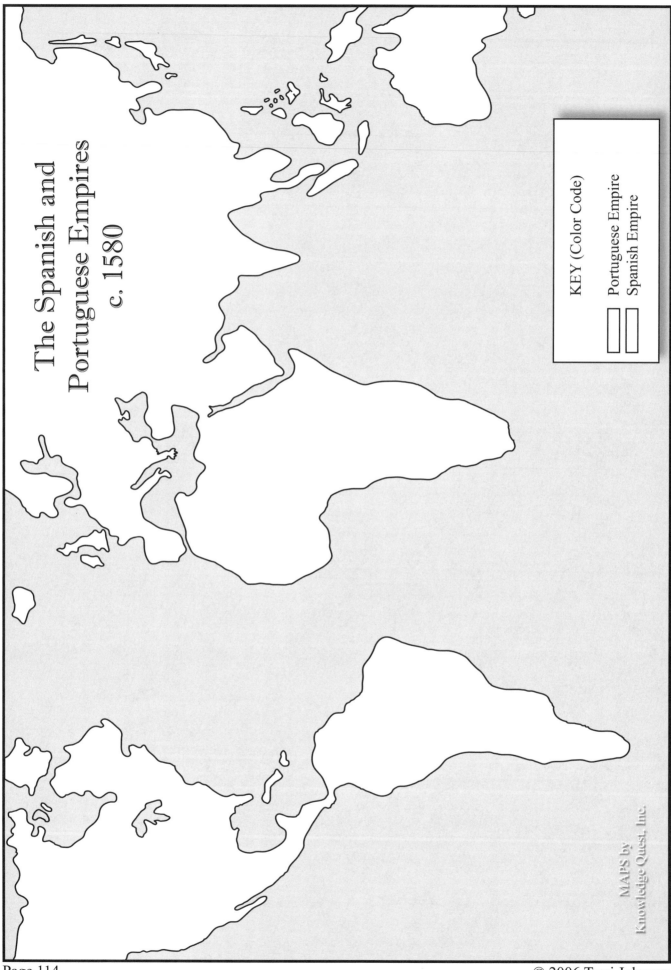

The Spanish and
Portuguese Empires
c. 1580

KEY (Color Code)

Portuguese Empire
Spanish Empire

MAPS by
Knowledge Quest, Inc.

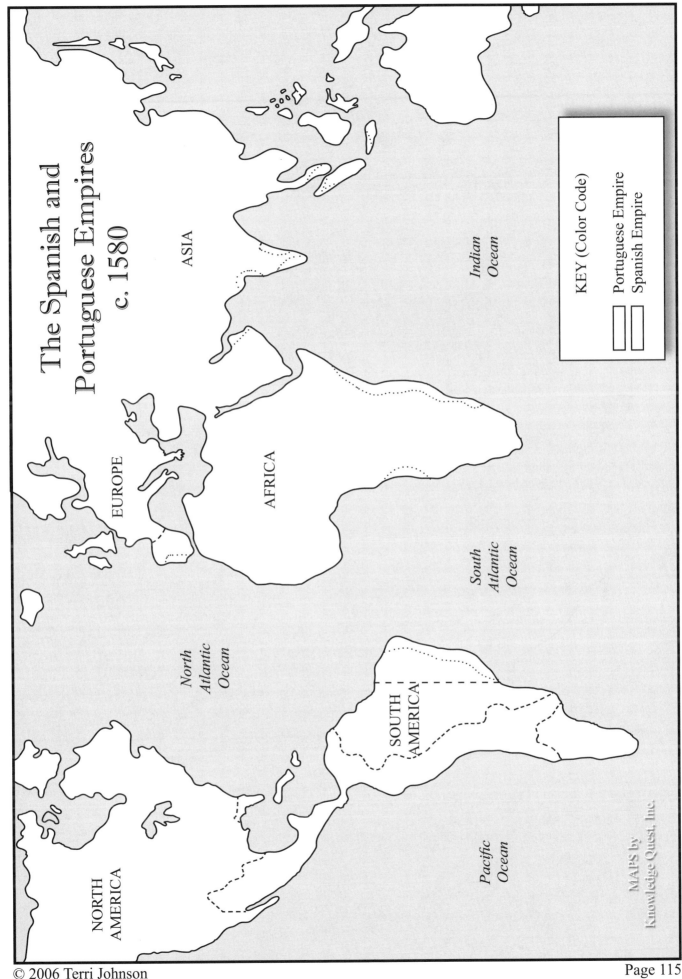

The Spanish and Portuguese Empires c. 1580

EUROPE

ASIA

AFRICA

NORTH AMERICA

SOUTH AMERICA

North Atlantic Ocean

South Atlantic Ocean

Indian Ocean

Pacific Ocean

KEY (Color Code)

Portuguese Empire
Spanish Empire

MAPS by
Knowledge Quest, Inc.

"The time for extracting a lesson from history is ever at hand for those who are wise.."

— Demosthenes

"Take hold of instruction; let her not go: keep her; for she is thy life."

— Proverbs 4:13

The New World
1600 - 1850

Lesson Plans

Discussion Questions:

1. **The Expansion of Russia – Page 125**
   - Label the country south of eastern Russia.
   - Label the two countries located on the peninsula northwest of Russia *(Sweden and Norway)*.
   - Color the Russian Empire by number *(date)* and then color-code your map key.
   - *Unlabeled map exercise: Label the countries surrounding Russia, including the islands on the right (east) side of your map. Label the four seas to the north of Russia (Barents, Kara, Laptev and East Siberian). Fill in the dates of expansion and then color by number.*

2. **African Exploitation – Page 127**
   - The Portuguese and Dutch primarily, as well as other countries, raided the African coasts for gold, slaves and other "valuables". The insert shows the area most heavily exploited.
   - Point to the Sahara Desert. What is a desert? Choose an appropriate color to fill in this area.
   - Label the island off the coast of Africa. Label the country on the east side of the Red Sea.
   - *Unlabeled map exercise: Label all bodies of water, including rivers. Label the Sahara desert and the places and people groups of the Benin region.*

3. **Native American Tribal Groups – Page 129**
   - Circle the Native American tribes which you have heard of and discuss why they are familiar to you.
   - If you live in the United States, find the tribes which used to *(or still)* live in your area and put a star by them.
   - Using a globe or wall map as your reference, label the five Great Lakes.
   - Label the country to the north of what is now the United States.
   - *Unlabeled map exercise: Label the locations of the Native American tribes when they first encountered European settlers.*

4. **Elizabethan London – Page 131**
   - Circle the names of places which are familiar to you or that you have heard about in books that you've read *(both fiction and nonfiction)*. Talk about why they are familiar to you *(ex: "I remember reading about Scotland Yard in my Sherlock Holmes book")*.
   - Find London on a larger map of England or on a globe.
   - *Unlabeled map exercise: Label the Thames River and the major landmarks of London. The Globe Theatre no longer exists, but record its location as well.*

5. The Reformation – Page 133

- Tell briefly what happened at Wittenberg. In which country is this city located?
- The dashed lines enclose the Protestant areas. Color them all one color.
- The solid lines enclose the Catholic regions *(most of Europe)*. Color this area all one color.
- The dotted line encircles the area in which lived both Catholics and Protestants. Color this small area with a combination of the two previous colors. Be creative.
- Color-code your key.
- *Unlabeled map exercise: Draw in the town of Wittenberg and label the major bodies of water on this map. Extra challenge: Label the larger countries of Europe. Use a globe for your reference or the map entitled, "Napoleon's Europe" on page 49.*

6. European Settlers in North America – Page 135

- Label the ocean through which Captain John Smith and his crew sailed, and later the Pilgrims on the Mayflower, to arrive at the New World.
- Before coloring your map, draw a picture or symbol at each settlement to remind you about who lived there and what happened there during its early years.
- *Unlabeled map exercise: Label the first three settlements in the New World. Label the three Great Lakes shown here and the mountain range. Approximately how long is Lake Erie?*

7. The Thirty Years' War – Page 137

- By referring to a globe, atlas or wall map, tell the modern day country in which this complex series of wars was fought.
- Draw a compass rose on your map with a minimum of the four main directional arrows *(N, S, E and W)*.
- Label the peninsula jutting up to the north just to the west of Sweden's southern tip.
- Label the island to the west of England *(hint: only a fraction of it is shown on this map)*.
- *Unlabeled map exercise: Label the significant battles of the Thirty Years' War. Label the countries surrounding Germany.*

8. Central and South American Colonization – Page 139

- Color lightly with yellow the three largest native civilizations shown on this map *(Maya, Aztec and Inca)*.
- Choose two more colors and again color lightly the colonies of the Spanish and Portuguese. Your coloring will begin to overlap the native empires, as did the European colonies when they settled and conquered in these regions.
- What is the equator? Find it on a globe.
- *Unlabeled map exercise: Label the Aztec, Maya and Inca Empires. Label the rivers and larger bodies of water surrounding Central and South America. Label Cape Horn at the southernmost tip of the continent.*

9. Republic of the United Netherlands – Page 141

- In 1550, the 17 provinces of the Netherlands were part of the Spanish Habsburg dynasty. Find Spain on a globe or wall map and then color the dotted region on your map in red.
- In 1581, after the Dutch Revolt, the seven northern provinces (the area north of the dashed line) declared themselves independent from Spain.
- By 1648, Spain finally recognized the Republic of the United Netherlands as an independent country. Color this northern section in purple or blue.
- *Unlabeled map exercise: Label the Holy Roman Empire and other surrounding countries. Label the rivers shown here and the sea to the northeast. Draw in and label the main cities in and near the Netherlands.*

10. Australia Discovered – Page 143

- Using an atlas or globe, label as many islands as you can.
- What ocean is this?
- One of the explorers named an island after himself. Who was it and which island did he name?
- *Unlabeled map exercise: Label Australia and all of the larger islands surrounding this island continent (include Sumatra, Java, Borneo, Celebes, the Philippines, New Guinea, and New Zealand). Label the large country to the northwest (China).*

11. The Expansion of Sweden – Page 145

- Color the area marked "Sweden" enclosed by solid lines in a color of your choice.
- The dotted lines show the area of Sweden's boundaries at its greatest extent. Color all of these areas with a different color.
- Much of the water shown on this map freezes over during the winter months. Color this water an icy blue.
- *Unlabeled map exercise: Label Sweden and the other countries shown here. Label the Baltic, North, Norwegian and Barents Seas.*

12. The Ming and Qing Dynasties of China – Page 147

- Using a ruler, make your own scale: 2" = 800 miles or 1,200 kilometers.
- Label the country to the north of China. Label the island kingdom to the east.
- Find Mt. Everest on a map or globe. Label its approximate location on this map.
- Color by number *(date)* and then color-code your key.
- *Unlabeled map exercise: Label the provinces of China at this time. Fill in the dates of expansion and color-code your map and key. Label the bodies of water and islands off the coast of China.*

13. The Mughal Empire – Page 149

- Draw a compass rose. Make this one more complex by added in four more directional symbols: NW, NE, SW and SE.
- Using an atlas or globe, find the country to the NE of India and label it.

- What is the name of the sea to the west of India?
- *Unlabeled map exercise: Draw the boundary lines of the Mughal Empire. Label the rivers and locate the four main cities. Label the island off the coast of India.*

14. The Isolated Kingdom of Japan – Page 151

- Using an atlas or a globe, find the sea to the west of Japan.
- Label the four main islands of Japan *(from top to bottom: Hokkaido, Honshu, Shikoku and Kyushu).*
- Using the scale as your guide, what is the approximate distance across the widest section of Hokkaido?
- *Unlabeled map exercise: Locate and label the five populous cities of Japan at this time. Label the bodies of water surrounding Japan.*

15. The Original 13 Colonies – Page 153

- Label the ocean and the three Great Lakes shown here.
- Draw in the Appalachian Mountain range.
- *Unlabeled map exercise: Label the 13 colonies of the new world.*

16. The Seven Years' War – Page 155

- Color the French territory in yellow, the British lands in red and the Spanish possessions in blue. This was how the land was divided before the Seven Years' War.
- Find the Mississippi River and lightly color red from the eastern edge of the river to the Atlantic coast, and lightly color blue from its western edge to the Pacific coast. This is how the land became divided after the war. The French had been squeezed out.
- The land to the south of the Ohio River was reserved as Indian Territory. Refer back to your map entitled "Native American Tribal Groups." How do you think this arrangement was accepted by the Native Americans?
- *Unlabeled map exercise: Label the six major rivers shown here. Label New France, Louisiana, Florida and the Thirteen Colonies. Label at least three bodies of water. Draw in Lake Thunder in Canada. (Just north of Lake Superior - refer to page 41)*

17. The American Revolution – Page 157

- Label the mountain range and the two Great Lakes.
- Using an atlas or a globe as needed, label the states using their two-letter abbreviations *(i.e.: Massachusetts = MA).*
- *Unlabeled map exercise: Label at least 10 major battles from the American Revolution.*

18. The French Revolution – Page 159

- Label the countries surrounding France. *(The Netherlands, Germany, Spain and England)* Label the Mediterranean Sea, the Bay of Biscay and the English Channel.
- Using a globe or atlas as your reference, draw the Seine River which flows through Paris.

- *Unlabeled map exercise: Locate the two towns of counter-revolutionary resistance and at least 10 towns ruled by revolutionary committees. Draw the Pyrenees Mountains at the southern border of France.*

19. Westward Expansion in the U.S. – Page 161

- Using a blue pencil or marker, trace over the three large rivers. Label the one that is not labeled *(St. Lawrence River)*.
- Label the two Great Lakes that have not been labeled on this map. Label the island of Cuba to the south of Florida.
- *Unlabeled map exercise: Label the Louisiana Purchase, Spanish Territory and Oregon Country. Label the Mississippi River which was the western boundary of the United States at that time.*

20. Napoleon's Europe – Page 163

- Label the three larger islands in the Mediterranean Sea. The three small islands off the coast of Spain are together known as the Balearic Islands. Label them.
- The areas enclosed by the dashes were under Napoleon's control. Was the island of Corsica controlled by Napoleon? How about the other islands in the Mediterranean? Was England under Napoleon's control? How about Denmark? Portugal?
- Label the island to the west of England.
- *Unlabeled map exercise: Label the Empires and countries of Europe at this time in history. Locate and label the Battle of Waterloo.*

21. Independence for Latin America – Page 165

- Label the two oceans on either side of South America.
- Which country is to the north of Mexico?
- Using an atlas or globe, find the countries whose names have changed and circle them. Draw in the equator.
- *Unlabeled map exercise: Label the countries of South America at this time in history.*

22. Slave vs. Free States – Page 167

- Label as many states as you can without looking at an atlas or globe *(use two letter abbreviations)*. Consult an atlas for the rest.
- Using similar colors *(red, orange, yellow, for example)*, color in the slave states and territories. Using different yet similar colors *(perhaps blues and greens)*, color in the free states and territories.
- *Unlabeled map exercise: Label the Northwest and Spanish Territories. Label all bodies of water shown on this map.*

23. Britain's Industrial Revolution – Page 169

- Color in the areas of heavy industrialization in one color.
- Referring to a history encyclopedia, list neatly on the front or back of your map the main products which England was manufacturing at this time.

- *Unlabeled map exercise: Label England, Wales and Scotland on your map in all capital letters. Locate and label at least 10 major industrial cities of Great Britain.*

24. Trails of Settlement and Exploration – Page 171
- Trace the five main trails with five different colors.
- Color-code your key.
- Label the two mountain ranges.
- *Unlabeled map exercise: Identify the cities shown here. Label the countries to the north and south of the United States. Label all bodies of water and mountain ranges.*

25. Goldrush in California – Page 173
- Trace the two sea routes in two different colors.
- Draw the most direct land route across the United States from New York to Sutter's Fort. This land route could take travelers anywhere from three to six months to reach their destination.
- Next to each route, record the approximate length of time it might take a 49er to complete the journey.
- *(Optional: Based on what you know about these three travel routes, decide which one you think is the best choice – safest, shortest, easiest – and trace over it with glue and sprinkle gold glitter on it.)*
- *Unlabeled map exercise: Label the countries and continents shown on this map. Locate and label the three major cities involved in the transportation of prospective miners to the gold fields. Label the site where gold was first discovered.*

Glossary of Terms Used

Atlas – a book containing a collection of maps.

Catholic – of the original Christian Church before the division - Orthodox.

Colony – a land or place settled by people from another country.

Compass Rose – a directional symbol on a chart used for navigation.

Desert – a large area of land where there is very little water and plants do not grow.

Empire – a kingdom which has been extended by military might to include countries which were originally independent.

Equator – the Earth's great line of latitude which divides the northern and southern hemispheres.

Expansion – to make larger or to increase.

Exploitation – to receive unjust profit from.

Explorer – one who travels through an unknown or little known region.

Globe – a spherical model of the earth or heavens.

Industrialization – the change from domestic industry to the factory system.

Island – a piece of land, smaller than a continent, entirely surrounded by water.

Kilometer – a unit of distance measurement equaling 1,000 meters.

Mile – a unit of distance measurement equaling 1,760 yards.

Ocean – the large bodies of salt water which comprise the majority (over ⅔) of the earth's surface.

Peninsula – a finger of land surrounded by sea on three sides.

Pilgrim – a person who makes a journey for religious purposes.

Protestant – a member of any Christian body which separated from the Catholic Church during or since the Reformation.

Province – the parts of a country beyond the capital.

Route – a course of travel, especially between two distant points.

Settlement – a place where travelers take up permanent residence.

Scale – a line on a map with marks dividing it to show proportional distance.

Tribe – a community of many families preserving its own customs and beliefs.

Geographical Regions Covered

London	Thames River	England	Ohio River
Denmark	Corsica	Mediterranean	Norway
Atlantic Ocean	Pacific Ocean	Newfoundland	China
Appalachian Mts.	Mississippi River	Sahara Desert	Sweden
North Sea	Mt. Everest	St. Lawrence R.	Red Sea
Estonia	Germany	Tasmania	Netherlands
Holland	Japan	India	Russia
Maya	Aztec	Inca	Australia
Great Lakes	Spain	United States	Portugal
Africa	California	S. America	Central Am.

Teacher or parent, you may choose to use these terms and geographical regions listed to put together an end of the year quiz. However, if you follow the lesson plans throughout the year, you may not feel that this is necessary.

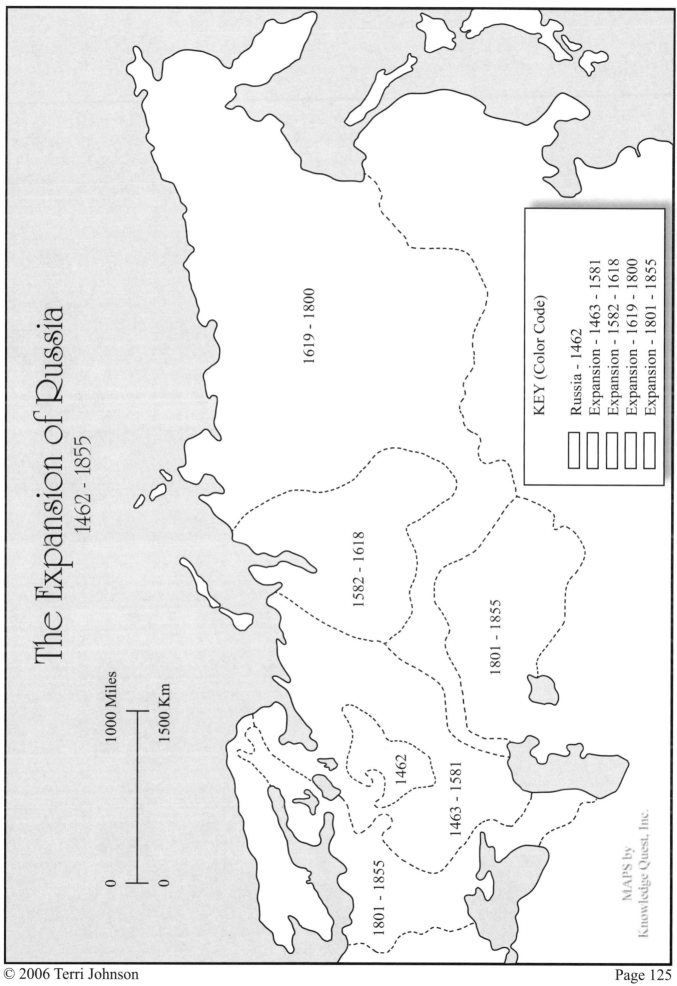

The Expansion of Russia
1462 - 1855

1000 Miles

1500 Km

1619 - 1800

1582 - 1618

1801 - 1855

1462

1463 - 1581

1801 - 1855

KEY (Color Code)

Russia - 1462
Expansion - 1463 - 1581
Expansion - 1582 - 1618
Expansion - 1619 - 1800
Expansion - 1801 - 1855

MAPS by
Knowledge Quest, Inc.

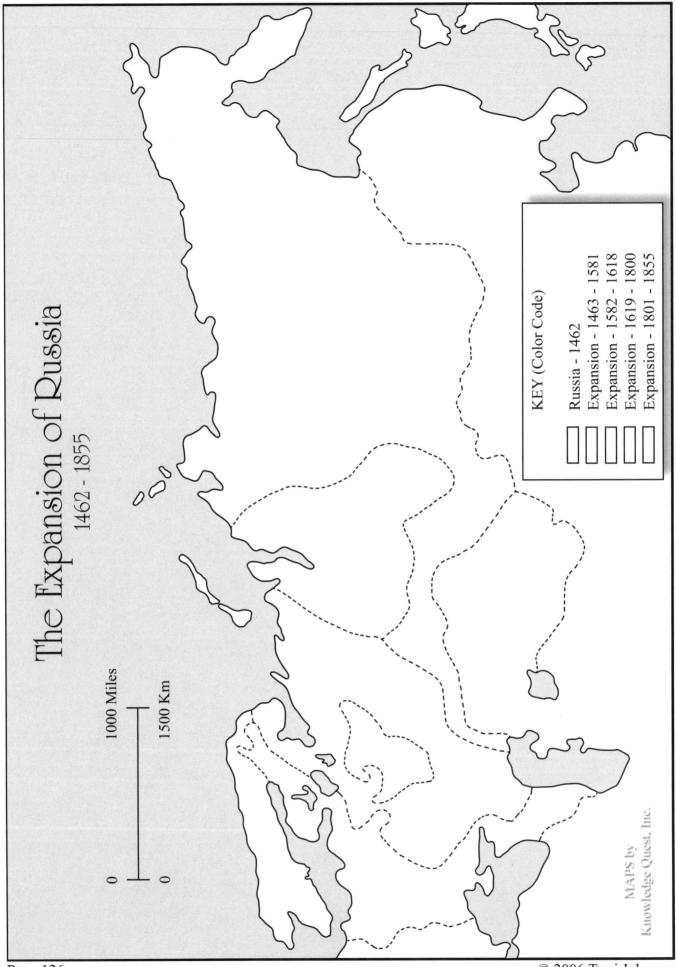

The Expansion of Russia
1462 - 1855

1000 Miles

1500 Km

0

0

KEY (Color Code)

Russia - 1462
Expansion - 1463 - 1581
Expansion - 1582 - 1618
Expansion - 1619 - 1800
Expansion - 1801 - 1855

MAPS by
Knowledge Quest, Inc.

Page 126

© 2006 Terri Johnson

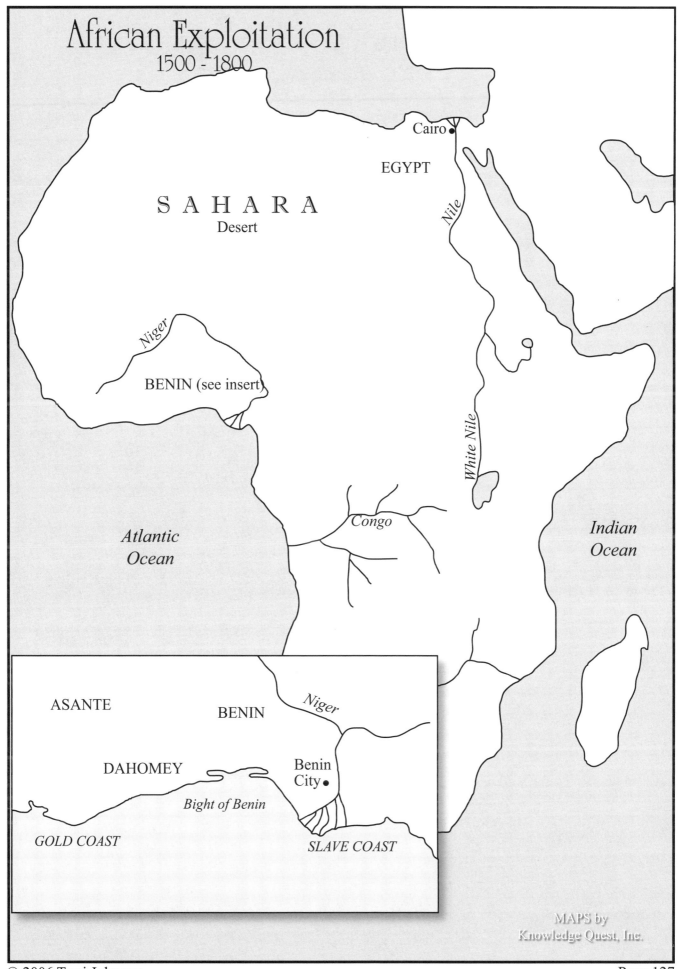

African Exploitation
1500 - 1800

Cairo

EGYPT

S A H A R A
Desert

Nile

Niger

BENIN (see insert)

White Nile

Congo

Atlantic
Ocean

Indian
Ocean

ASANTE

BENIN

Niger

DAHOMEY

Benin
City

Bight of Benin

GOLD COAST

SLAVE COAST

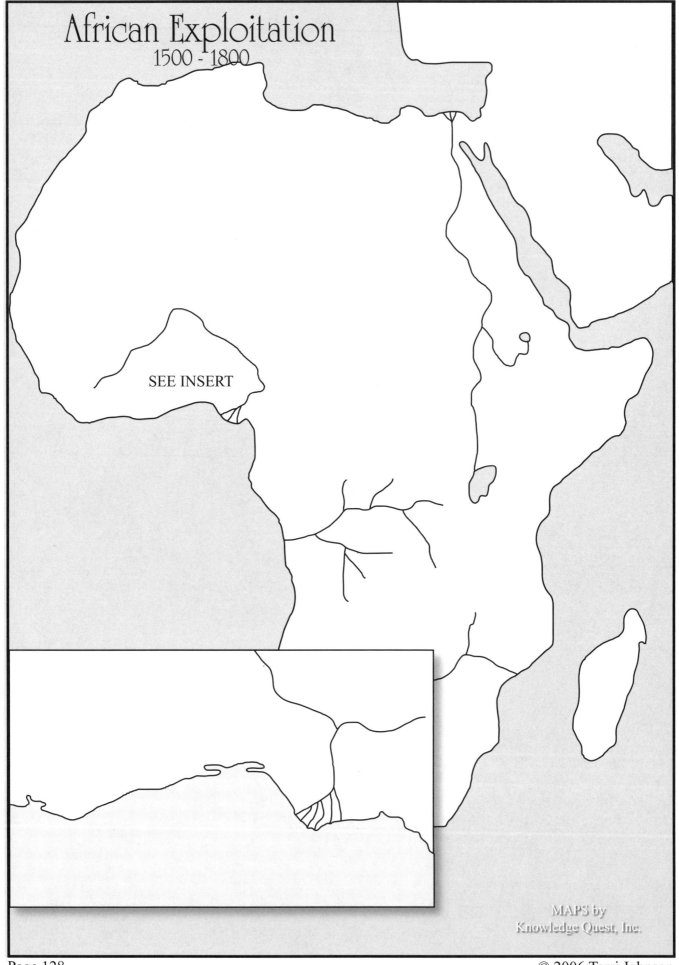

African Exploitation
1500 - 1800

SEE INSERT

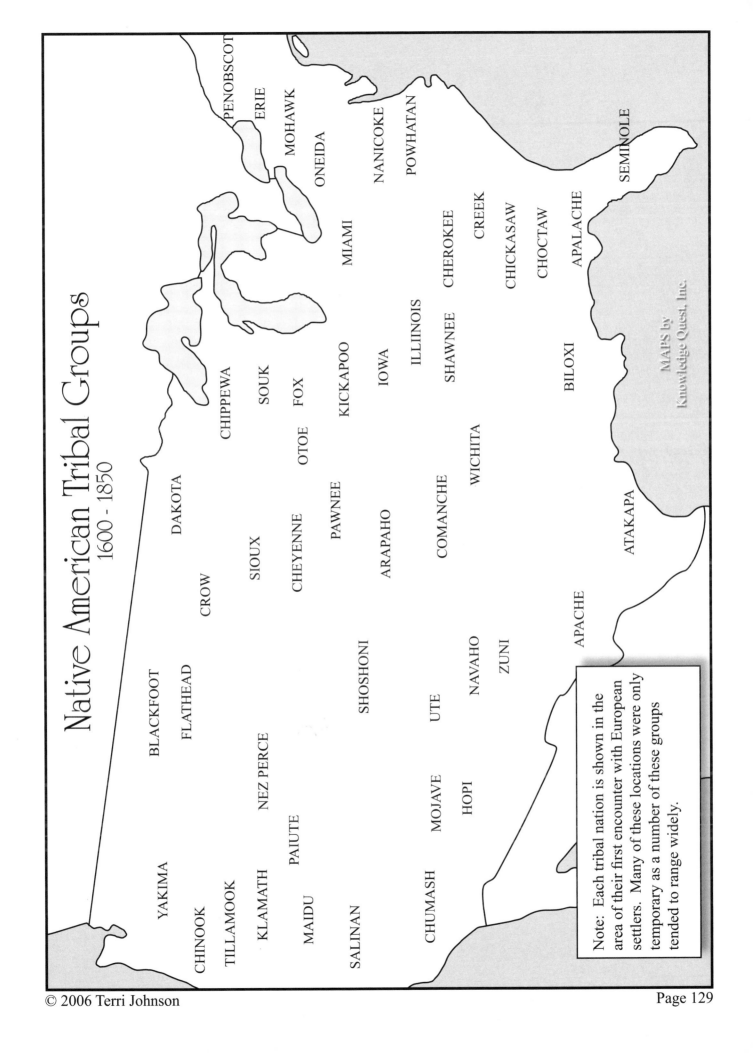

Native American Tribal Groups
1600 - 1850

PENOBSCOT
ERIE
MOHAWK
ONEIDA
NANICOKE
POWHATAN
SEMINOLE

CREEK
CHEROKEE
CHICKASAW
CHOCTAW
APALACHE

MIAMI

CHIPPEWA
SOUK
FOX
OTOE
KICKAPOO
IOWA
ILLIINOIS
SHAWNEE
WICHITA
BILOXI

DAKOTA
SIOUX
CHEYENNE
PAWNEE
ARAPAHO
COMANCHE
ATAKAPA

CROW
SHOSHONI
UTE
NAVAHO
ZUNI
APACHE

BLACKFOOT
FLATHEAD
NEZ PERCE
PAIUTE
MOJAVE
HOPI

YAKIMA
CHINOOK
TILLAMOOK
KLAMATH
MAIDU
SALINAN
CHUMASH

MAPS by
Knowledge Quest, Inc.

Note: Each tribal nation is shown in the area of their first encounter with European settlers. Many of these locations were only temporary as a number of these groups tended to range widely.

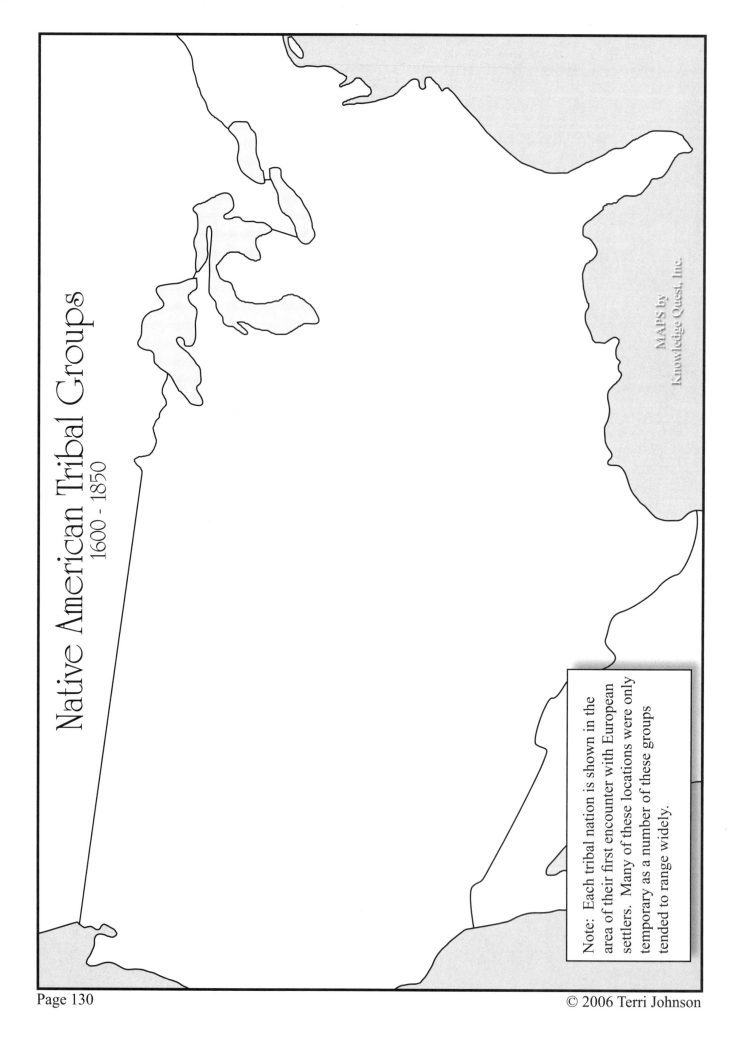

Native American Tribal Groups
1600 - 1850

MAPS by
Knowledge Quest, Inc.

Note: Each tribal nation is shown in the area of their first encounter with European settlers. Many of these locations were only temporary as a number of these groups tended to range widely.

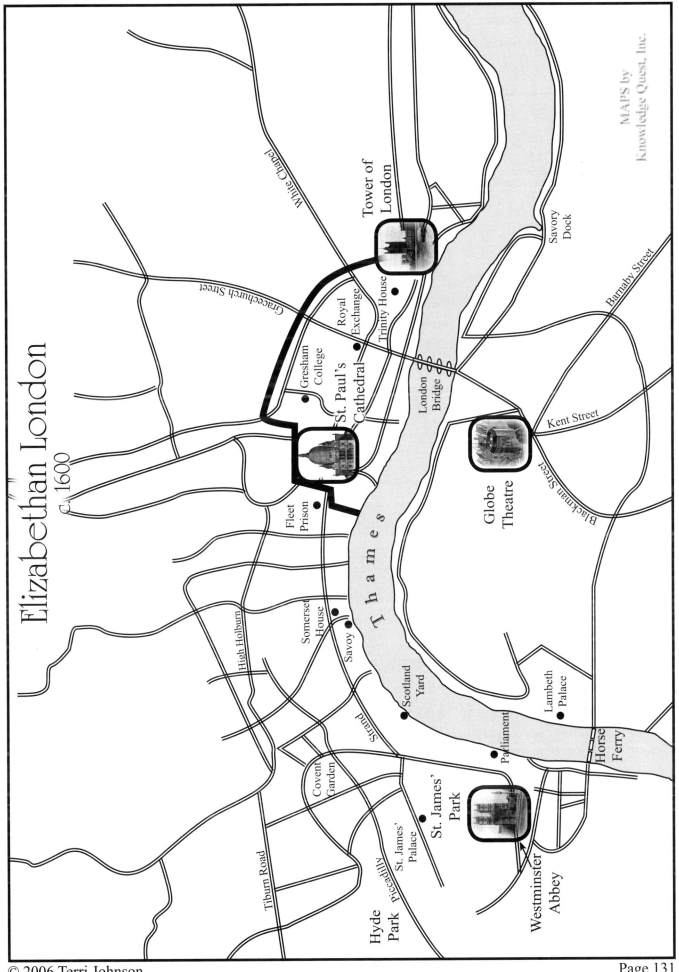

Elizabethan London
c. 1600

Tower of London

White Chapel

Gracechurch Street

Royal Exchange

Trinity House

Gresham College

St. Paul's Cathedral

Fleet Prison

Globe Theatre

Kent Street

Barnaby Street

Savory Dock

Blackman Street

Thames

London Bridge

High Holburn

Somerset House

Savoy

Scotland Yard

Lambeth Palace

Strand

Covent Garden

Parliament

Horse Ferry

Tiburn Road

Piccadilly

St. James' Palace

St. James' Park

Westminster Abbey

Hyde Park

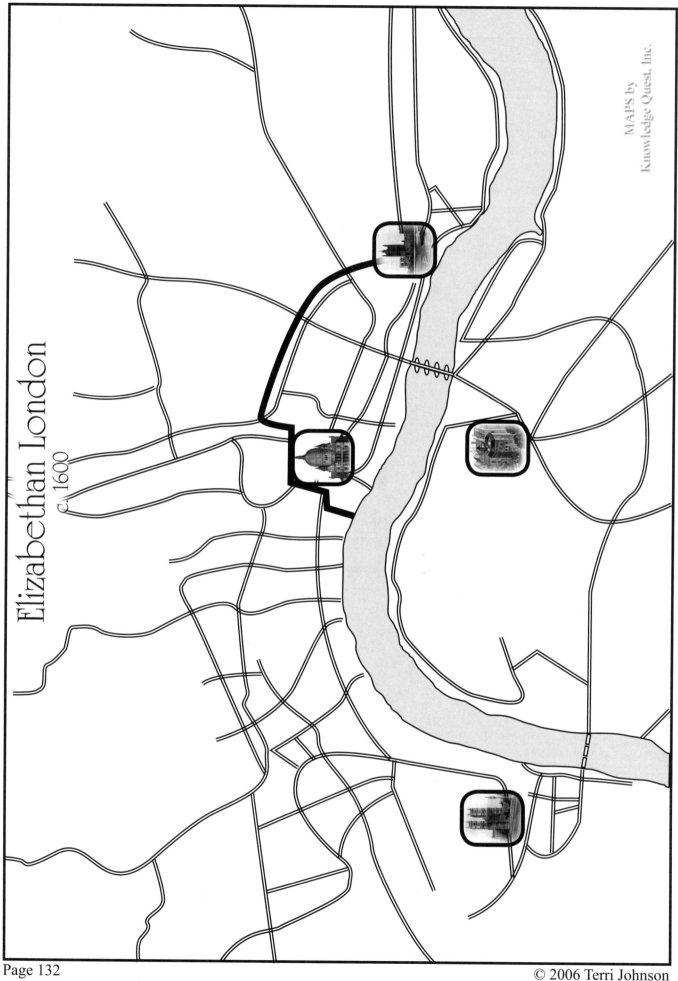

Elizabethan London
c. 1600

MAPS by
Knowledge Quest, Inc.

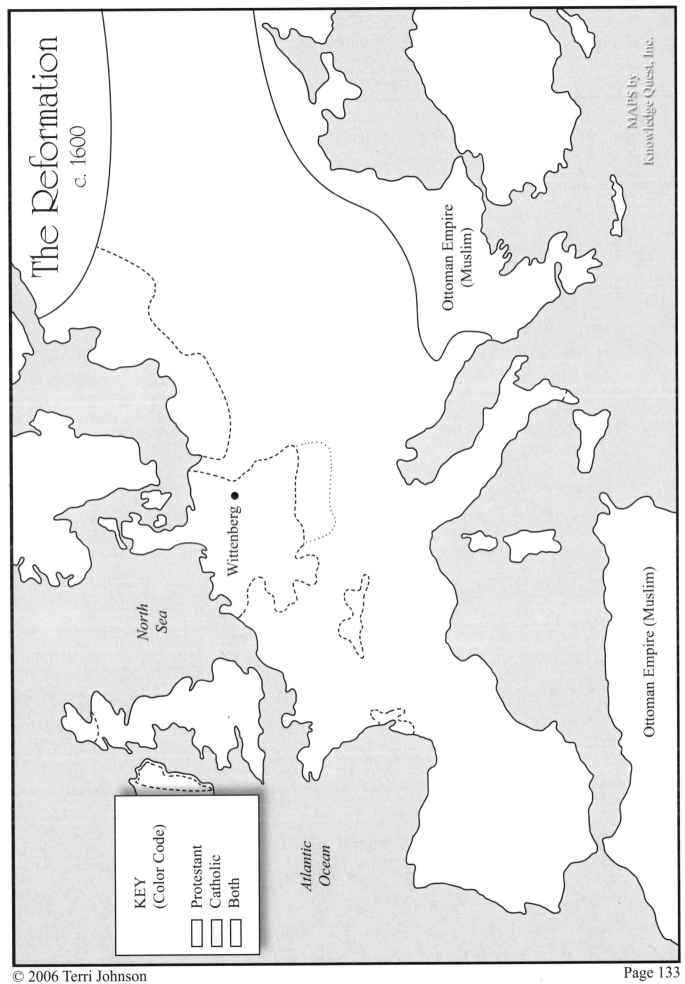

The Reformation
c. 1600

MAPS by Knowledge Quest, Inc.

Ottoman Empire (Muslim)

Ottoman Empire (Muslim)

North Sea

Wittenberg

Atlantic Ocean

KEY
(Color Code)

Protestant

Catholic

Both

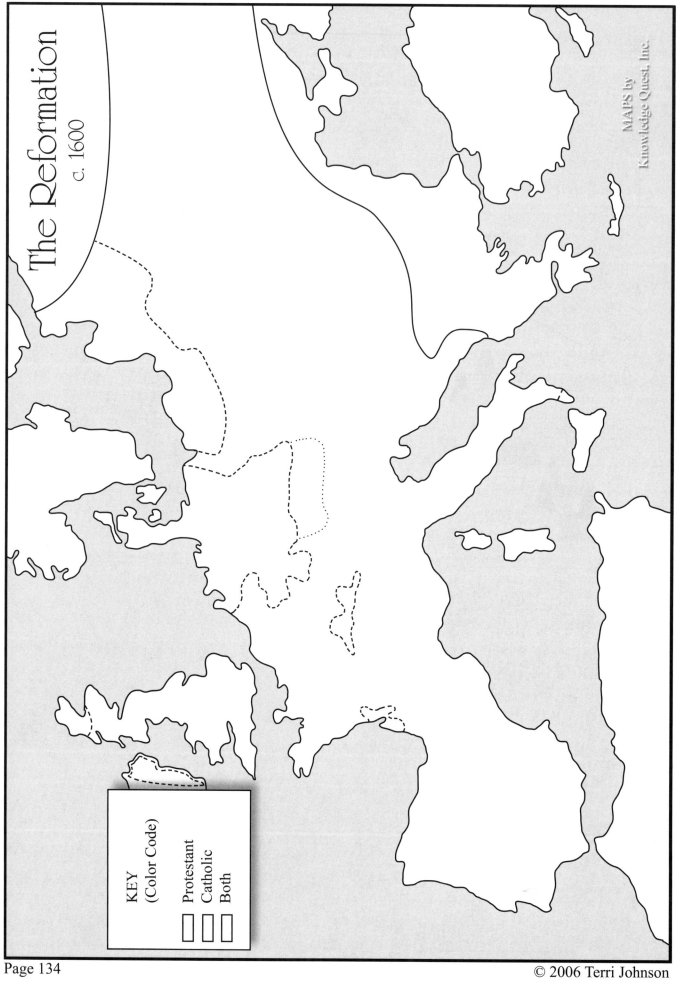

The Reformation
c. 1600

KEY
(Color Code)

Protestant
Catholic
Both

MAPS by
Knowledge Quest, Inc.

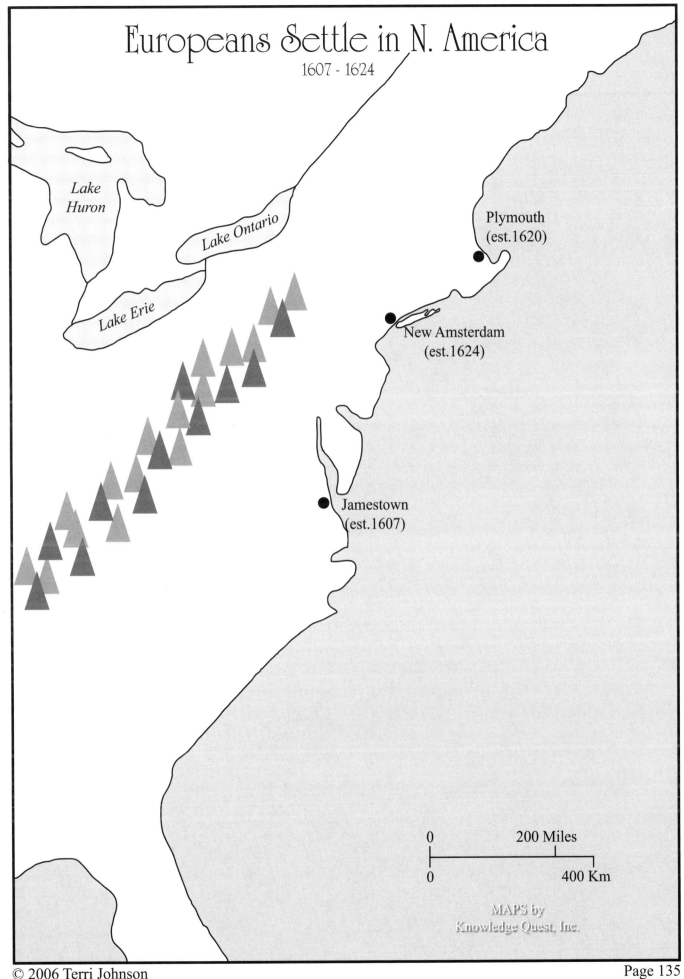

Europeans Settle in N. America

1607 - 1624

Lake Huron

Lake Ontario

Lake Erie

Plymouth
(est.1620)

New Amsterdam
(est.1624)

Jamestown
(est.1607)

0   200 Miles

0   400 Km

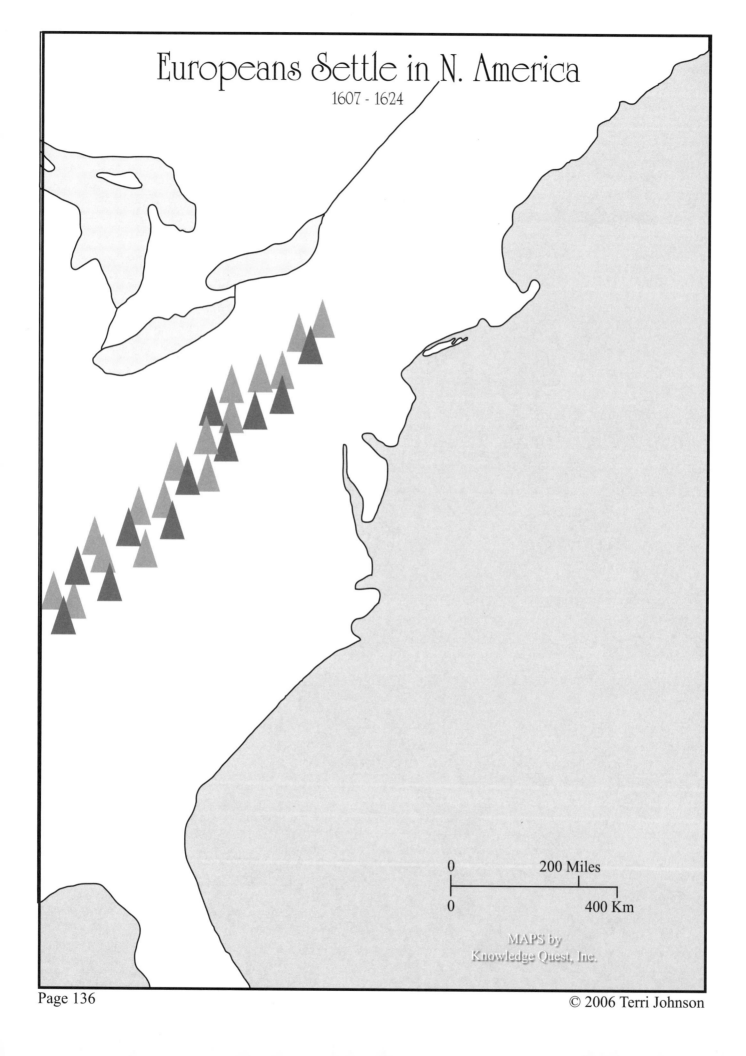

Europeans Settle in N. America
1607 - 1624

0   200 Miles

0   400 Km

SWEDEN

Kiterbog
1644

Dessau
1628

Breitenfeld
1631,1642

Lutzen
1632

ENGLAND

Wolgast
1628

Triebel
1647

Rakonitz
1620

White Mtn.
1620

Schweidnitz
1642

Domitz
1845

Rhine R.

Racroi
1643

Thionville
1643

Nordlingen
1634

Zusmarshausen
1643

Jankau
1646

Neuhausel
1626

Danube R.

FRANCE

Donauworth
1632

The Thirty Years' War
1618 - 1648

KEY

Site of important
battle with date

SPAIN

Tiber R.

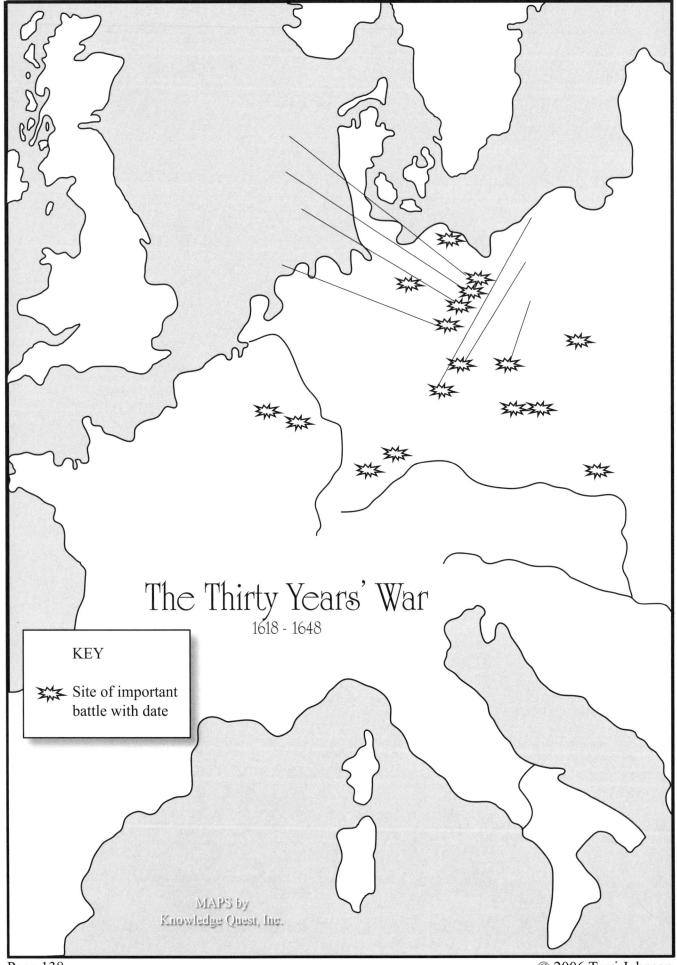

The Thirty Years' War

1618 - 1648

KEY

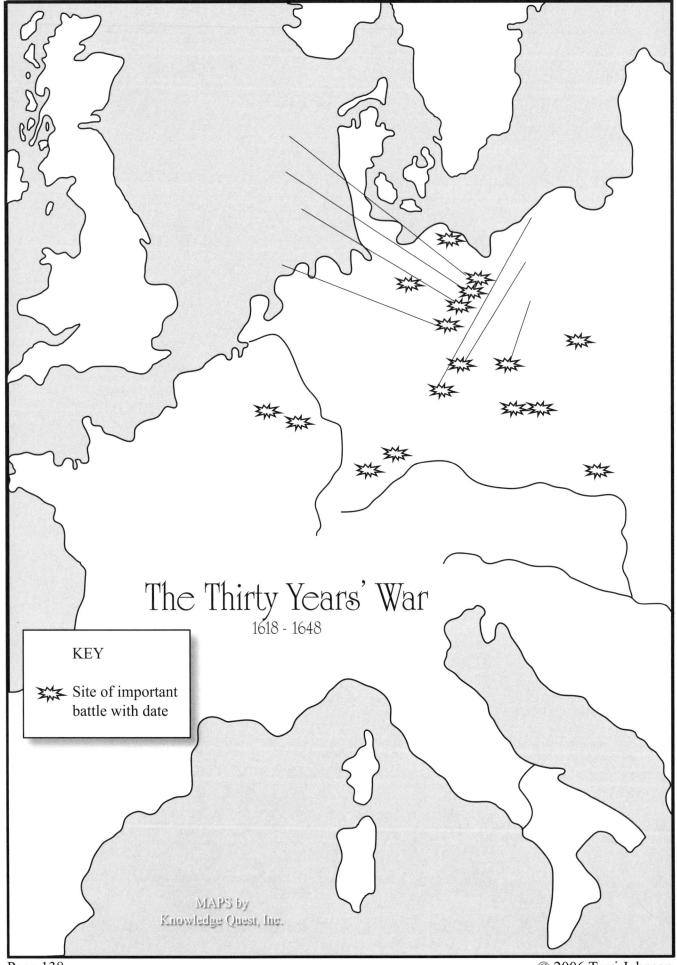 Site of important
battle with date

MAPS by
Knowledge Quest, Inc.

Central and South American Colonization

c. 1640

MAYA

AZTECS

Panama

DUTCH GUIANA

EQUATOR

Amazon

Lima

INCA EMPIRE

JESUIT MISSION

São Francisco

Rio de Janiero

Buenos Aires

KEY

- - - - Spanish Settlement
- - - Portuguese Settlement
······· Inca Empire

Central and South American Colonization

c. 1640

KEY

----- Spanish Settlement
- - - Portuguese Settlement
.... Inca Empire

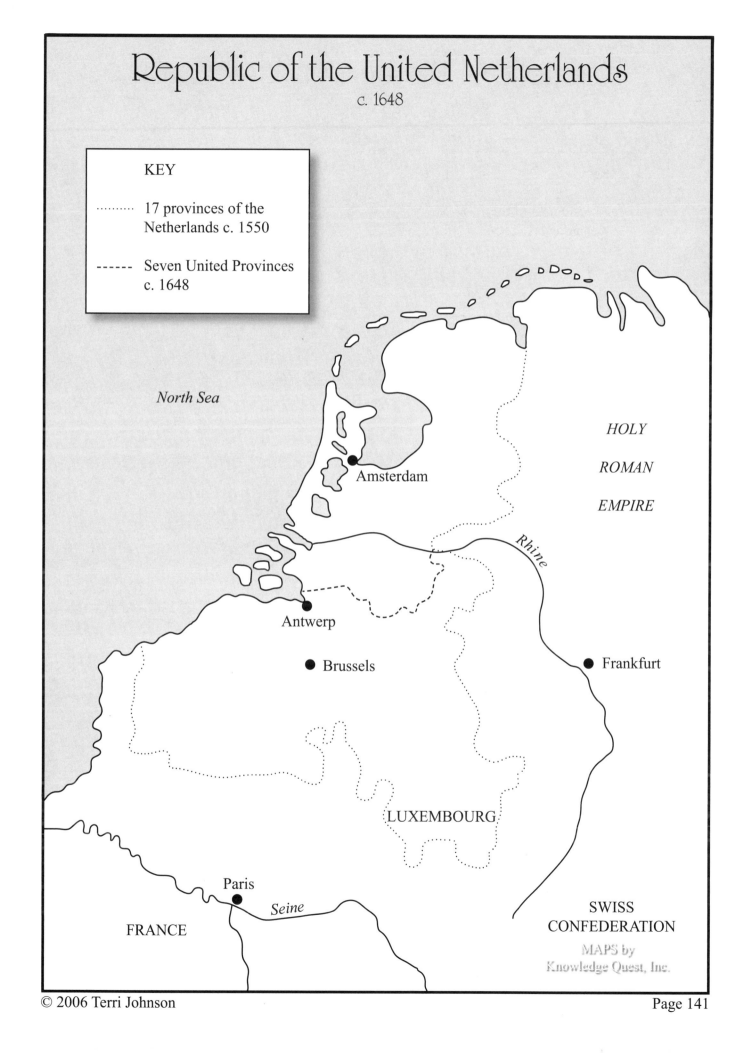

Republic of the United Netherlands

c. 1648

KEY

.... 17 provinces of the
Netherlands c. 1550

------ Seven United Provinces
c. 1648

North Sea

HOLY

ROMAN

EMPIRE

● Amsterdam

Rhine

● Antwerp

● Brussels

● Frankfurt

LUXEMBOURG

SWISS
CONFEDERATION

Paris
●

Seine

FRANCE

Republic of the United Netherlands

c. 1648

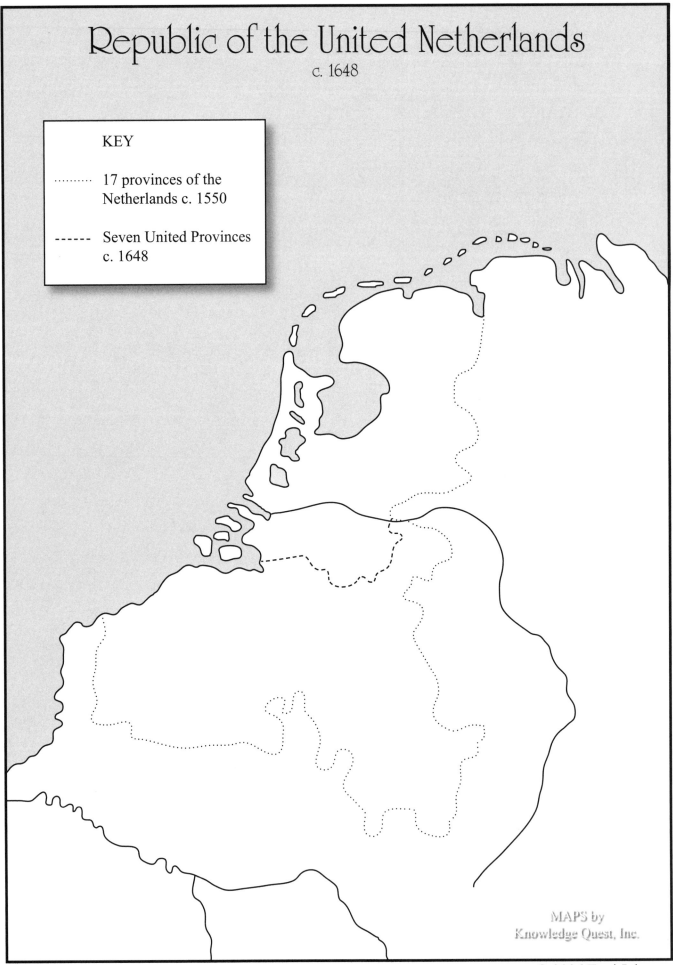

KEY

.... 17 provinces of the
Netherlands c. 1550

------ Seven United Provinces
c. 1648

MAPS by
Knowledge Quest, Inc.

Australia Discovered
1640 - 1800

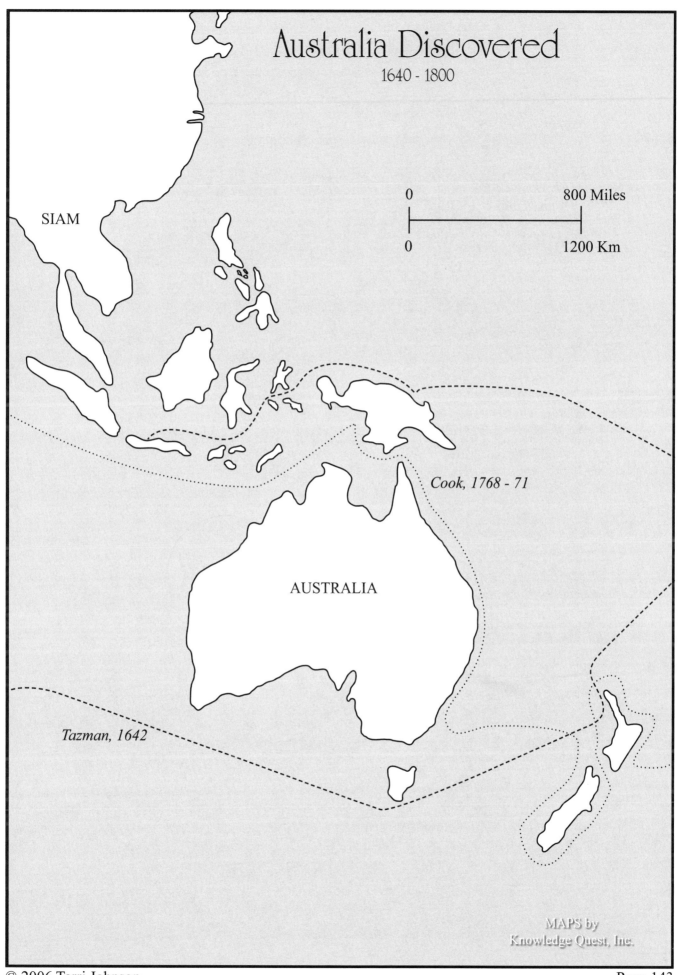

SIAM

0   800 Miles

0   1200 Km

Cook, 1768 - 71

AUSTRALIA

Tazman, 1642

Australia Discovered
1640 - 1800

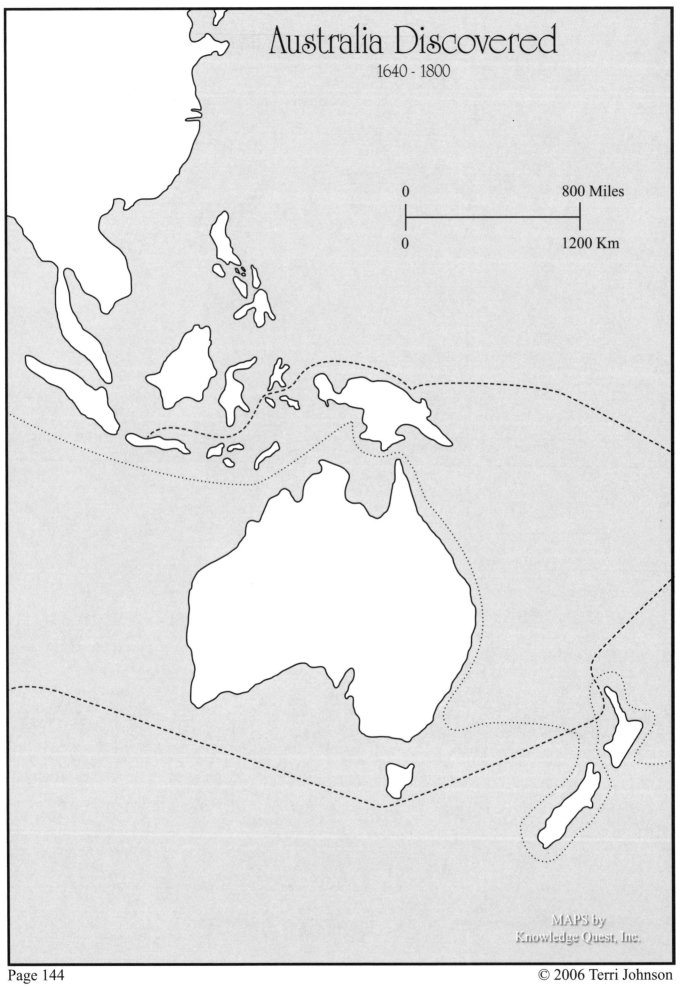

The Expansion of Sweden
c. 1660

LAPLAND

SWEDEN

DENMARK - NORWAY

CARELLA

FINLAND

INGRIA

ESTONIA

Stockholm

LIVONIA

RUSSIA

Riga

COURLAND

LITHUANIA

Kőnigsberg

Danzig

PRUSSIA

Hamburg

POLAND

BRANDENBURG

The Expansion of Sweden
c. 1660

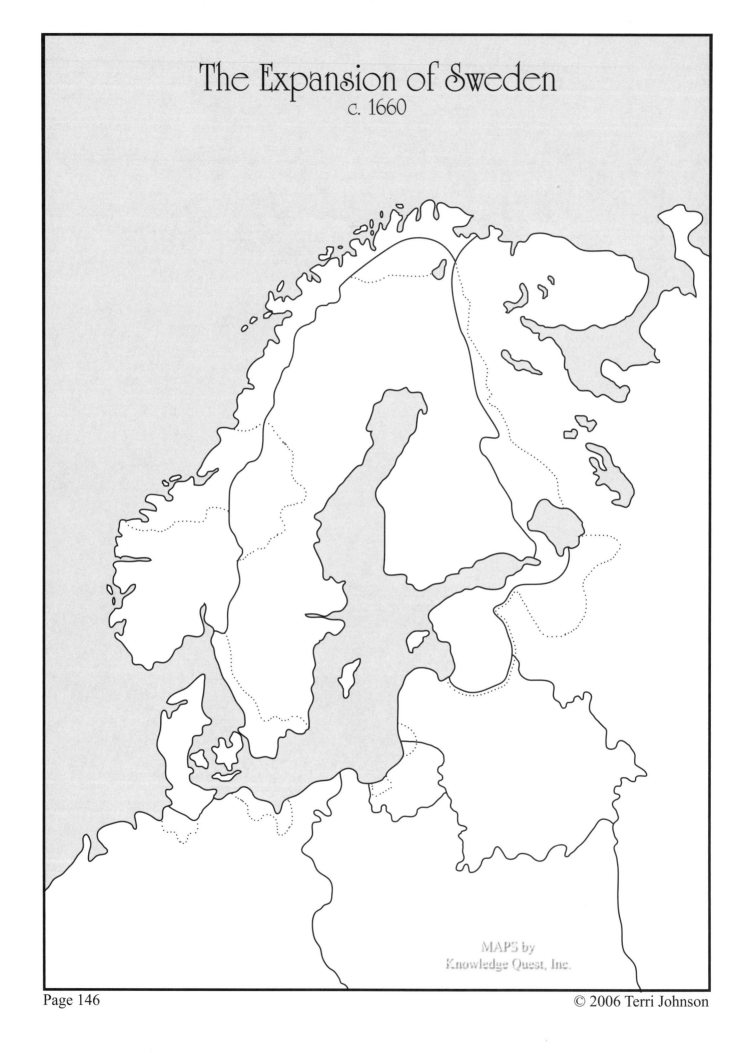

MAPS by
Knowledge Quest, Inc.

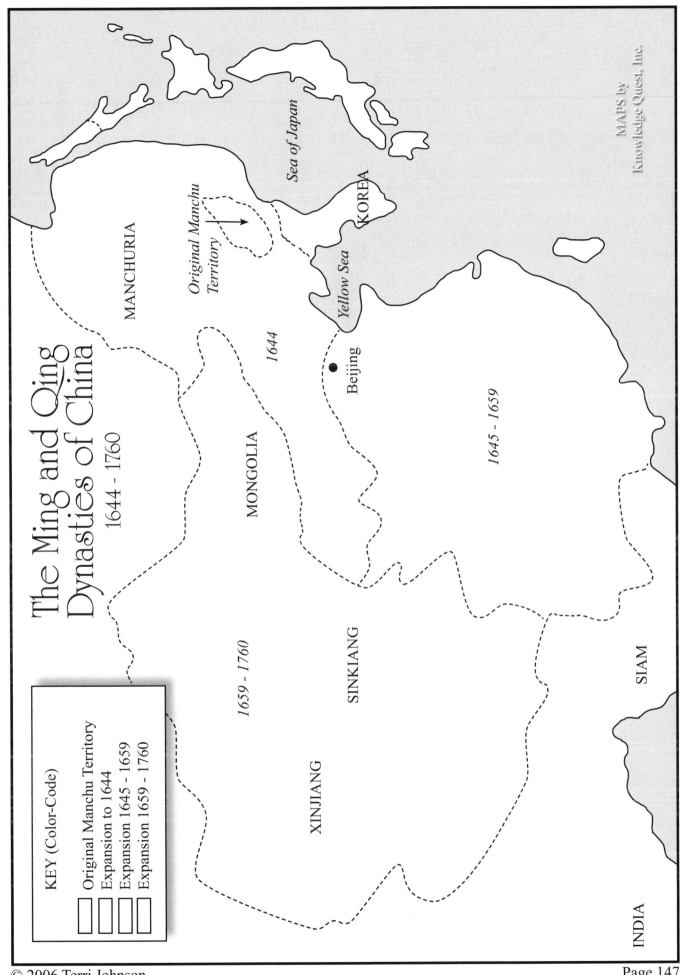

The Ming and Qing Dynasties of China
1644 - 1760

KEY (Color-Code)

Original Manchu Territory
Expansion to 1644
Expansion 1645 - 1659
Expansion 1659 - 1760

MANCHURIA

Original Manchu Territory

Sea of Japan

KOREA

Yellow Sea

1644

● Beijing

MONGOLIA

1645 - 1659

1659 - 1760

SINKIANG

XINJIANG

SIAM

INDIA

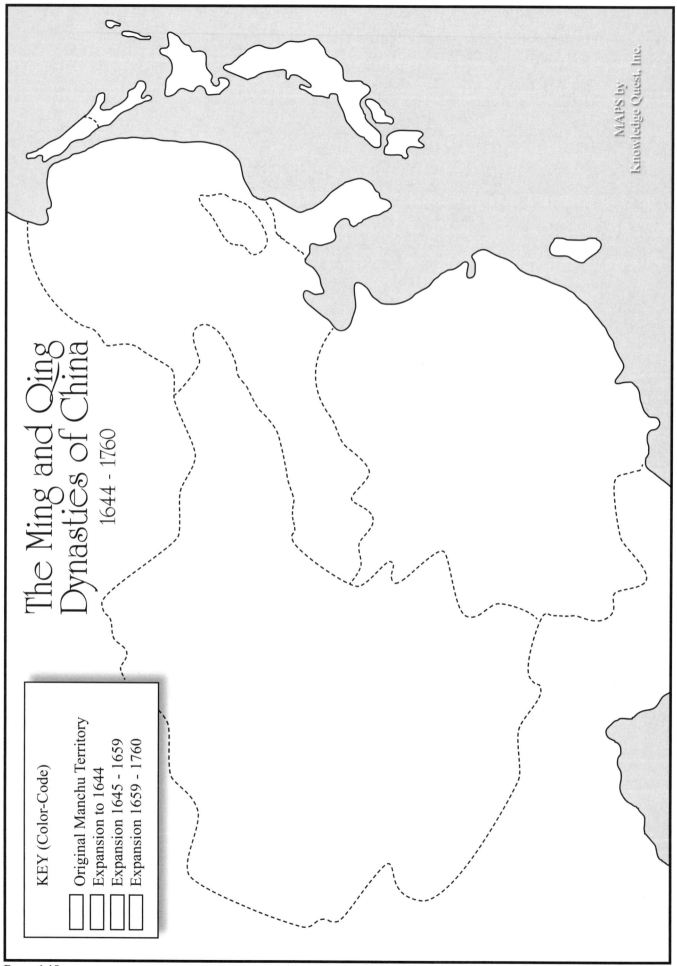

The Ming and Qing Dynasties of China
1644 - 1760

KEY (Color-Code)

Original Manchu Territory

Expansion to 1644

Expansion 1645 - 1659

Expansion 1659 - 1760

MAPS by Knowledge Quest, Inc.

The Mughal Empire
c. 1700

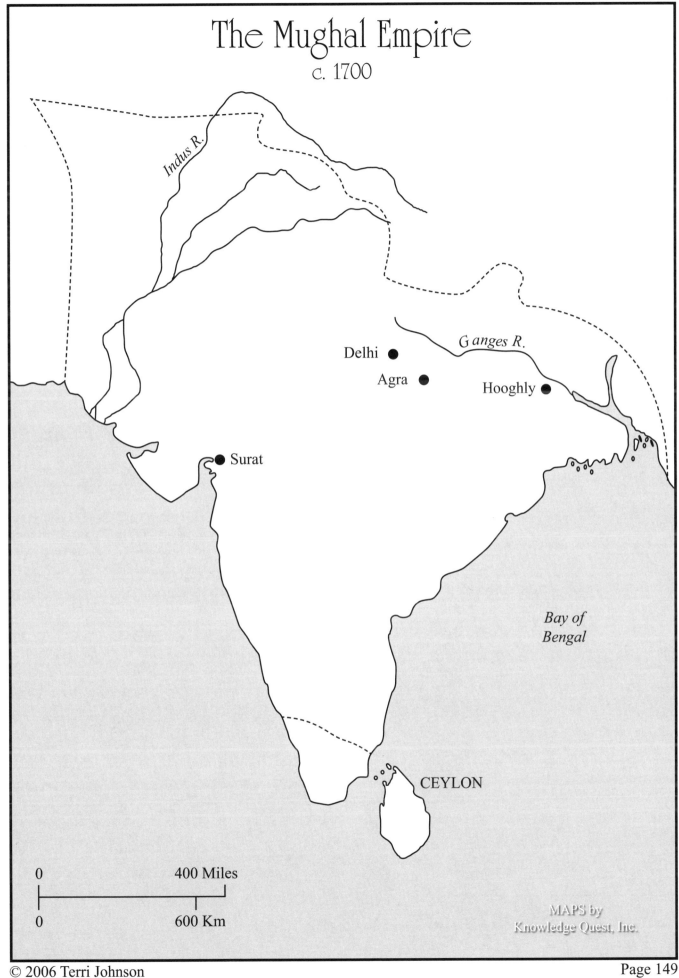

Indus R.

Delhi ●

Ganges R.

Agra ●

Hooghly ●

● Surat

Bay of Bengal

CEYLON

0   400 Miles

0   600 Km

MAPS by
Knowledge Quest, Inc.

The Mughal Empire
c. 1700

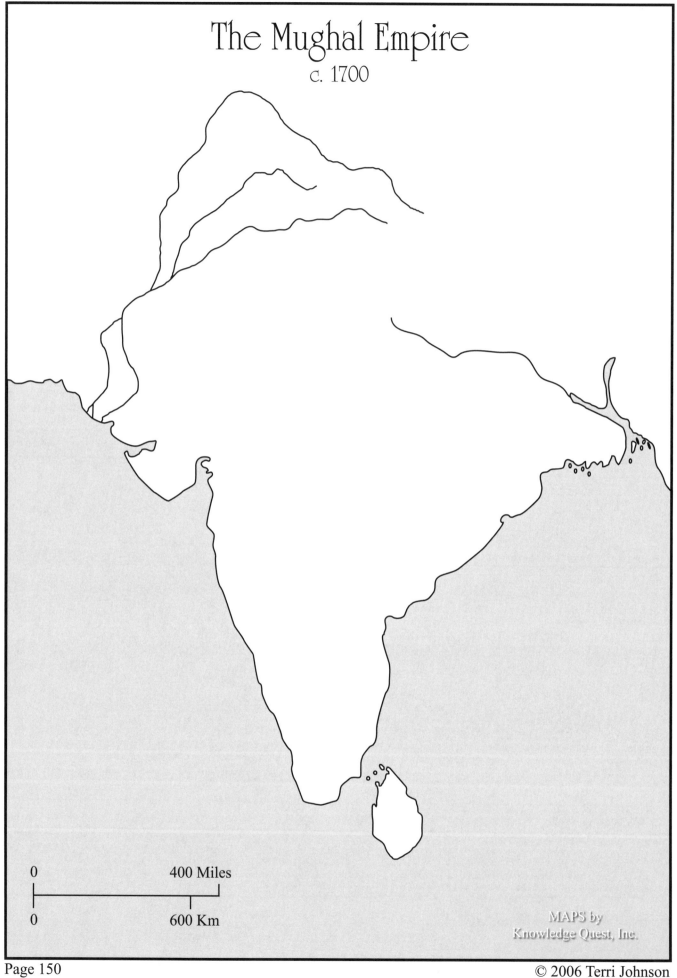

0
400 Miles

0
600 Km

The Isolated Kingdom of Japan

c. 1700

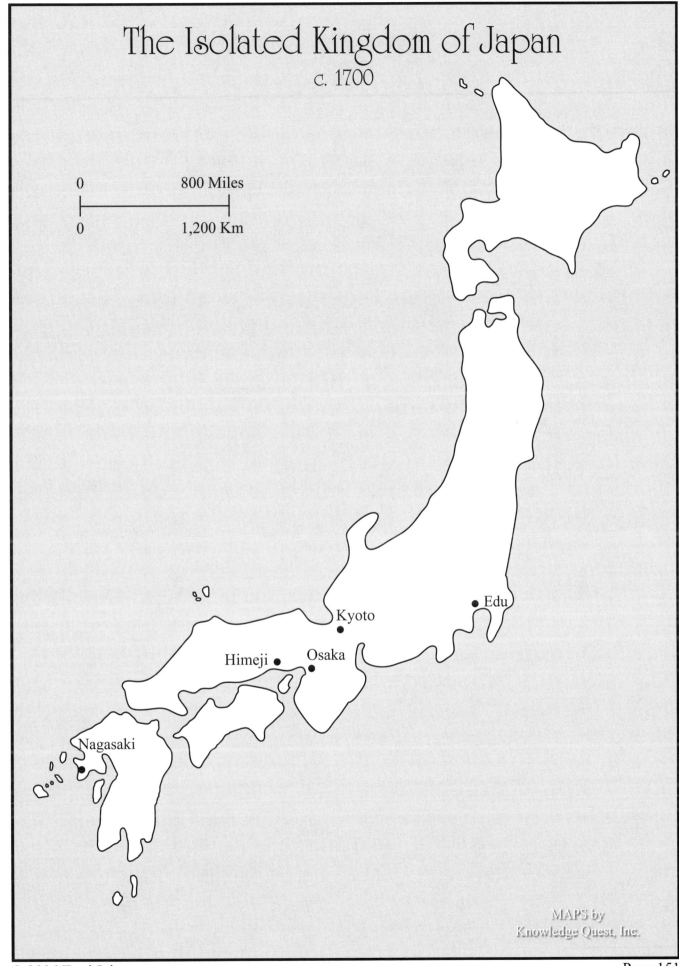

0   800 Miles

0   1,200 Km

Edu

Kyoto

Himeji   Osaka

Nagasaki

The Isolated Kingdom of Japan
c. 1700

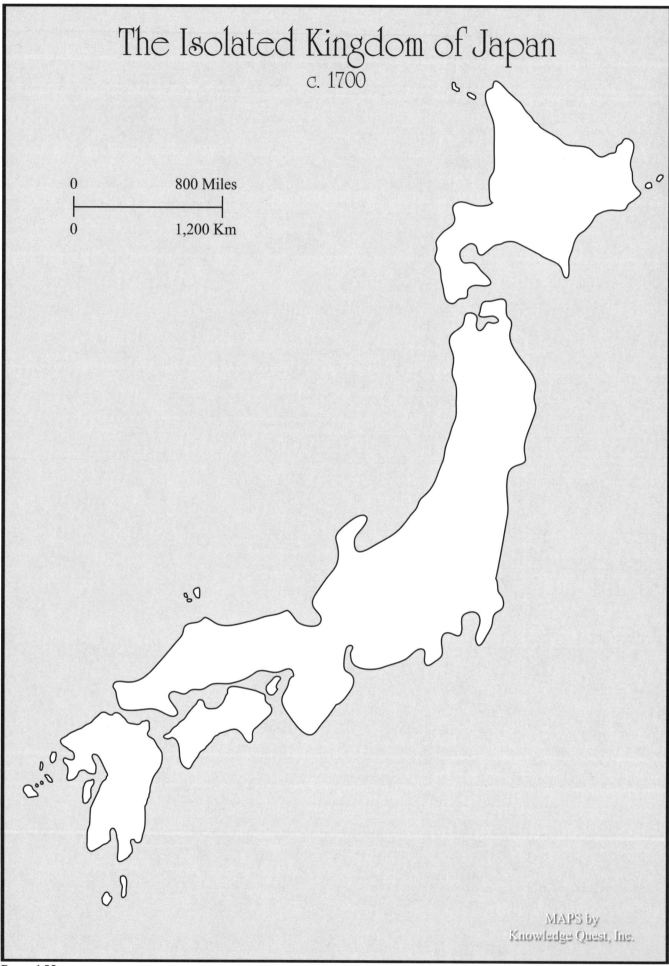

0   800 Miles

0   1,200 Km

The Original 13 Colonies
c. 1750

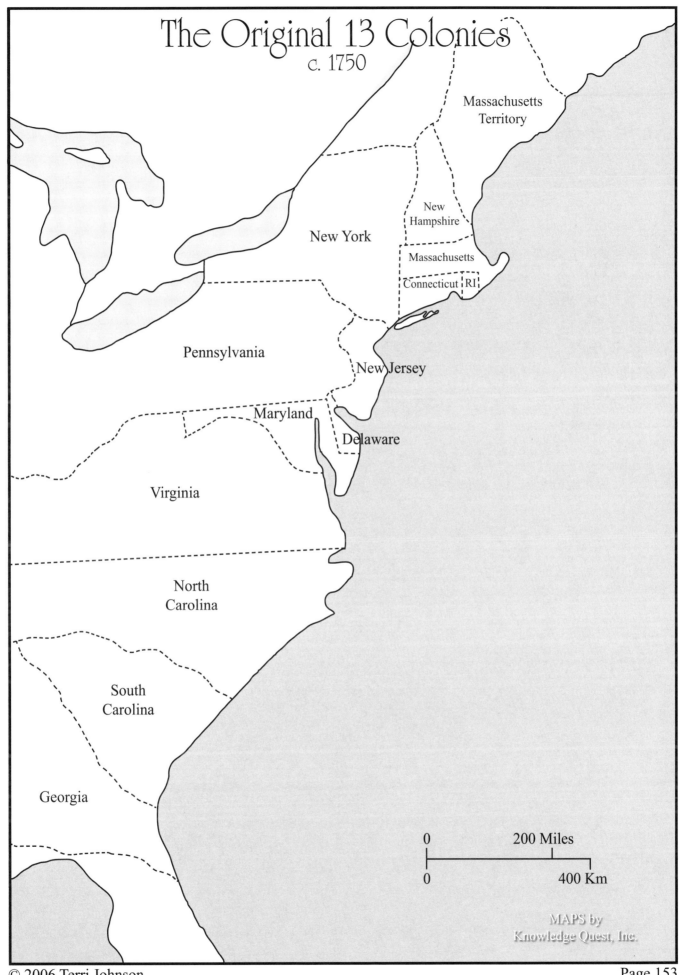

Massachusetts
Territory

New York

New
Hampshire

Massachusetts

Connecticut   RI

Pennsylvania

New Jersey

Maryland

Delaware

Virginia

North
Carolina

South
Carolina

Georgia

0   200 Miles

0   400 Km

MAPS by
Knowledge Quest, Inc.

The Original 13 Colonies
c. 1750

0   200 Miles

0   400 Km

MAPS by
Knowledge Quest, Inc.

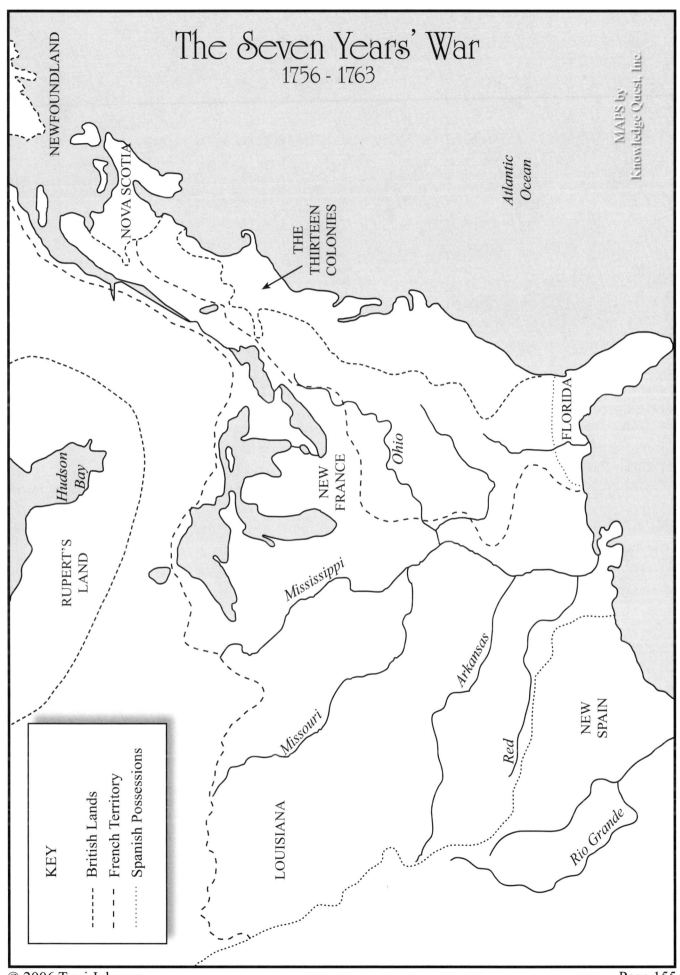

The Seven Years' War
1756 - 1763

NEWFOUNDLAND

NOVA SCOTIA

THE THIRTEEN COLONIES

Atlantic Ocean

FLORIDA

Hudson Bay

RUPERT'S LAND

NEW FRANCE

Ohio

Mississippi

Arkansas

Red

NEW SPAIN

Missouri

LOUISIANA

Rio Grande

KEY

- - - British Lands
- - - French Territory
.... Spanish Possessions

The Seven Years' War
1756 - 1763

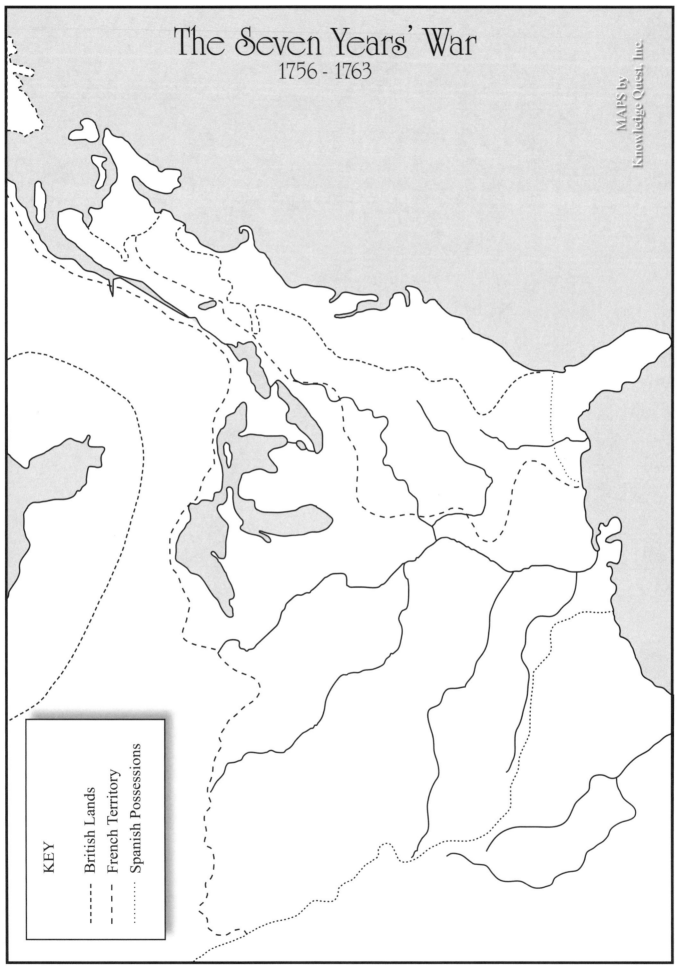

KEY

----- British Lands

- - - French Territory

·········· Spanish Possessions

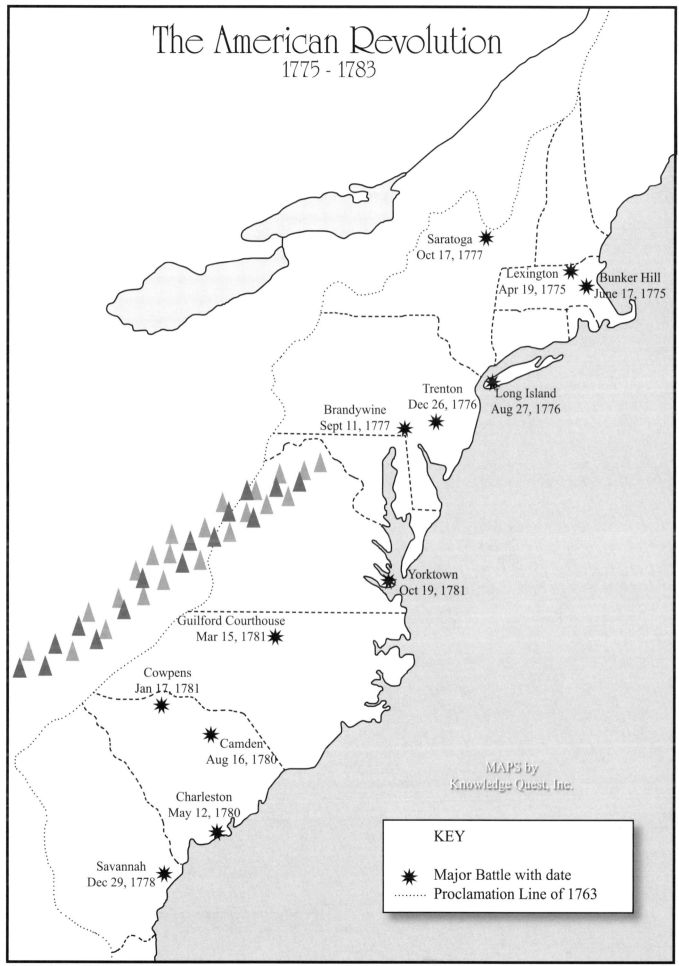

The American Revolution
1775 - 1783

Saratoga
Oct 17, 1777

Lexington
Apr 19, 1775

Bunker Hill
June 17, 1775

Trenton
Dec 26, 1776

Long Island
Aug 27, 1776

Brandywine
Sept 11, 1777

Yorktown
Oct 19, 1781

Guilford Courthouse
Mar 15, 1781

Cowpens
Jan 17, 1781

Camden
Aug 16, 1780

Charleston
May 12, 1780

Savannah
Dec 29, 1778

MAPS by
Knowledge Quest, Inc.

KEY

✴ Major Battle with date

⋯⋯ Proclamation Line of 1763

The American Revolution
1775 - 1783

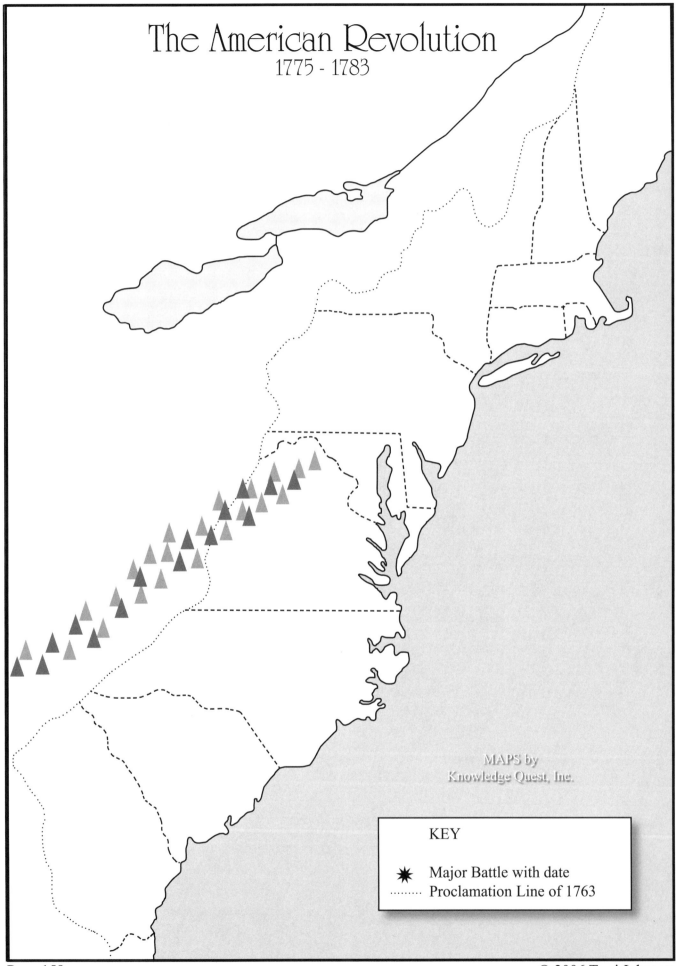

KEY

✸ Major Battle with date

⋯⋯ Proclamation Line of 1763

MAPS by
Knowledge Quest, Inc.

The French Revolution
1789 - 1794

KEY

- - - Areas of sustained counter-revolutionary resistance - 1793

● Towns ruled by revolutionaries

F R A N C E

Rouen

Caen

Strasbourg

Paris

Brest

Rennes

Troyes

Dijon

Nantes

Sancerre ●
Bourges ●

Poitiers

Lyons

Bordeaux

MAPS by
Knowledge Quest, Inc.

Nimes

Montpelier

Marseilles

P Y R E N E E S

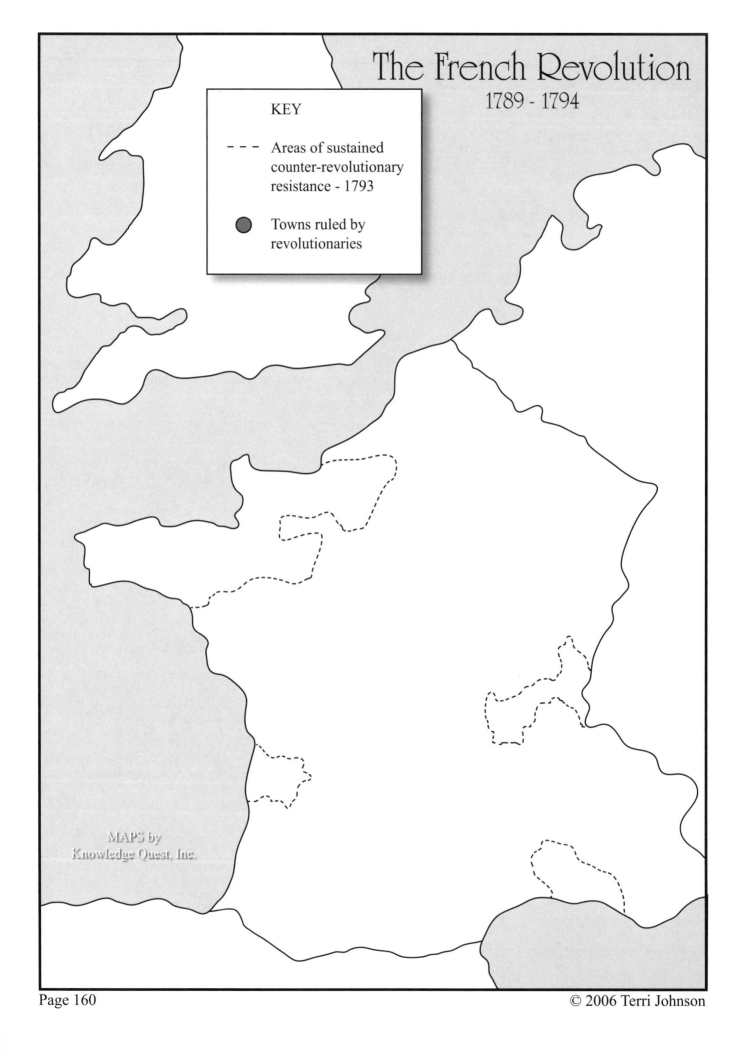

The French Revolution
1789 - 1794

KEY

– – – Areas of sustained counter-revolutionary resistance - 1793

● Towns ruled by revolutionaries

MAPS by
Knowledge Quest, Inc.

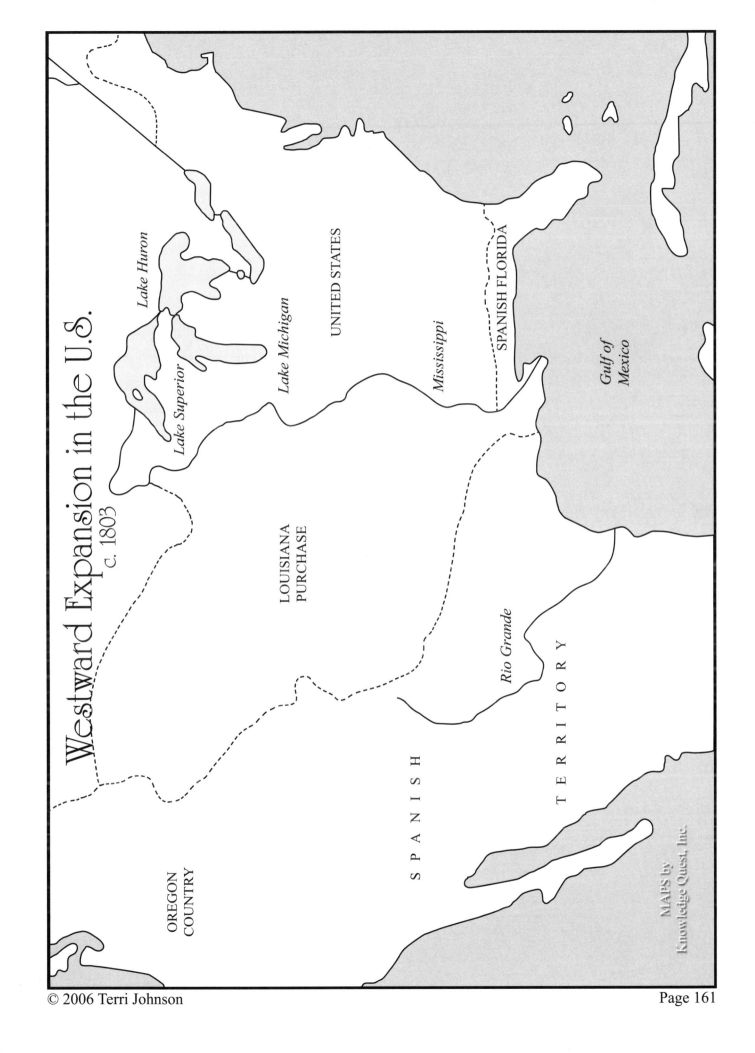

Westward Expansion in the U.S.
c. 1803

Lake Huron

Lake Superior

Lake Michigan

UNITED STATES

Mississippi

SPANISH FLORIDA

Gulf of Mexico

LOUISIANA PURCHASE

Rio Grande

S P A N I S H

T E R R I T O R Y

OREGON COUNTRY

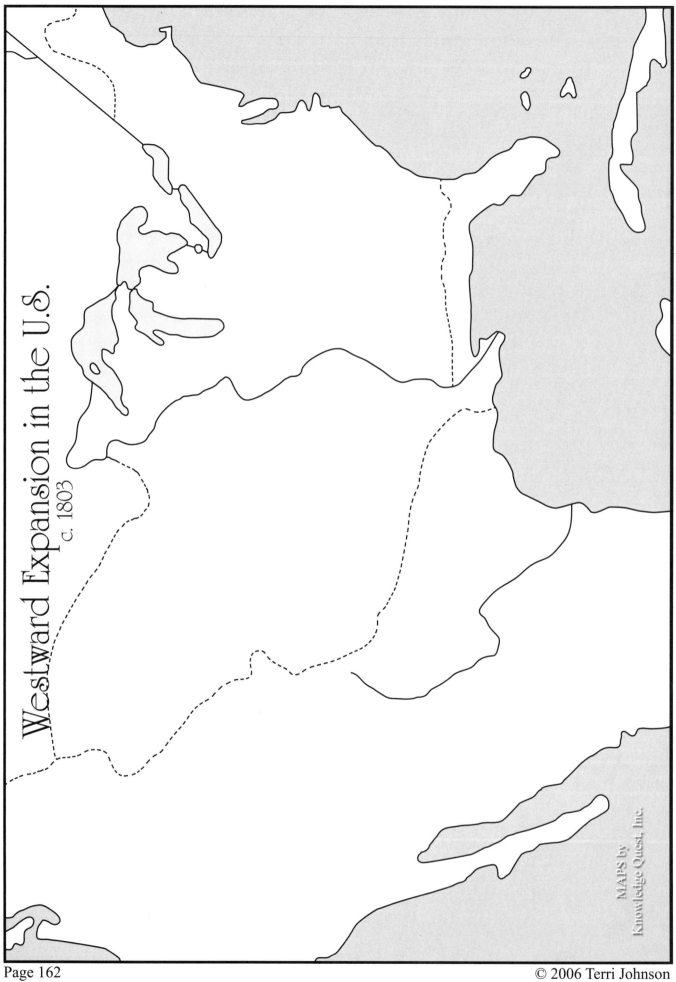

Westward Expansion in the U.S.
c. 1803

MAPS by
Knowledge Quest, Inc.

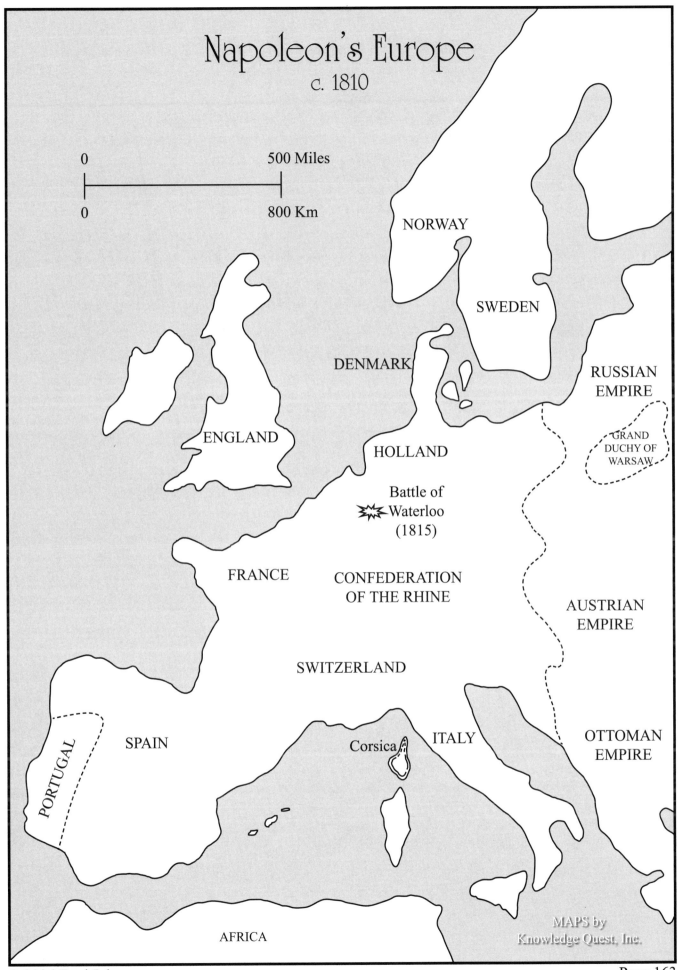

Napoleon's Europe
c. 1810

0   500 Miles

0   800 Km

NORWAY

SWEDEN

DENMARK

RUSSIAN EMPIRE

GRAND DUCHY OF WARSAW

ENGLAND

HOLLAND

Battle of Waterloo (1815)

FRANCE

CONFEDERATION OF THE RHINE

AUSTRIAN EMPIRE

SWITZERLAND

PORTUGAL

SPAIN

Corsica

ITALY

OTTOMAN EMPIRE

AFRICA

MAPS by Knowledge Quest, Inc.

Napoleon's Europe

c. 1810

0   500 Miles

0   800 Km

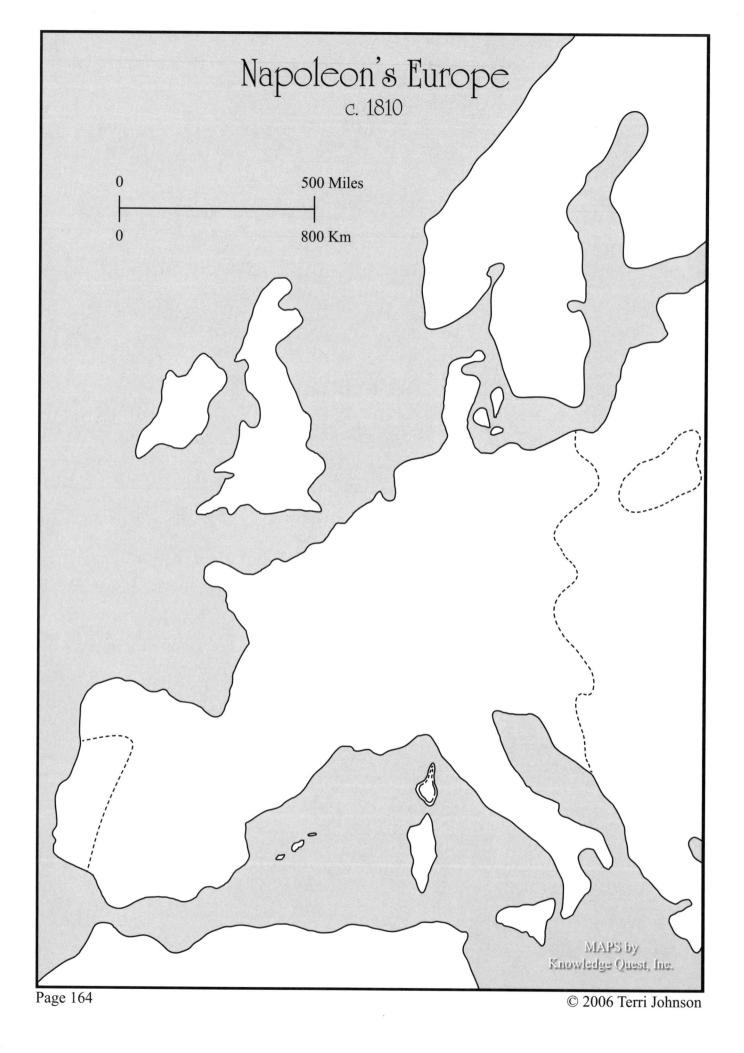

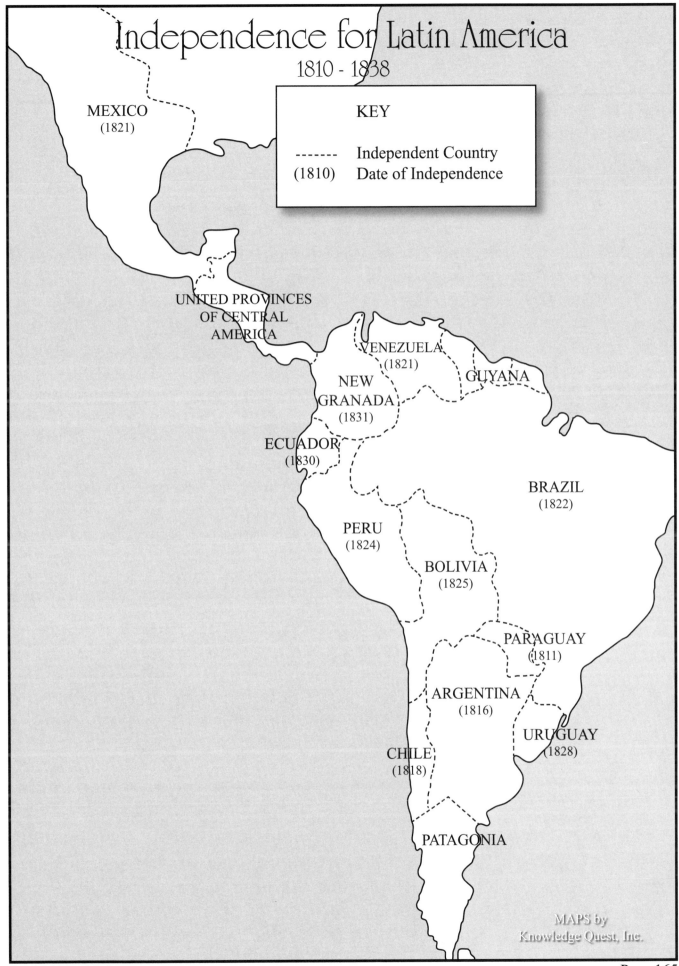

Independence for Latin America
1810 - 1838

MEXICO
(1821)

KEY

------- Independent Country
(1810) Date of Independence

UNITED PROVINCES
OF CENTRAL
AMERICA

VENEZUELA
(1821)

GUYANA

NEW
GRANADA
(1831)

ECUADOR
(1830)

BRAZIL
(1822)

PERU
(1824)

BOLIVIA
(1825)

PARAGUAY
(1811)

ARGENTINA
(1816)

URUGUAY
(1828)

CHILE
(1818)

PATAGONIA

MAPS by
Knowledge Quest, Inc.

Independence for Latin America
1810 - 1838

KEY

- - - - - Independent Country
(1810)   Date of Independence

MAPS by
Knowledge Quest, Inc.

Slave vs. Free States

c. 1820

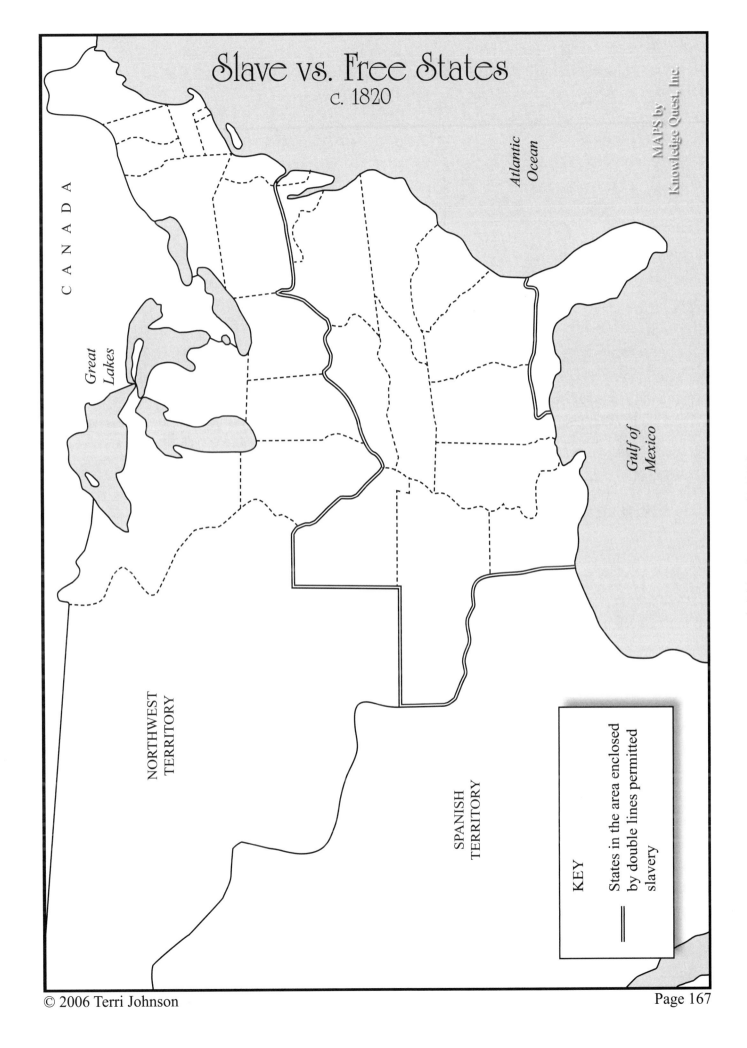

CANADA

Atlantic Ocean

Great Lakes

Gulf of Mexico

NORTHWEST TERRITORY

SPANISH TERRITORY

MAPS by Knowledge Quest, Inc.

KEY

States in the area enclosed by double lines permitted slavery

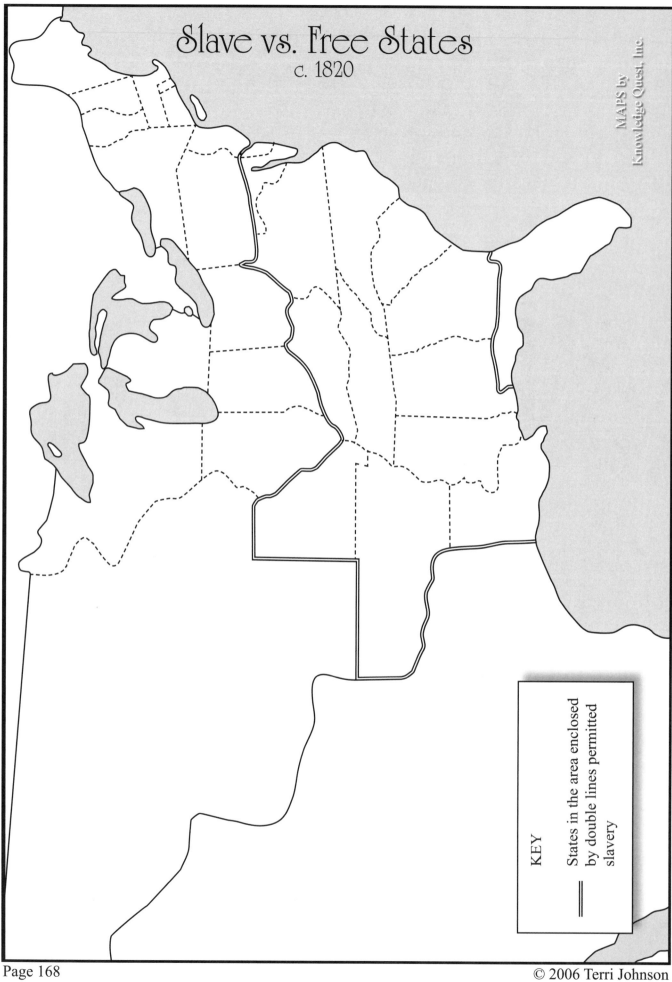

Slave vs. Free States

c. 1820

KEY

— States in the area enclosed by double lines permitted slavery

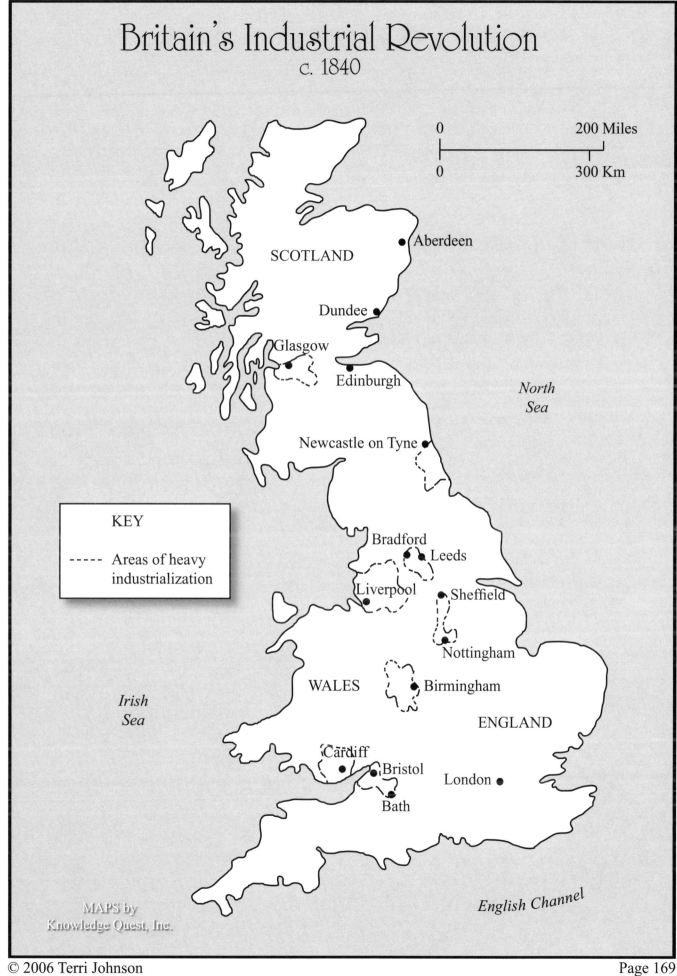

Britain's Industrial Revolution
c. 1840

0   200 Miles

0   300 Km

SCOTLAND

Aberdeen

Dundee

Glasgow

Edinburgh

North Sea

Newcastle on Tyne

KEY

----- Areas of heavy industrialization

Bradford

Leeds

Liverpool

Sheffield

Nottingham

WALES

Birmingham

ENGLAND

Irish Sea

Cardiff

Bristol

London

Bath

English Channel

Britain's Industrial Revolution
c. 1840

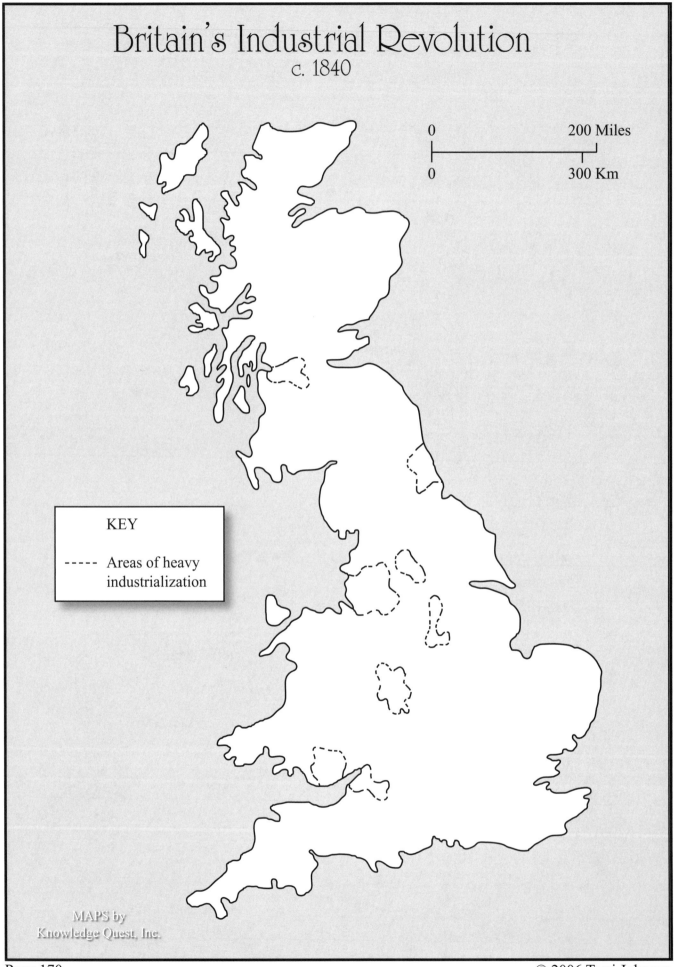

0   200 Miles

0   300 Km

KEY

----- Areas of heavy industrialization

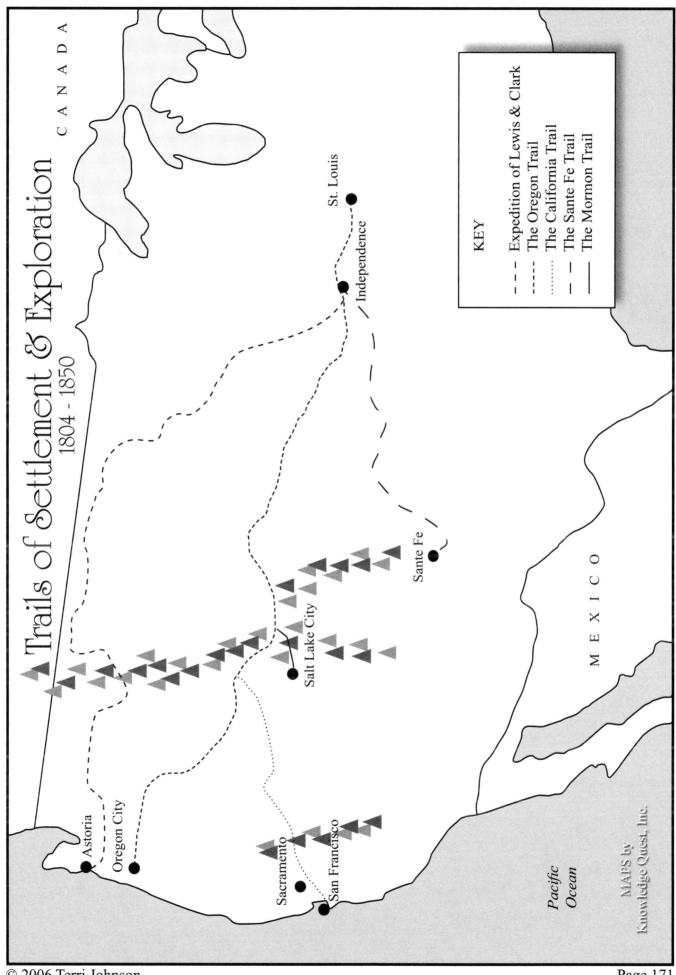

Trails of Settlement & Exploration
1804 - 1850

CANADA

MEXICO

Pacific
Ocean

KEY
- - - Expedition of Lewis & Clark
- - - The Oregon Trail
...... The California Trail
- - The Sante Fe Trail
—— The Mormon Trail

St. Louis

Independence

Sante Fe

Salt Lake City

Astoria

Oregon City

Sacramento

San Francisco

MAPS by
Knowledge Quest, Inc.

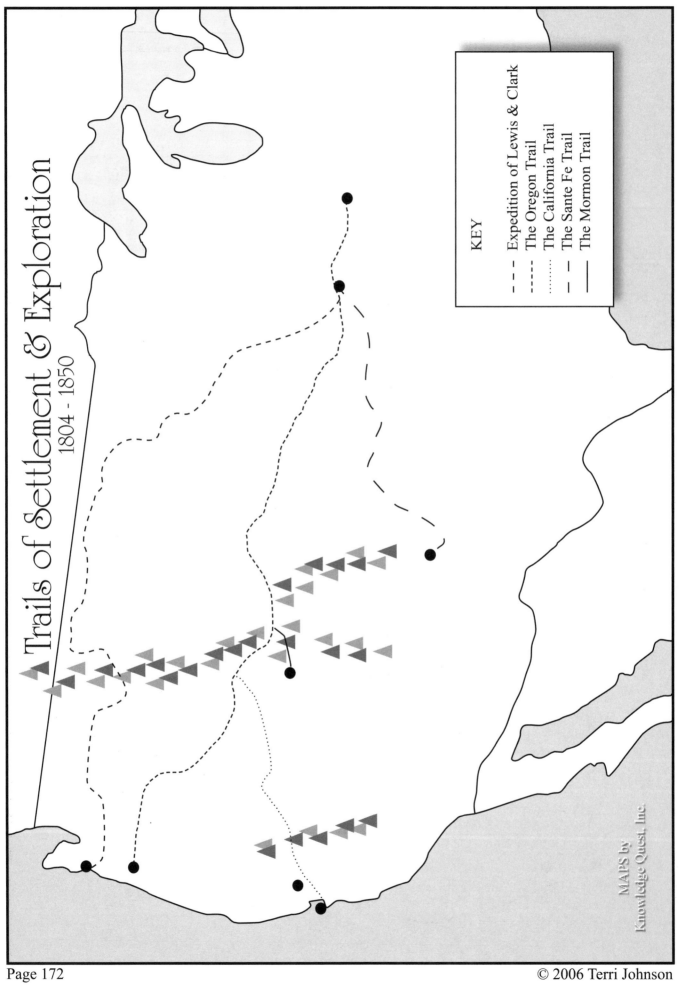

Trails of Settlement & Exploration
1804 - 1850

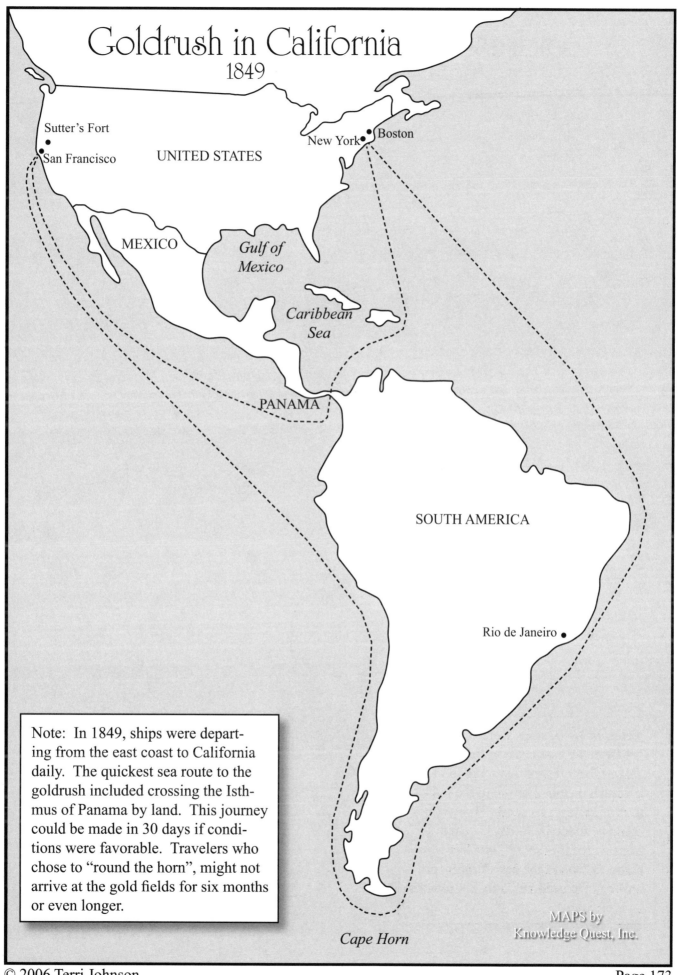

Goldrush in California
1849

Sutter's Fort

San Francisco

UNITED STATES

New York • Boston

MEXICO

Gulf of Mexico

Caribbean Sea

PANAMA

SOUTH AMERICA

Rio de Janeiro •

Note: In 1849, ships were departing from the east coast to California daily. The quickest sea route to the goldrush included crossing the Isthmus of Panama by land. This journey could be made in 30 days if conditions were favorable. Travelers who chose to "round the horn", might not arrive at the gold fields for six months or even longer.

Cape Horn

MAPS by
Knowledge Quest, Inc.

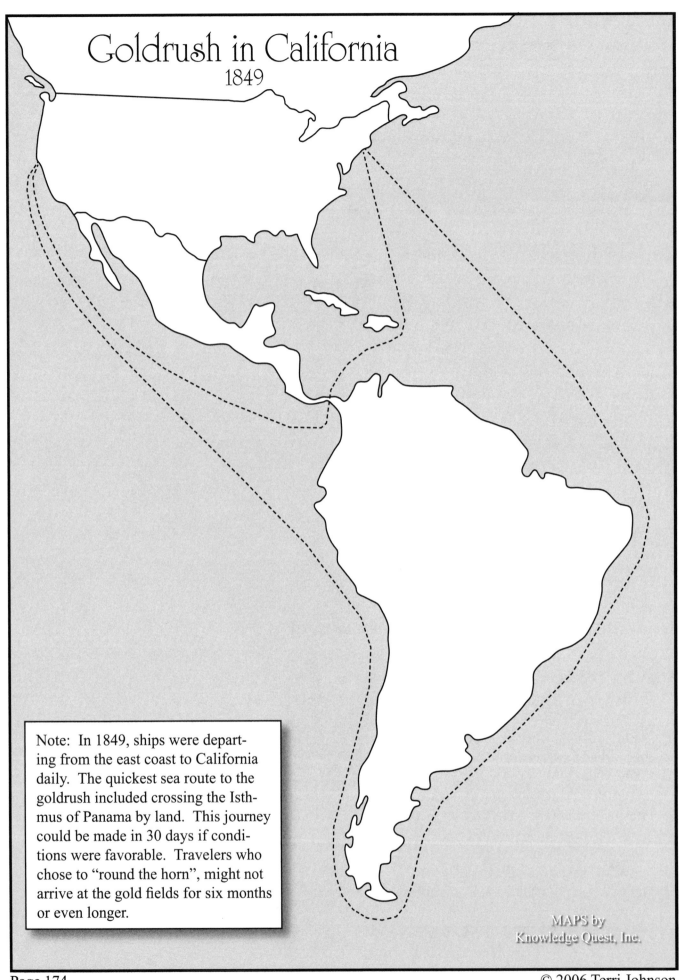

Goldrush in California
1849

Note: In 1849, ships were departing from the east coast to California daily. The quickest sea route to the goldrush included crossing the Isthmus of Panama by land. This journey could be made in 30 days if conditions were favorable. Travelers who chose to "round the horn", might not arrive at the gold fields for six months or even longer.

MAPS by
Knowledge Quest, Inc.

Lesson Plans

Discussion Questions:

1. The Crimean War – Page 184
   - Which two empires primarily were fighting for control over the Crimean peninsula on the Black Sea and the surrounding region?
   - Two other countries came to the aid of the Ottoman Turks to help drive out the Russians. Who were they? *(Great Britain and France)* Draw arrows on your map to show the direction their armies would have marched. Label the arrows with the names of the aiding countries.
   - *Unlabeled map exercise: Label the major battles of the Crimean War. Label the bodies of water, countries and empires surrounding the Crimean peninsula.*

2. Japan Opens to Trade – Page 186
   - Find Japan on a wall map, atlas or globe. Label the four main islands *(north to south: Hokkaido, Honshu, Shikoku and Kyushu).*
   - Which large country is located to the left of your map? Draw an arrow pointing that direction and write the name of the country next to the arrow.
   - *Unlabeled map exercise: Locate and label the major ports and cities of Japan at this time in history. Label the surrounding bodies of water. Consult an atlas to find the location of Mt. Fuji and mark it on your map.*

3. The American Civil War – Page 188
   - Label the states where the battles shown on your map were fought.
   - Choose colors close to each other on the color wheel to help differentiate the divided states of the nation. For example, color all of the Confederate states warm colors such as red, orange and yellow. Use the cool colors (purple, blue and green) to color the states of the Union to the north.
   - Label the country to the north of the United States.
   - *Unlabeled map exercise: Label the major battles of the Civil War. Record dates beside them if you have this information. Locate the capitals of both the Union and the Confederacy and label them on your map.*

4. Italy United – Page 190
   - All of the Italian states were united under Piedmont by 1870, except for three. These were Savoy, Nice and Corsica. These states were ceded to France. Draw an arrow from each one to the country of France.
   - Label the main body of water that surrounds the peninsula of Italy and its islands.
   - *Unlabeled map exercise: Label the Italian states at this time in history. Label the islands and bodies of water surrounding Italy. Label the Tiber River.*

5. The Dominion of Canada – Page 192
   - Circle the two directional symbols on your map. Can you explain why north is pointing in two different directions? Now wrap your map around a globe (or a medium sized ball) with the north symbols pointing to the top. Does this make it easier to understand? Flat maps are always distorted to a certain degree. The only truly accurate map must be spherical (in other words, a globe).
   - Label the area of land in the northwest corner of Canada. Which country does this belong to? Label the large island to the east of Canada *(Greenland)*.
   - *Unlabeled map exercise: Label the provinces of Canada. Label the Hudson Bay and at least five of the islands to the north.*

6. The German Confederation – Page 194
   - Look on a wall map, atlas or globe and determine which country now occupies a large portion of the areas then known as Prussia and Bavaria.
   - Discuss some of the reasons why a country might change its name or become a different size or disappear altogether *(wars, treaties, alliances, surrenders, etc.)*. As you continue to study modern history, notice how the boundaries of the European Nations change tremendously over the next 100 years.
   - Label the following on your map: Sweden, Denmark and the Baltic Sea.
   - *Unlabeled map exercise: Label Prussia and the surrounding countries and bodies of water.*

7. The Scramble for Africa – Page 196
   - Color-code your map by coloring all British colonies one color, all French territories another color, etc. until all of the African countries are filled in. Which one country is left? The Congo was the only country claimed by Belgium. Color it a different color than all of the rest.
   - *Unlabeled map exercise: Label the countries of Africa at this time in history. Compare on a current map or globe how the countries have changed from then until now.*

8. India under the Rule of the British East India Company – Page 198
   - The small unlabeled area in the center of your map was called Bundelkhand. Label it on your map. Label the country north of Nepal. Label the country to the west of Afghanistan. Consult your globe or wall map for the answers.
   - The areas enclosed by the dashed lines were dependent Indian states, governed by Indian rulers. The British Empire had acquired the rest of India. Color your map accordingly, and then color-code your key.
   - *Unlabeled map exercise: Label the states and regions of India. Label the surrounding countries and bodies of water.*

9. The British Empire – Page 200
   - By 1914, the British Empire had spread into every continent and occupied many islands around the world. Label the five continents show here *(Australia is already labeled and Antarctica is not shown)*.

- Color all of the areas of British occupation one color.
- Label the large island of Greenland. On this map, it appears larger than Australia. Consult your globe to find out if this is so. As mentioned earlier under lesson plan 5, distortion occurs whenever one attempts to convert a spherical shape onto a flat surface. This distortion can occur in distance, shape or size. This map's distortion is mostly in the size of the areas closest to the poles.
- *Unlabeled map exercise: Label the British colonies. New Zealand was also a colony of the British Empire. Find its location and draw the two islands onto your map.*

10. The Commonwealth of Australia – Page 202
- Find Australia in an atlas or on a globe. Locate the Gulf of Carpentaria and label it on your blackline map.
- What is the Great Barrier Reef? Look it up in the dictionary or an encyclopedia to find out. Note on your map the length of this coral reef *(approximately 1250 miles or 2000 kilometers),* which is the longest in the world.
- *Unlabeled map exercise: Label the six territories of Australia. Consult your globe to determine if these political boundaries have changed. Label the deserts, the oceans and the Great Barrier Reef.*

11. The Boxer Rebellion in China – Page 204
- Label the region south of Russia and north of China *(Mongolia).*
- Consult your atlas or globe to determine the modern name for the country of Siam. Label it in parenthesis next to the word "Siam". *(Thailand)*
- Label the ocean shown here.
- After coloring in the map, color-code your key.
- *Unlabeled map exercise: Label these five large cities in China. Label the countries bordering China.*

12. The Balkan Wars – Page 206
- Label and color the body of water to the east of Bulgaria and Romania.
- Draw in and label the city of Constantinople, the capital of the Ottoman Empire.
- What is the name of the island on the left side of your map, just off the coast of Italy? *(Sicily)* To what country does it belong? *(Italy)*
- *Unlabeled map exercise: Label the countries of the Balkan Peninsula at this time in history. Label the surrounding seas and islands. What is the **Bosporus**? Look it up in the dictionary or encyclopedia and label it on your map.*

13. World War I – Page 208
- Referring to the previous map "The Balkan Wars – Page 34", find and label the small country of Montenegro.
- Using a black pen or pencil, draw a line connecting the lower portion of the Black Sea to the lower part of the Caspian Sea. At its midway point, draw a line perpendicular down to the bottom of your map. This most southeast corner which you have defined on your map is the country of Persia. Label it and print an N beside it, for Persia

remained neutral during this war.

- Color all neutral countries one color, Central Powers another color and Allied Powers a third color. Color-code your key.
- *Unlabeled map exercise: Label the countries as they existed before and during the 1ˢᵗ World War.*

14. The Russian Revolution – Page 210

- Label the two countries to the west of Finland.
- Draw a scale on your map. The widest distance across the Black Sea is approximately 700 miles (or 1100 km).
- Notice how radically the boundary of Russia fluxuated between the years 1914 and 1922. About how far did Germany advance during WWI into what was then the Russian Empire? How much of their territory did they gain back as the newly governed U.S.S.R.?
- *Unlabeled map exercise: Label Russia and the countries bordering her. Label all bodies of water. **Extra challenge:** Referring to your previous map "World War I" on page 36, draw in some of the European countries in the war-torn Europe region.*

15. The Division of Ireland – Page 212

- Locate Ireland on a wall map, atlas or globe. What island nation lies just to the east?
- Label the bodies of water surrounding the island of Ireland. *(Irish Sea, Celtic Sea and Atlantic Ocean)*
- Color Northern Ireland a different color than the Irish Free State as they became divided in 1922.
- *Unlabeled map exercise: Label at least five cities in Ireland. Draw in the division between the Irish Free State and Northern Ireland. Label the Shannon River and the seas surrounding Ireland.*

16. Europe, Post WWI – Page 214

- Label the island countries to the north of France. Label the two rivers flowing from the Caspian Sea up into the U.S.S.R. *(Consult map on page 36 for river names)*
- Compare this map to the one titled "World War I". First, color the countries that did not exist previously. What countries disappeared altogether? Which countries changed the most in size?
- *Unlabeled map exercise: Label the countries of Europe, Post WWI. Label all bodies of water shown on this map.*

17. China's Long March – Page 216

- Label these bodies of water: *(Consult an atlas or globe as necessary).*
  - The sea between Japan and Korea
  - The sea between Korea and China
  - The bay touching India and Burma
  - The ocean on the right side of your map
- *Unlabeled map exercise: Draw in the route taken by Mao Zedong when he led his Chinese army on the Long March. Label the countries on China's borders.*

18. China and Japan at War – Page 218
   - Color the areas occupied by the Japanese Empire by 1932 using one color. Using a second color, fill in the additional areas occupied by Japan in 1941. Finally, with a third color, fill in the areas still under China's control.
   - Label the four islands of Japan *(refer to discussion questions for map #2 – Japan Opens to Trade)*.
   - *Unlabeled map exercise: Label China and its surrounding countries. Label all bodies of water shown on this map.*

19. World War II – Page 220
   - Referring to the previous map "Europe, Post WWI", label the countries that are not labeled.
   - Find Ireland, Sweden, Portugal, Spain, Morocco and Turkey. Print a capital letter N on these countries for they remained neutral during the war. Color them all the same color.
   - Color all the countries within the dots another color. This entire area was under German/Axis control by 1941.
   - The remaining countries formed the Allied Forces.
   - *Unlabeled map exercise: See point #1 above. Label all bodies of water. Draw in the Ural Mountains.*

20. Italy and the Balkan Peninsula – Page 222
   - Label the two larger islands in the Mediterranean Sea shown here.
   - What was the previous name of the city of Istanbul in Turkey?
   - Compare this map with map #12 "The Balkan Wars" on page 34. How have the country divisions changed?
   - *Unlabeled map exercise: Label Italy and Greece and the surrounding countries. Label the islands and bodies of water. Locate and label the city of Istanbul (previously named Constantinople).*

21. Independence for India – Page 224
   - Using an atlas or globe, find the island of Sri Lanka. Draw it onto your map and label it. Find and number the lines of latitude and longitude using your globe as your reference. *(Remember that longitude lines stretch from pole to pole and latitude lines run parallel to the equator.)*
   - Draw a compass rose on your map. Label the country to the west of Pakistan and to the north of Afghanistan.
   - *Unlabeled map exercise: Label India along with its surrounding countries and seas. Number the lines of latitude and longitude (Use the degree° symbol).*

22. The Nation of Israel – Page 226
   - Label the river running up through Egypt.
   - Using an atlas or globe, find and label the cities of Jerusalem, Tel Aviv, Beirut and

Cairo. Label the country to the north of Syria and Iraq. Label the island off the southern coast of Turkey.

- *Unlabeled map exercise: Label Israel and the surrounding countries. Label the bodies of water, including the river flowing up through Egypt.*

23. The 50 United States of America – Page 228

- Point to each state and name it.
- Label the countries to the north and south of the United States.
- Consult a globe to determine which state is the furthest from the lower 48 – Alaska or Hawaii?
- *Unlabeled map exercise: Label all states with their two letter abbreviation (ie: Texas = TX). Label the countries to the north and south of the United States.*

24. The Cold War – Page 230

- Using your previous map "Europe, Post WWI" as a reference, label the three countries north of Poland.
- Color Warsaw Pact *(W)* countries all the same color, NATO *(N)* countries another color, and neutral countries a third color.
- Using a bold marker, draw a line along the western-most boundary of the Warsaw Pact nations. This boundary line between the free and communist states was deemed "The Iron Curtain."
- *Unlabeled map exercise: Label the countries of Europe as they were at this time in history. Consult a current globe or map to see how they have changed since 1989, when the "Iron Curtain" came down.*

25. The Wars in Asia – Page 232

- Label as many islands and island chains that you know. Consult your atlas or globe for the rest.
- Both Korea and Vietnam were divided nations at this time. The northern halves of each were communist countries. Color these halves the same color, and their southern counterparts a different color.
- Using your globe as a reference, number the lines of latitude and longitude.
- *Unlabeled map exercise: Label North and South Vietnam and North and South Korea. Number the lines of latitude and longitude shown here on this map. Label the surrounding oceans and seas.*

26. The Gulf War – Page 234

- Label the countries on either side of Iraq, using your globe as your reference.
- *(Your student may not remember this war. In fact, s/he may not even have been born yet. Share your memories from this recent war in the Middle East with your student/s, include your age and whether or not you were married or had children at this time in your life.)*
- *Unlabeled map exercise: Label the countries of the Middle East shown on this map. Label all bodies of water.*

27. The Attack on the United States – Page 236
- Label the state to the east of New York. Label the island to the east. Label the ocean shown on this map.
- *(Discuss the events most memorable to you on this day in history. What events followed this tragic terrorist attack on American soil?)*
- *Unlabeled map exercise: Label the states shown here on this map. Locate and label the cities of New York and Washington, DC.*

28. The Conflict in Iraq – Page 238
- Label the four countries bordering Iraq that have been left blank.
- Label the body of water on the southeast tip of Iraq.
- What was/is the goal of this war?
- On December 13, 2003, Saddam Hussein was pulled out of a hole outside of his hometown of Tikrit. Locate this site on your map.
- *Unlabeled map exercise: Label the Persian Gulf and the two main rivers flowing from it. Draw in some of the major battle sites from this recent conflict. Using an atlas or globe, label some of the major cities in Iraq. Label the countries bordering Iraq.*

Glossary of Terms Used

Allied Powers – the 23 countries allied against the Central Powers in WWI and the 49 countries allied against the Axis in the 2nd World War.

Atlas – a book containing a collection of maps.

Axis, the – the alliance of Bulgaria, Finland, Germany, Hungary, Italy, Japan and Romania during the 2nd World War.

Central Powers – the alliance between Germany, Austria-Hungary, Bulgaria and Turkey during the 1st World War.

Colony – a land or place settled by people from another country.

Confederate States of America – the government formed (1861-1865) by the southern states of the United States after they had seceded from the Union.

Continent – one of the seven great land masses of the world – *Europe, Asia, Africa, North America, South America, Australia and Antarctica.*

Empire – a kingdom which has been extended by military might to include countries which were originally independent.

Globe – a spherical model of the earth or heavens.

Island – a piece of land, smaller than a continent, entirely surrounded by water.

Kilometer – a unit of distance measurement equaling 1,000 meters.

Latitude – the distance of a place on the earth's surface from the equator as measured in degrees, the equator being 0° latitude and the poles *(N or S)* being 90°.

Longitude – the distance between the meridian passing through a given point on the earth's surface and the poles, measured in degrees. The standard meridian is at Greenwich, England.

Mile – a unit of distance measurement equaling 1,760 yards.

NATO – North Atlantic Treaty Organization (April 4, 1949) – an alliance set up by the U.S., Great Britain, and 10 other countries in an effort to defend one another in the event of another war or attack on these lands.

Ocean – the large bodies of salt water which comprise the majority (over ⅔) of the earth's surface.

Revolution – the overthrow of an established government.

Scale – a line on a map with marks dividing it to show proportional distance.

Terrorism – using acts inspiring terror as a method of ruling or of conducting political oppression.

Union, the – the 23 northern states which opposed the Confederate states in the Civil War (1861-1865)

Warsaw Pact – a treaty signed by the U.S.S.R. and seven other countries in response to the formation of NATO.

Geographical Regions Covered

Crimea	Black Sea	Russia	Japan
China	Italy	Corsica	France
Canada	Germany	Prussia	Bavaria
The Congo	India	Britain	Australia
Mongolia	Thailand	Bulgaria	Romania
Istanbul	Sicily	Montenegro	Caspian Sea
Persia	Finland	Ireland	Korea
Burma	Sweden	Portugal	Spain
Morocco	Turkey	Mediterranean	Sri Lanka
Israel	Egypt	United States	Alaska
Hawaii	Vietnam	New York	

Teacher or parent, you may choose to use these terms and geographical regions listed to put together an end of the year quiz. However, if you follow the lesson plans throughout the year, you may not feel that this is necessary.

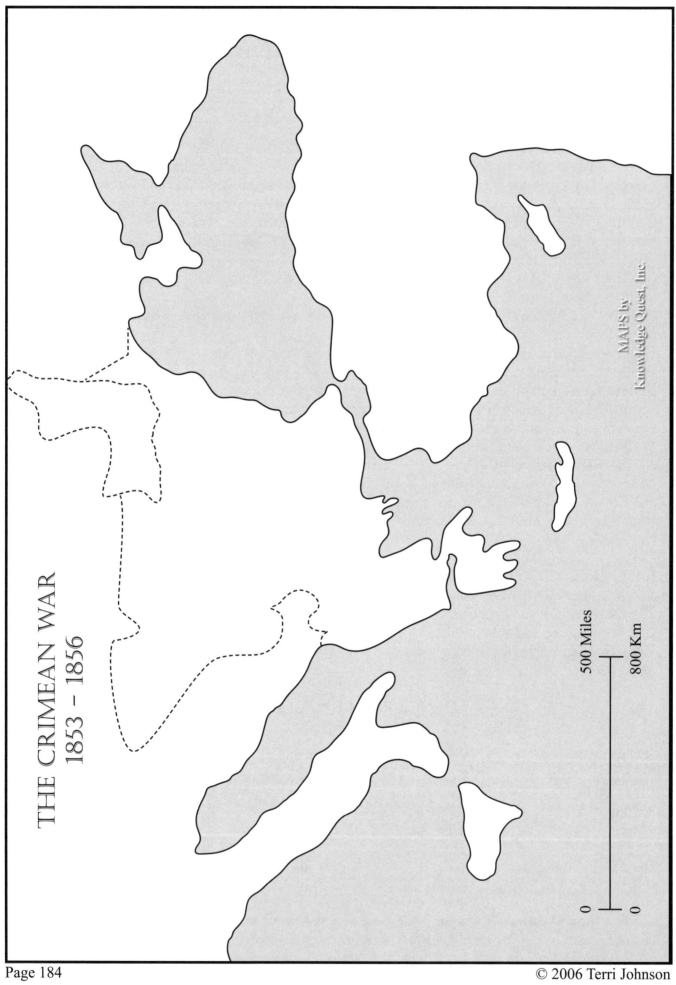

THE CRIMEAN WAR
1853 – 1856

500 Miles

800 Km

0

0

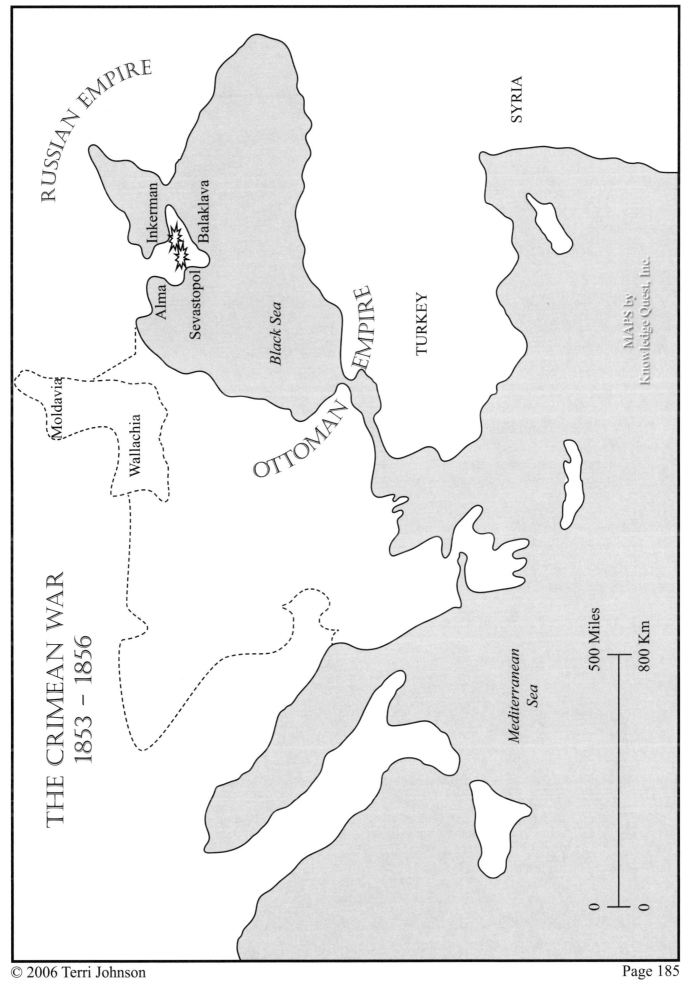

THE CRIMEAN WAR
1853 – 1856

RUSSIAN EMPIRE

Inkerman

Balaklava

Alma

Sevastopol

Black Sea

Moldavia

Wallachia

OTTOMAN EMPIRE

TURKEY

SYRIA

Mediterranean Sea

MAPS by Knowledge Quest, Inc.

500 Miles

800 Km

0

0

JAPAN OPENS TO TRADE
1854

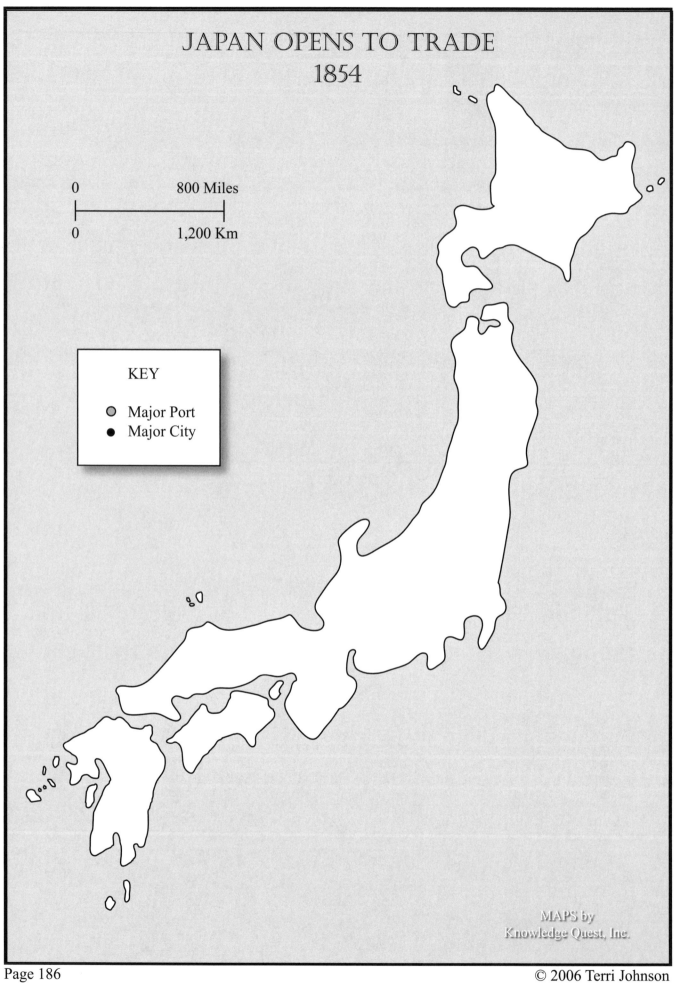

KEY

○ Major Port
● Major City

0   800 Miles

0   1,200 Km

MAPS by
Knowledge Quest, Inc.

JAPAN OPENS TO TRADE
1854

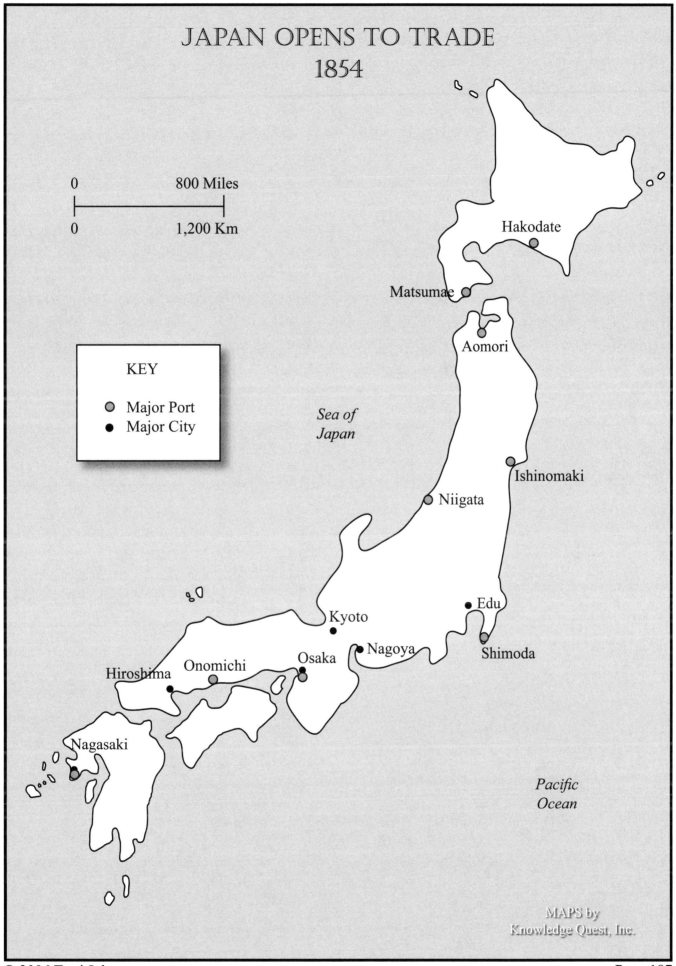

KEY

Major Port

Major City

Hakodate

Matsumae

Aomori

Sea of
Japan

Ishinomaki

Niigata

Kyoto

Edu

Shimoda

Osaka

Nagoya

Onomichi

Hiroshima

Nagasaki

Pacific
Ocean

0   800 Miles

0   1,200 Km

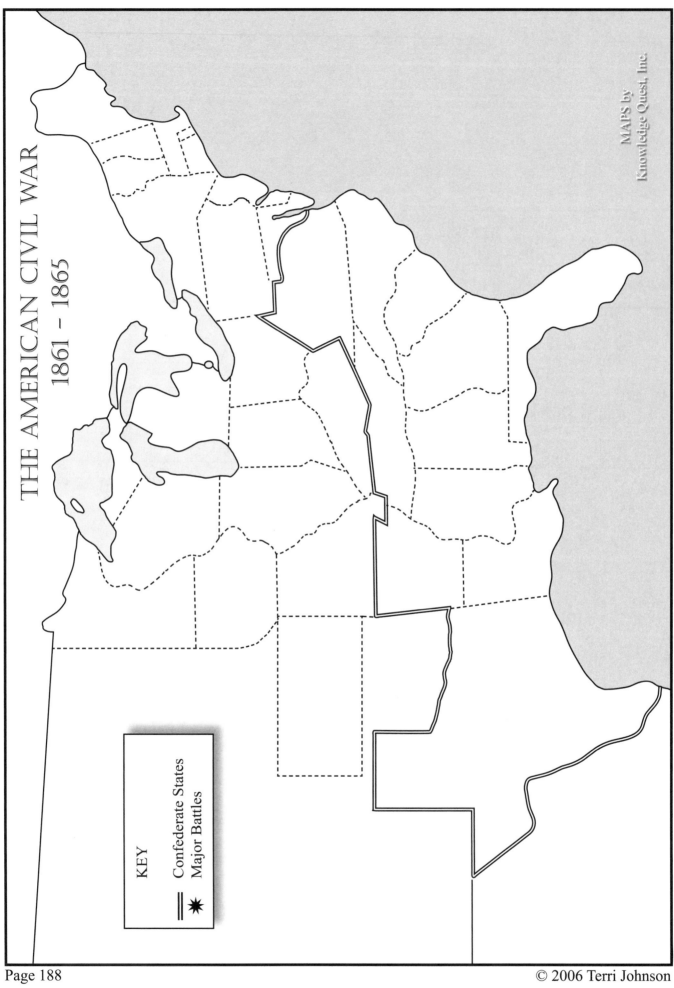

THE AMERICAN CIVIL WAR
1861 – 1865

MAPS by
Knowledge Quest, Inc.

KEY
Confederate States
Major Battles

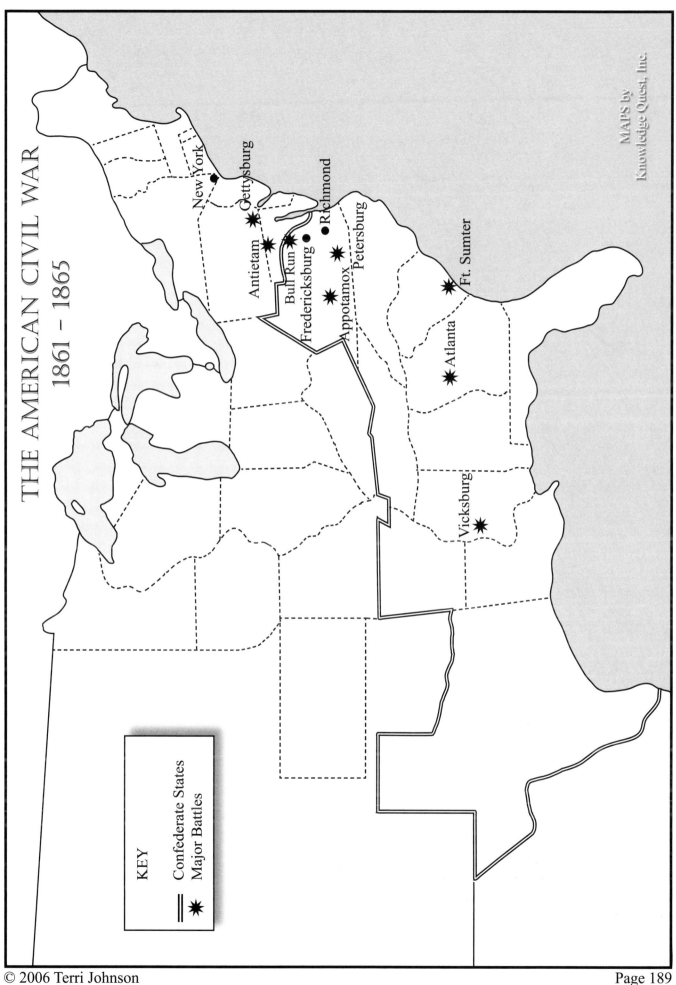

THE AMERICAN CIVIL WAR
1861 – 1865

New York

Gettysburg

Antietam

Bull Run

Fredericksburg

Richmond

Appotamox

Petersburg

Ft. Sumter

Atlanta

Vicksburg

KEY

Confederate States

Major Battles

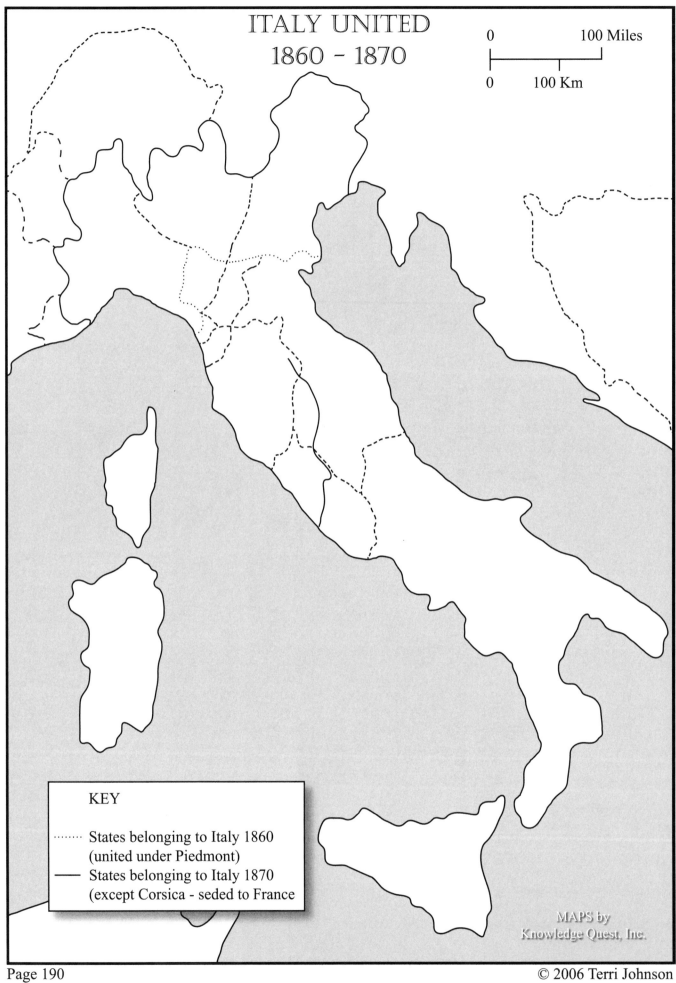

ITALY UNITED
1860 – 1870

0   100 Miles

0   100 Km

KEY

.... States belonging to Italy 1860
(united under Piedmont)

——— States belonging to Italy 1870
(except Corsica - seded to France

MAPS by
Knowledge Quest, Inc.

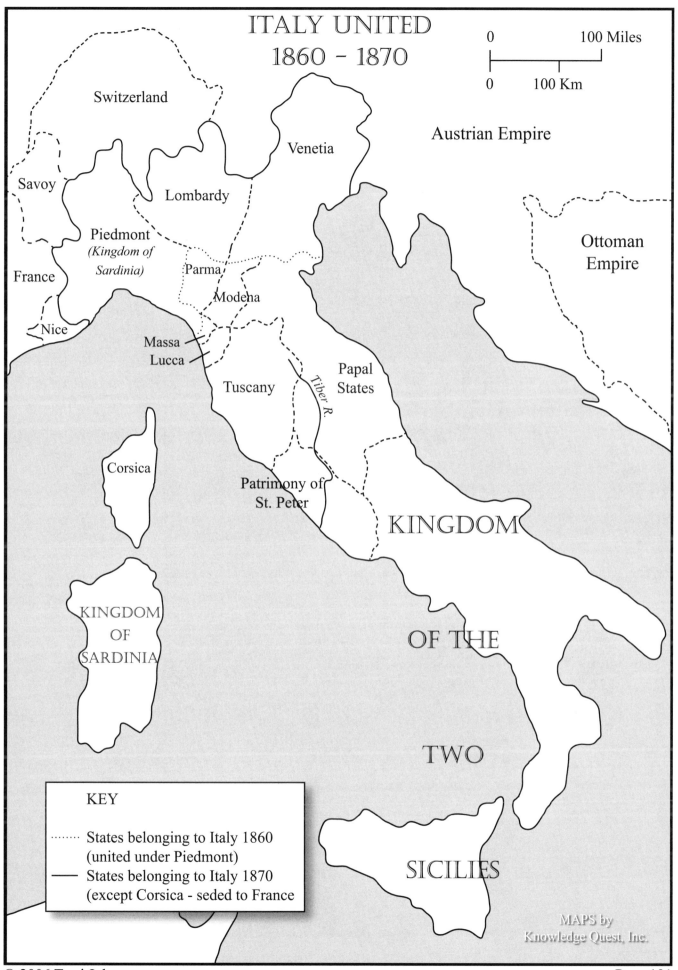

ITALY UNITED
1860 – 1870

0   100 Miles

0   100 Km

Switzerland

Austrian Empire

Venetia

Savoy

Lombardy

Ottoman
Empire

Piedmont
*(Kingdom of
Sardinia)*

France

Parma

Modena

Nice

Massa

Lucca

Papal
States

Tiber R.

Tuscany

Corsica

Patrimony of
St. Peter

KINGDOM

KINGDOM
OF
SARDINIA

OF THE

TWO

KEY

.... States belonging to Italy 1860
(united under Piedmont)

———— States belonging to Italy 1870
(except Corsica - seded to France

SICILIES

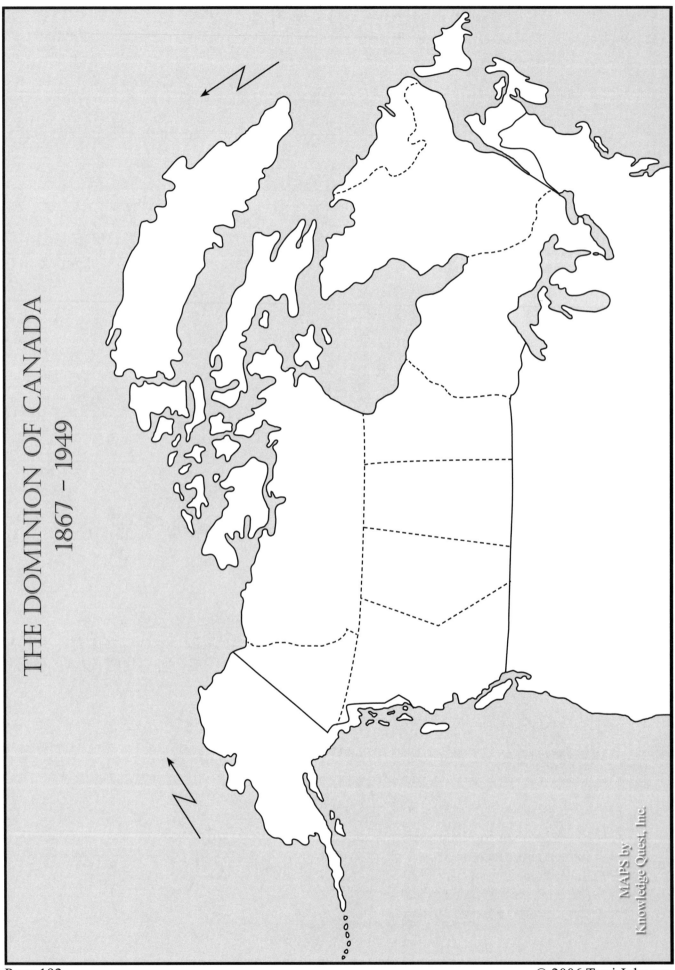

THE DOMINION OF CANADA
1867 – 1949

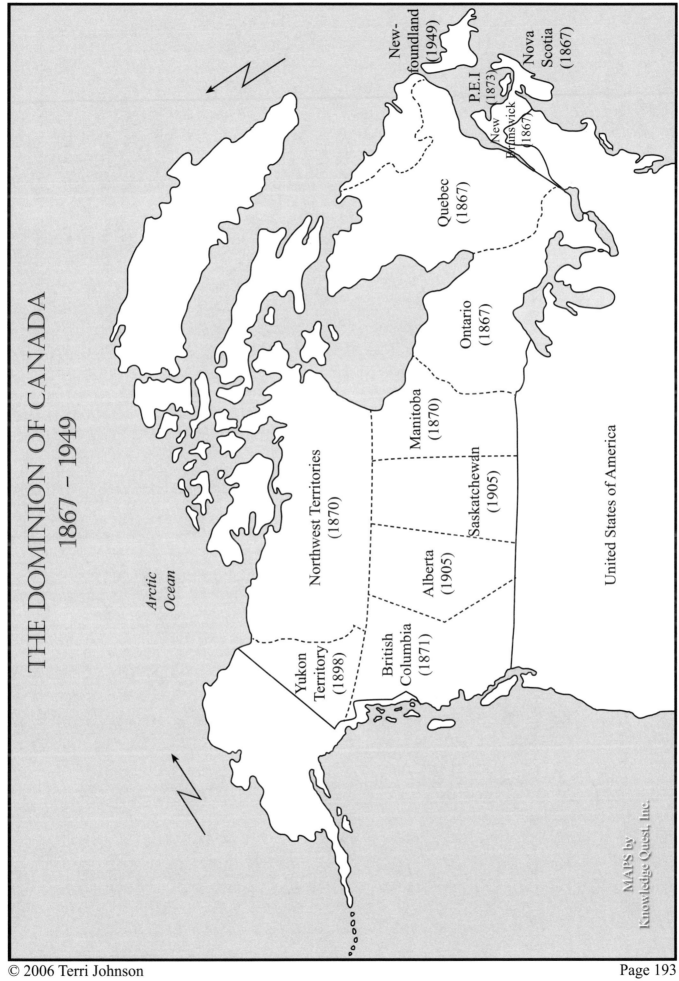

THE DOMINION OF CANADA
1867 – 1949

Arctic Ocean

New-foundland (1949)

Nova Scotia (1867)

P.E.I (1873)

New Brunswick (1867)

Quebec (1867)

Ontario (1867)

Manitoba (1870)

Saskatchewan (1905)

Alberta (1905)

Northwest Territories (1870)

Yukon Territory (1898)

British Columbia (1871)

United States of America

MAPS by Knowledge Quest, Inc.

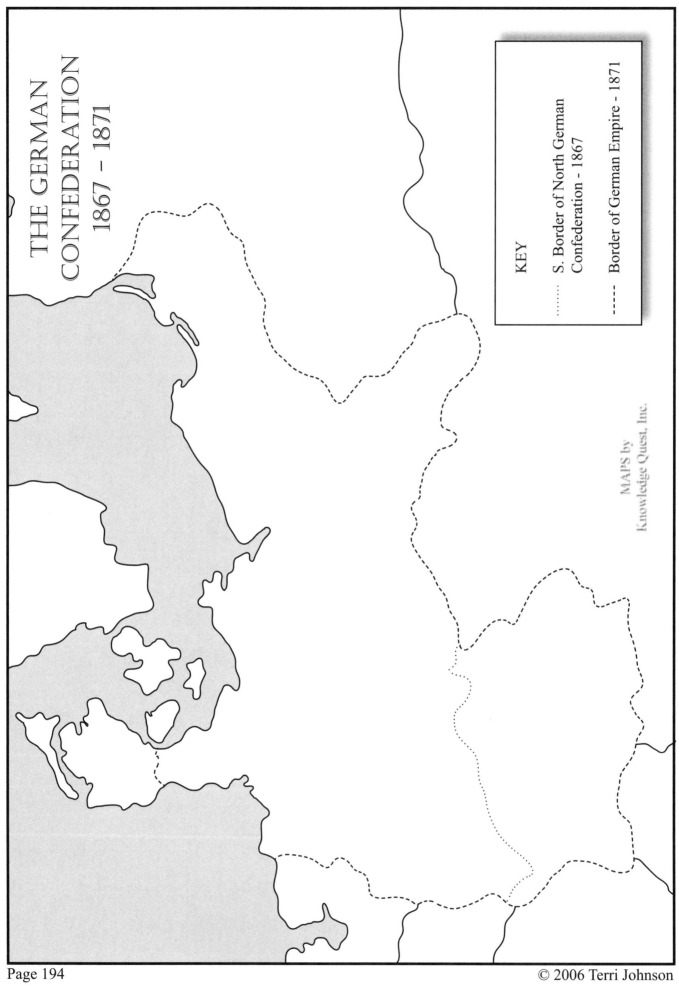

THE GERMAN
CONFEDERATION
1867 – 1871

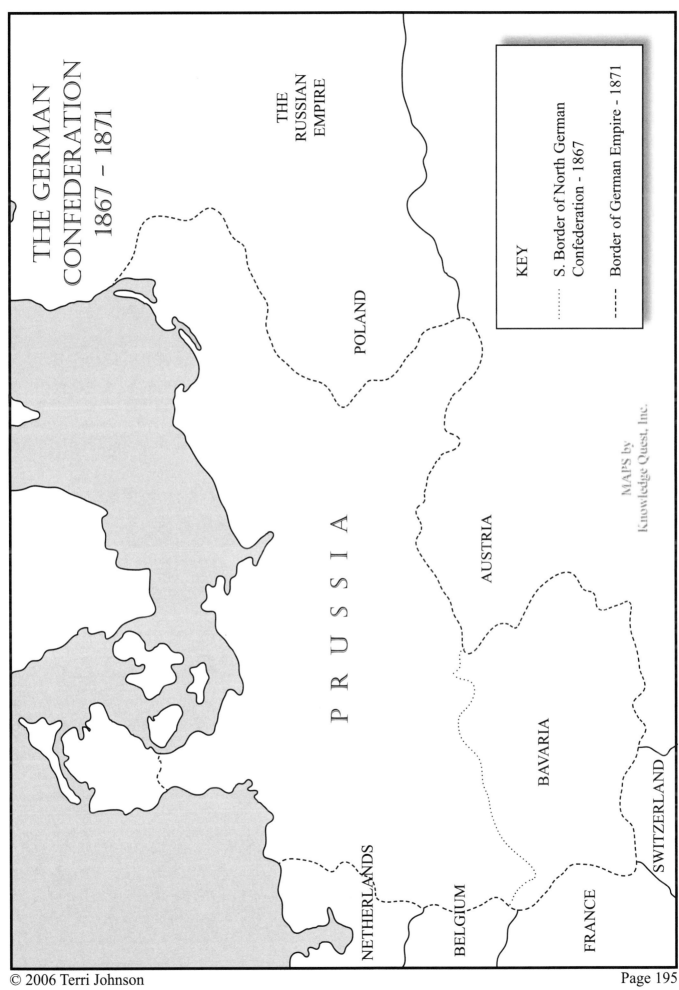

THE GERMAN
CONFEDERATION
1867 – 1871

THE
RUSSIAN
EMPIRE

POLAND

PRUSSIA

AUSTRIA

BAVARIA

NETHERLANDS

BELGIUM

FRANCE

SWITZERLAND

KEY

.... S. Border of North German
Confederation - 1867

----- Border of German Empire - 1871

MAPS by
Knowledge Quest, Inc.

© 2006 Terri Johnson

THE SCRAMBLE FOR AFRICA
1884

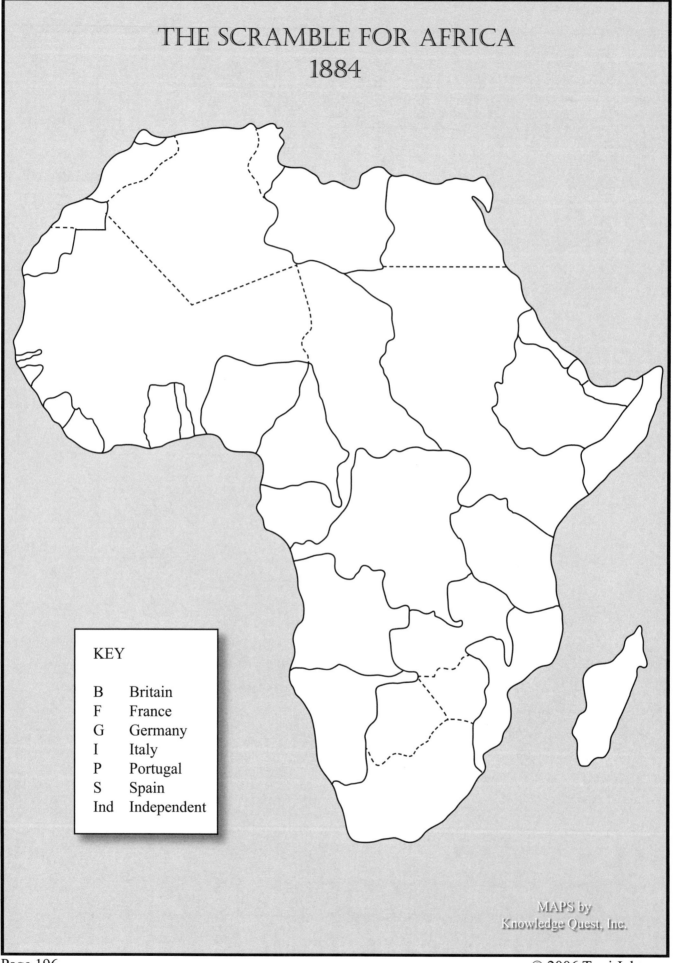

KEY

B Britain
F France
G Germany
I Italy
P Portugal
S Spain
Ind Independent

THE SCRAMBLE FOR AFRICA
1884

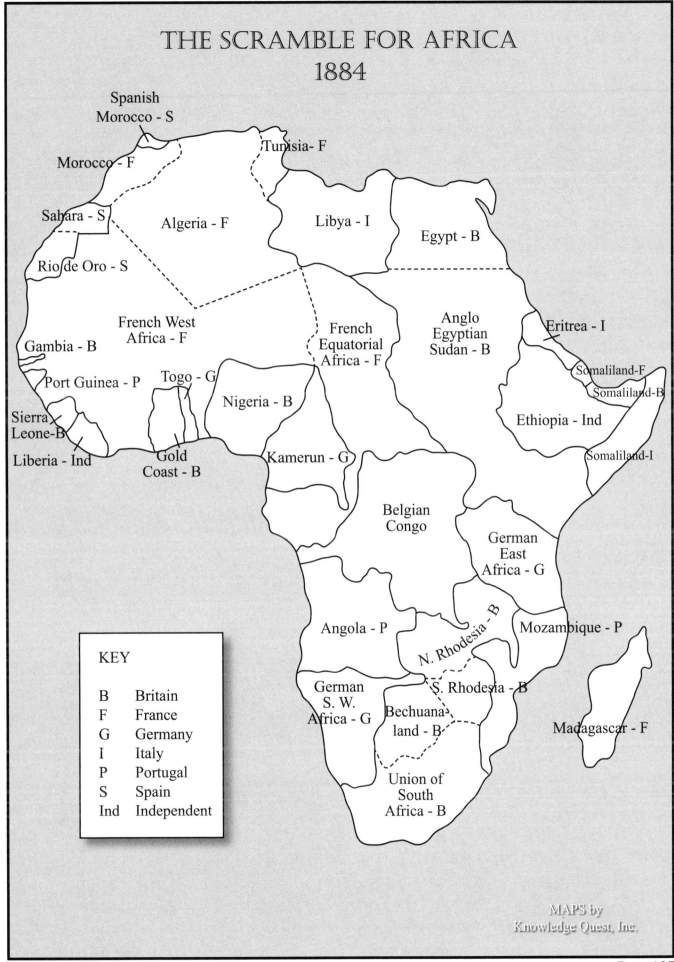

KEY

B	Britain
F	France
G	Germany
I	Italy
P	Portugal
S	Spain
Ind	Independent

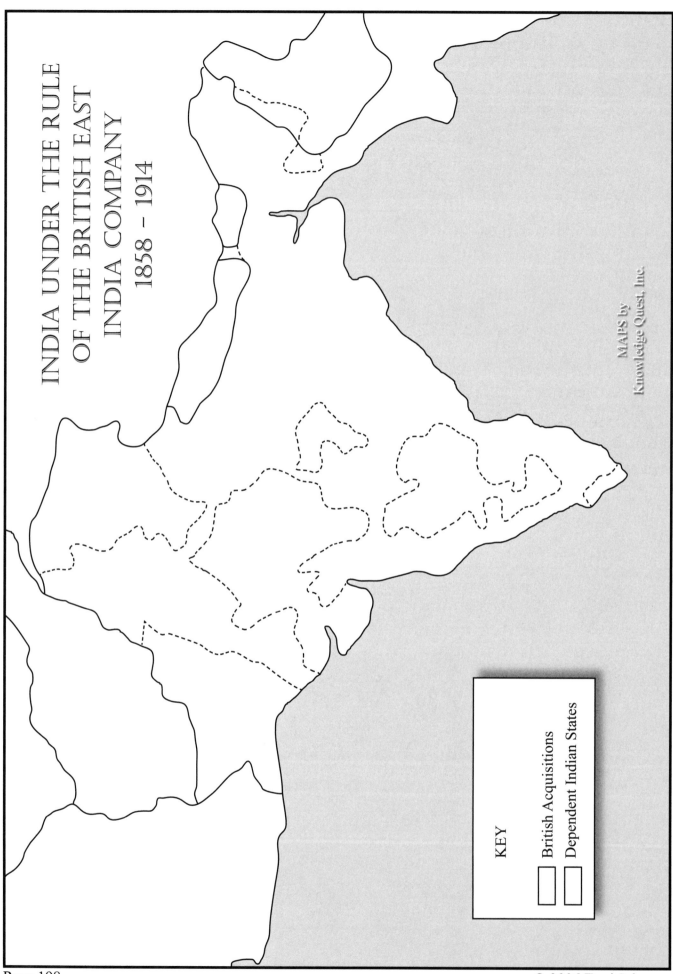

INDIA UNDER THE RULE
OF THE BRITISH EAST
INDIA COMPANY
1858 – 1914

MAPS by
Knowledge Quest, Inc.

KEY

British Acquisitions
Dependent Indian States

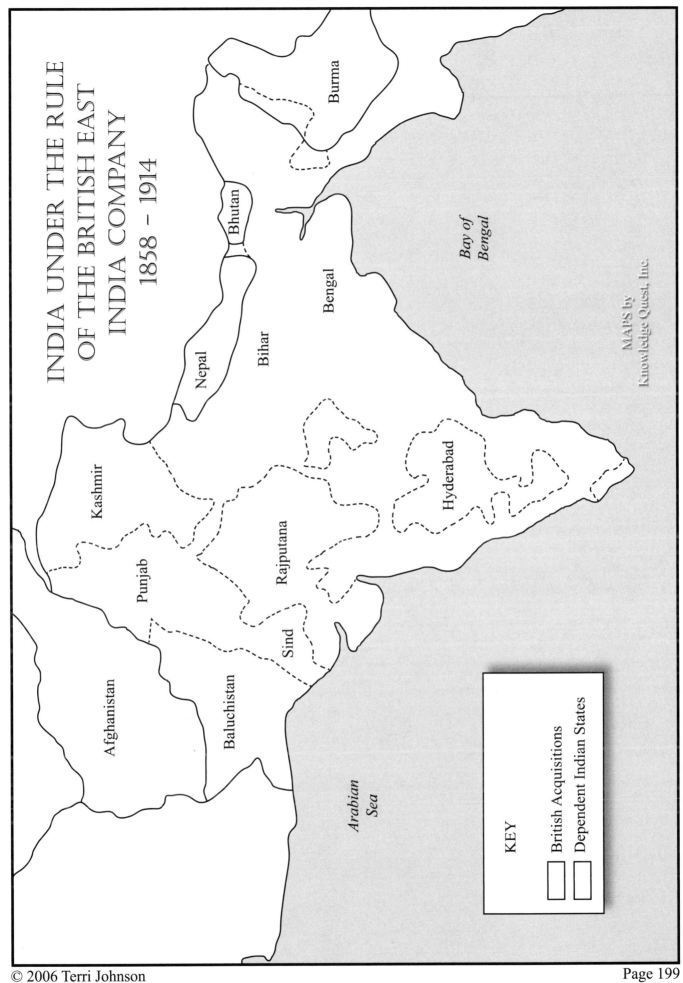

INDIA UNDER THE RULE OF THE BRITISH EAST INDIA COMPANY 1858 – 1914

Burma

Bhutan

Nepal

Bihar

Bengal

Bay of Bengal

Kashmir

Punjab

Rajputana

Hyderabad

Afghanistan

Baluchistan

Sind

Arabian Sea

KEY

British Acquisitions

Dependent Indian States

MAPS by Knowledge Quest, Inc.

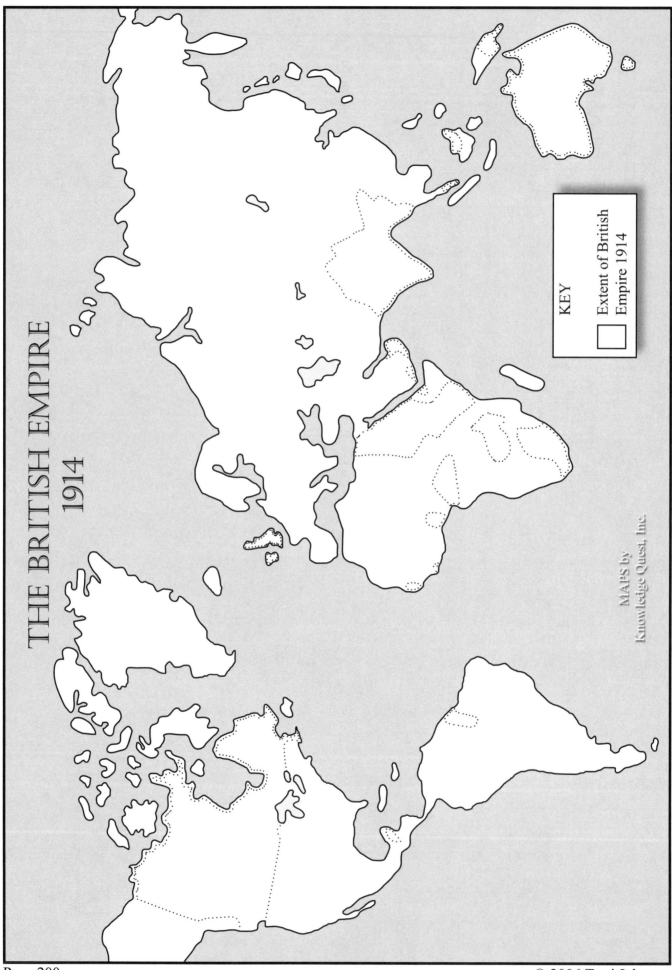

THE BRITISH EMPIRE
1914

KEY

Extent of British
Empire 1914

MAPS by
Knowledge Quest, Inc.

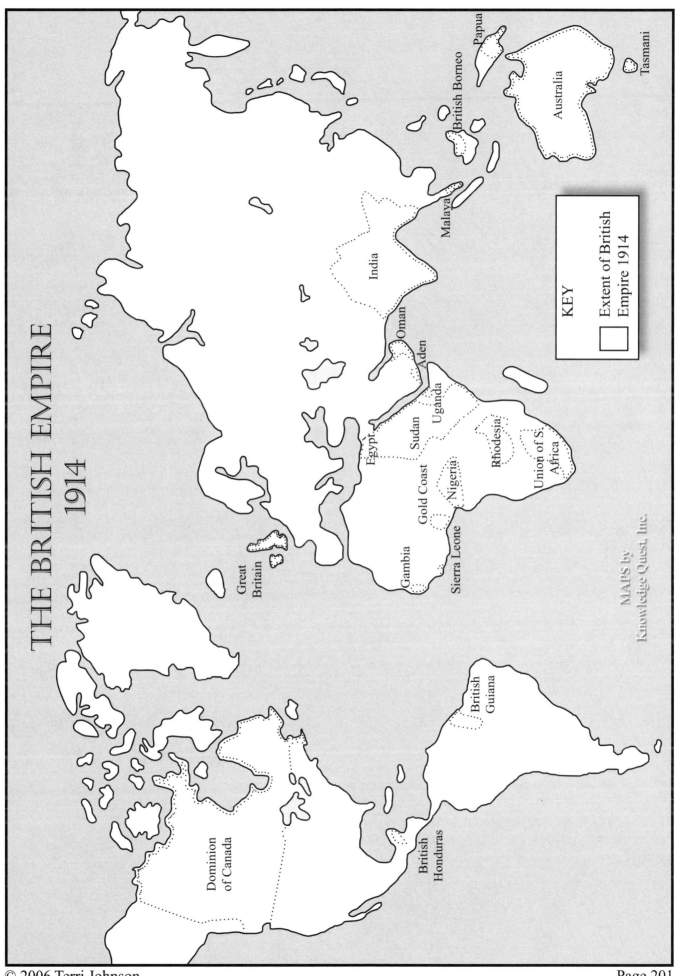

THE BRITISH EMPIRE 1914

KEY

Extent of British Empire 1914

Papua
British Borneo
Tasmani
Australia
Malaya
India
Oman
Aden
Uganda
Egypt
Sudan
Gold Coast
Nigeria
Rhodesia
Union of S. Africa
Gambia
Sierra Leone
Great Britain
British Guiana
Dominion of Canada
British Honduras

MAPS by
Knowledge Quest, Inc.

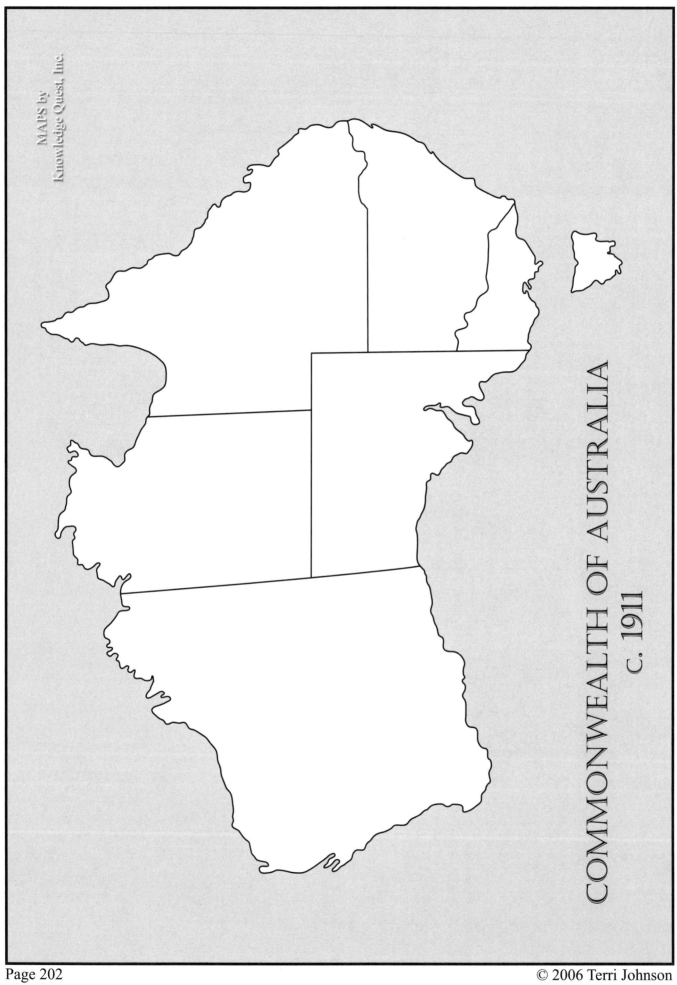

COMMONWEALTH OF AUSTRALIA
c. 1911

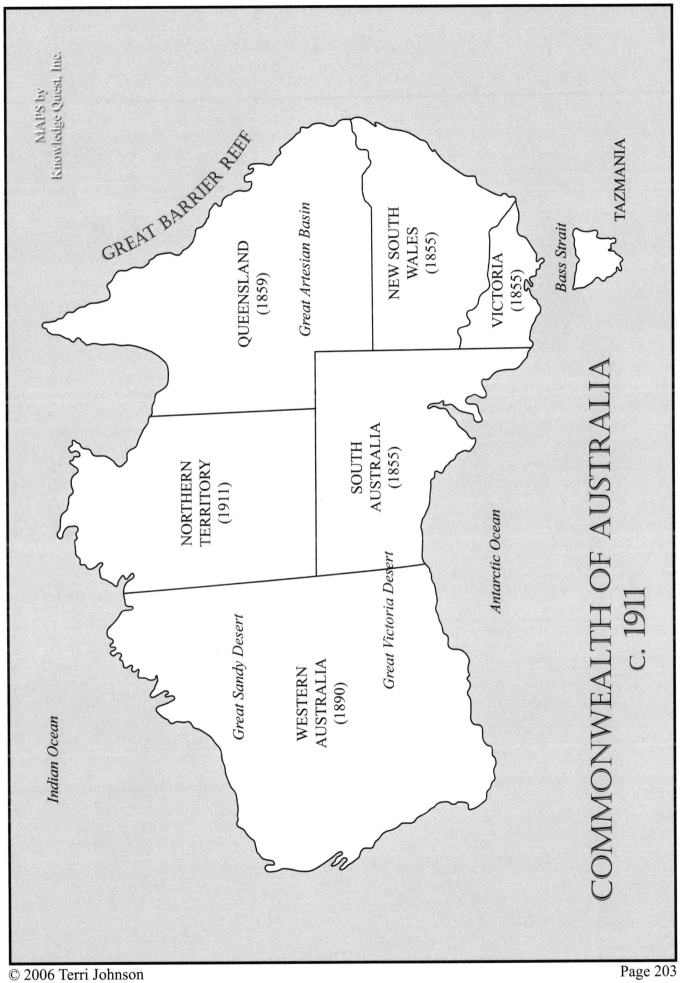

GREAT BARRIER REEF

Indian Ocean

QUEENSLAND
(1859)

Great Artesian Basin

NEW SOUTH
WALES
(1855)

VICTORIA
(1855)

TAZMANIA

Bass Strait

NORTHERN
TERRITORY
(1911)

SOUTH
AUSTRALIA
(1855)

Great Sandy Desert

WESTERN
AUSTRALIA
(1890)

Great Victoria Desert

Antarctic Ocean

COMMONWEALTH OF AUSTRALIA
c. 1911

THE BOXER REBELLION IN CHINA
1900 – 1911

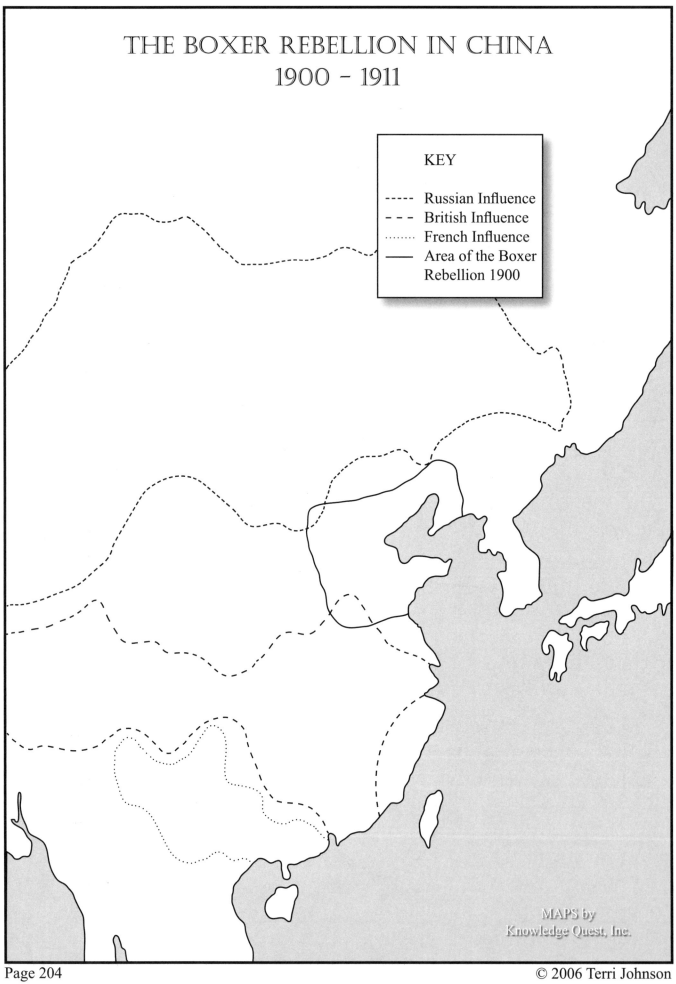

KEY

---- Russian Influence
--- British Influence
······ French Influence
—— Area of the Boxer
Rebellion 1900

MAPS by
Knowledge Quest, Inc.

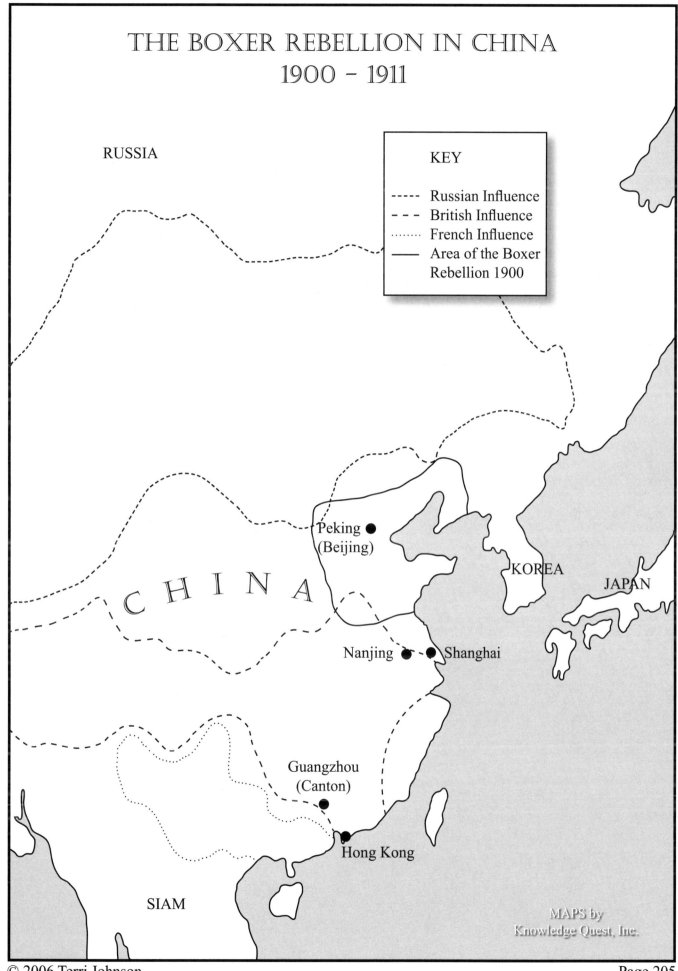

THE BOXER REBELLION IN CHINA
1900 – 1911

RUSSIA

KEY

- - - - Russian Influence
- - - British Influence
.... French Influence
——— Area of the Boxer
Rebellion 1900

CHINA

Peking
(Beijing)

KOREA

JAPAN

Nanjing ● ● Shanghai

Guangzhou
(Canton)

Hong Kong

SIAM

MAPS by
Knowledge Quest, Inc.

THE BALKAN WARS
1912 – 1914

KEY

----- Border of Country - 1912

——— Border of Country - 1914

(1913) Date of Independence
from Ottoman Empire

MAPS by
Knowledge Quest, Inc.

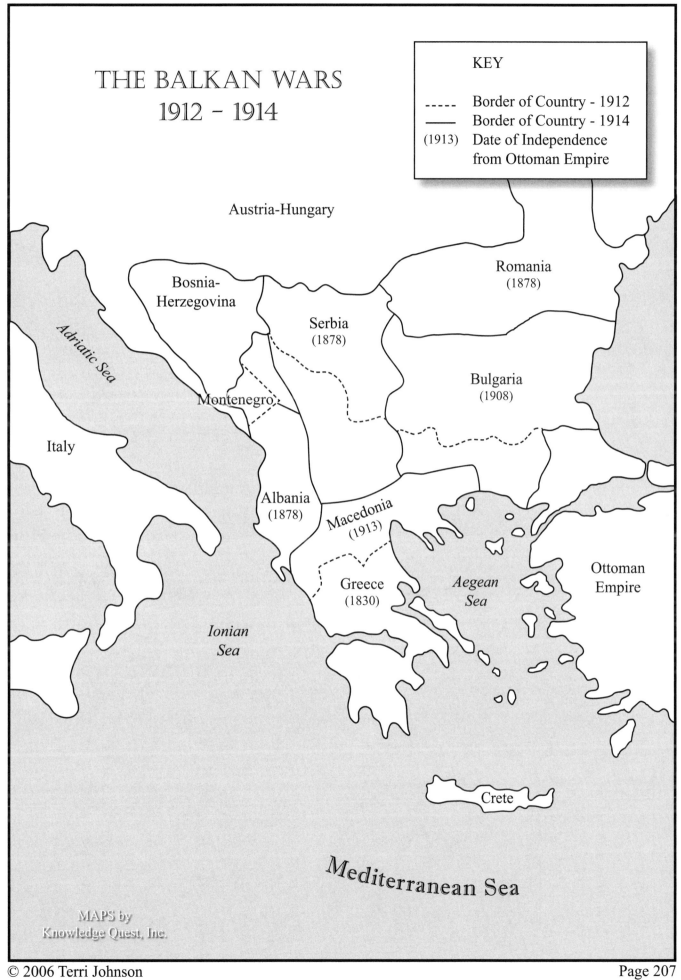

THE BALKAN WARS
1912 – 1914

KEY

----- Border of Country - 1912

——— Border of Country - 1914

(1913) Date of Independence from Ottoman Empire

Austria-Hungary

Romania
(1878)

Bosnia-
Herzegovina

Serbia
(1878)

Adriatic Sea

Bulgaria
(1908)

Montenegro

Italy

Albania
(1878)

Macedonia
(1913)

Greece
(1830)

*Aegean
Sea*

Ottoman
Empire

*Ionian
Sea*

Mediterranean Sea

Crete

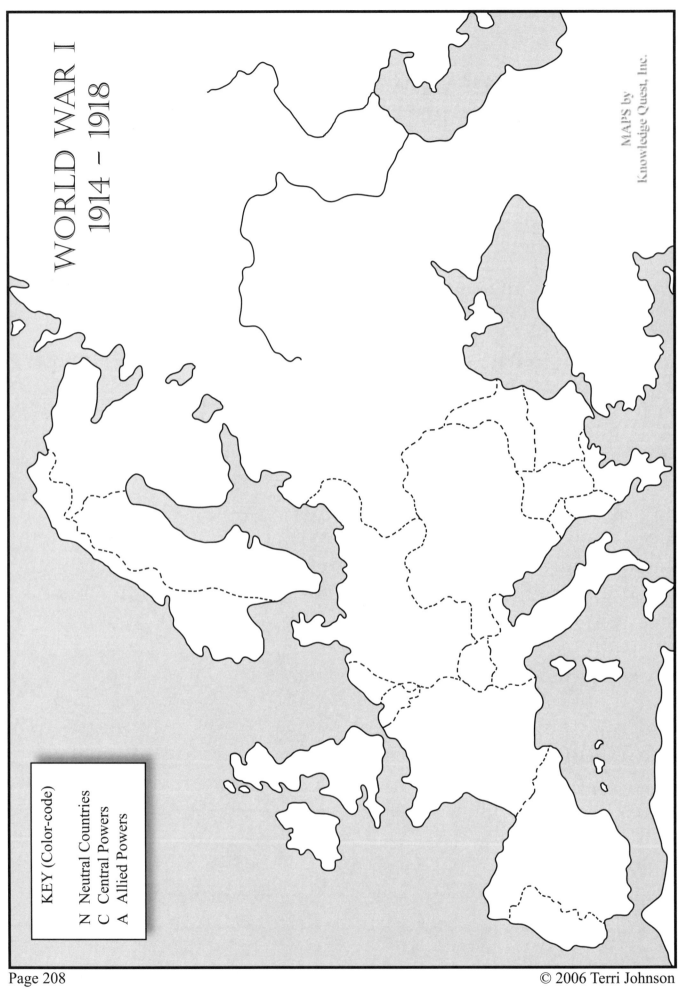

WORLD WAR I
1914 – 1918

MAPS by
Knowledge Quest, Inc.

KEY (Color-code)

N Neutral Countries
C Central Powers
A Allied Powers

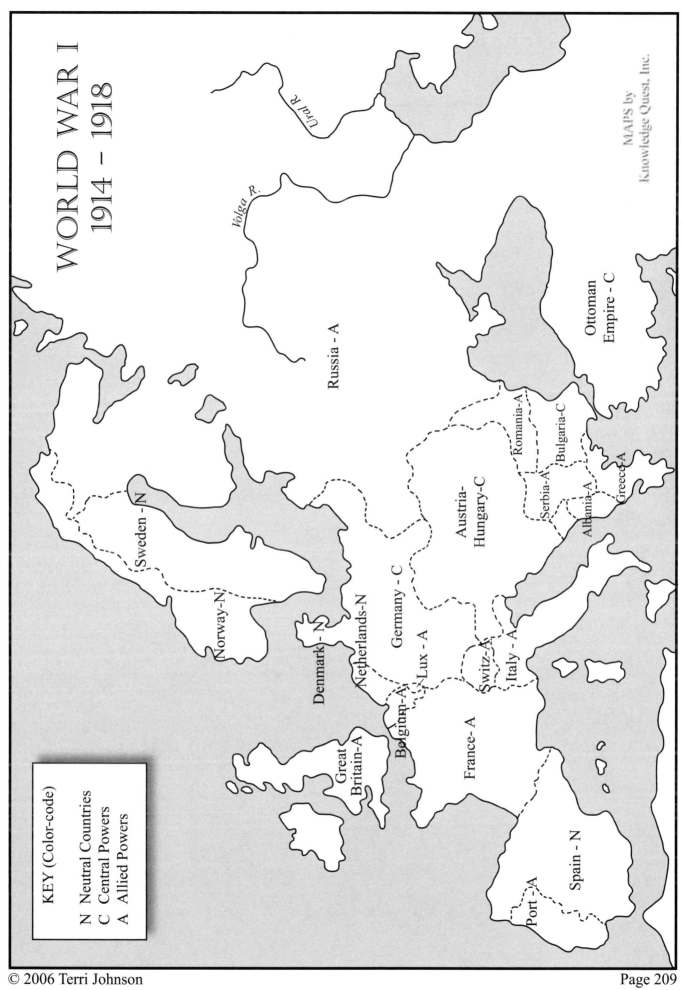

WORLD WAR I
1914 – 1918

MAPS by
Knowledge Quest, Inc.

KEY (Color-code)

N Neutral Countries
C Central Powers
A Allied Powers

Ural R.

Volga R.

Russia - A

Ottoman
Empire - C

Sweden – N

Norway-N

Denmark- N

Netherlands-N

Germany - C

Austria-
Hungary-C

Romania-A

Bulgaria-C

Serbia-A

Albania-A

Greece-A

Lux - A

Switz-A

Italy - A

Belgium-A

France - A

Great
Britain-A

Spain - N

Port -A

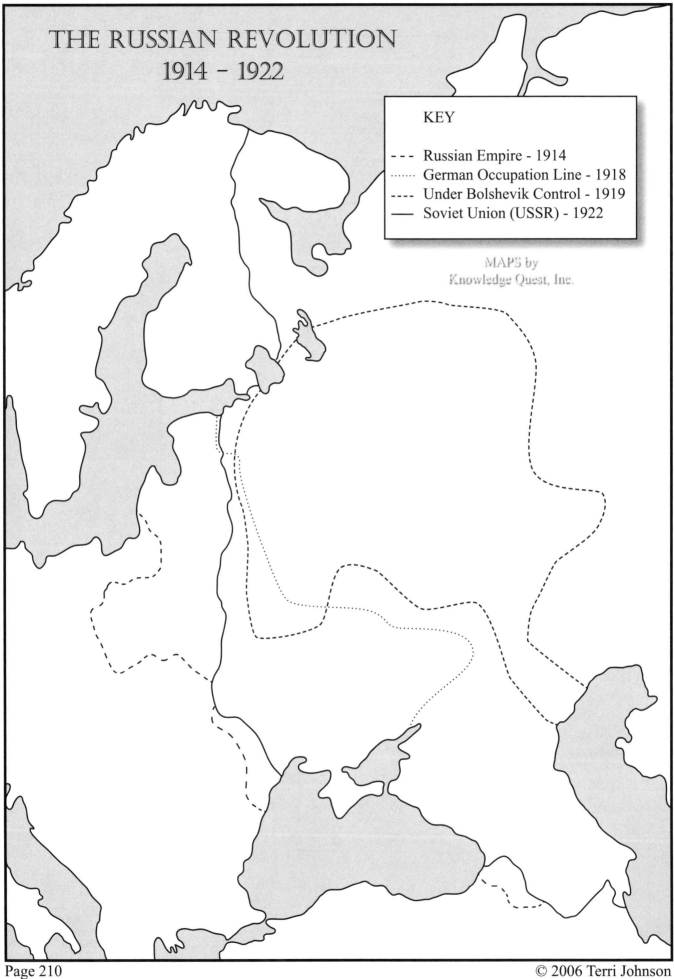

THE RUSSIAN REVOLUTION
1914 – 1922

KEY

- - - Russian Empire - 1914
.... German Occupation Line - 1918
- - - Under Bolshevik Control - 1919
——— Soviet Union (USSR) - 1922

MAPS by
Knowledge Quest, Inc.

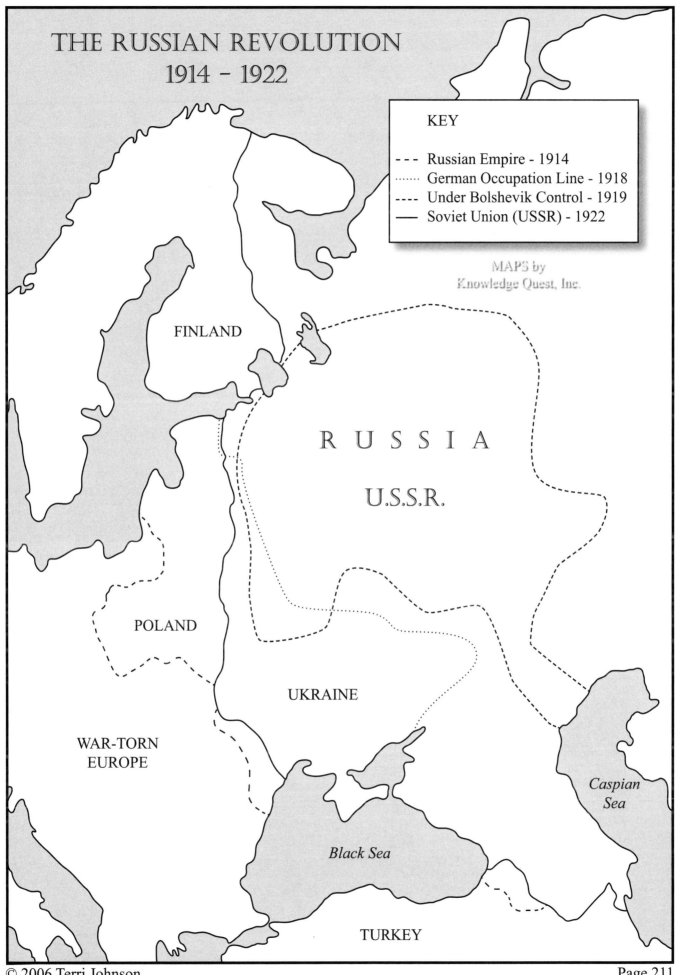

THE RUSSIAN REVOLUTION
1914 – 1922

KEY

--- Russian Empire - 1914
...... German Occupation Line - 1918
– – Under Bolshevik Control - 1919
—— Soviet Union (USSR) - 1922

MAPS by
Knowledge Quest, Inc.

FINLAND

R U S S I A

U.S.S.R.

POLAND

UKRAINE

WAR-TORN
EUROPE

Caspian
Sea

Black Sea

TURKEY

THE DIVISION OF IRELAND
1922

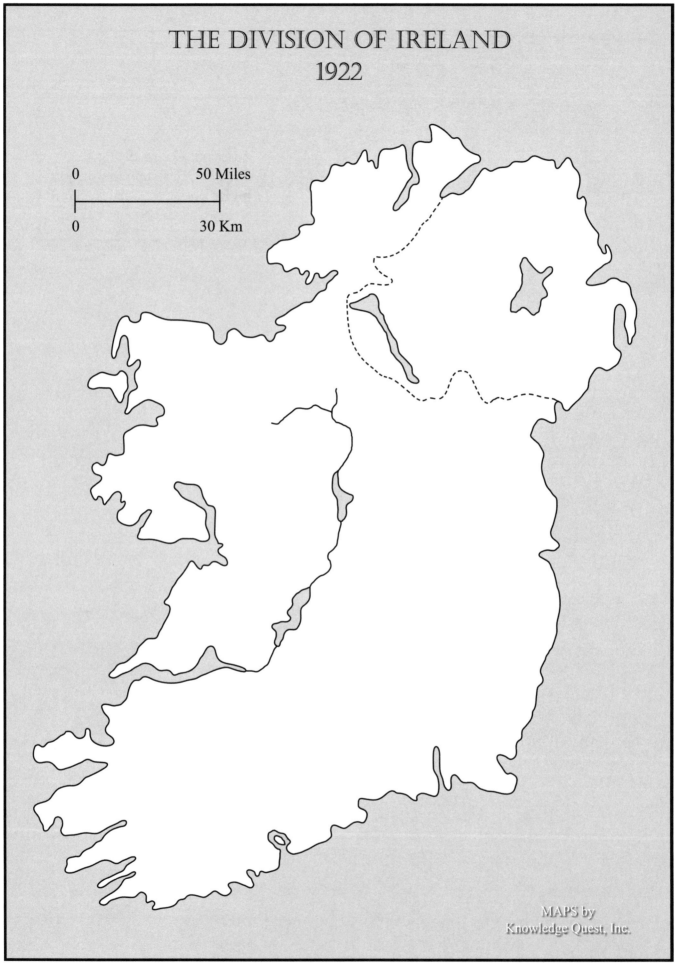

0   50 Miles

0   30 Km

MAPS by
Knowledge Quest, Inc.

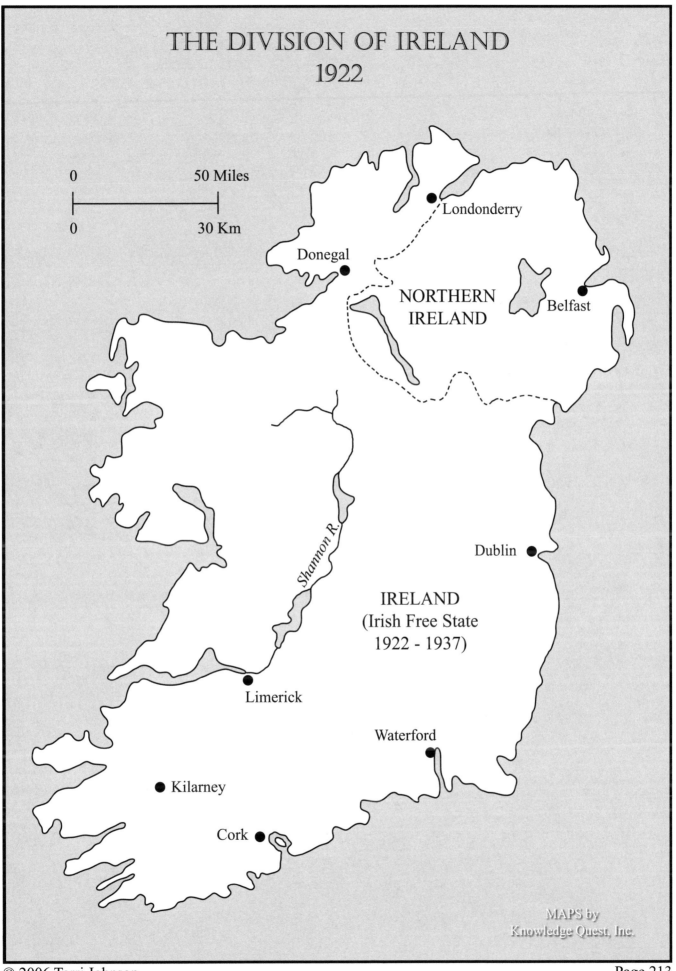

THE DIVISION OF IRELAND
1922

0   50 Miles

0   30 Km

Londonderry

Donegal

NORTHERN
IRELAND

Belfast

Shannon R.

Dublin

IRELAND
(Irish Free State
1922 - 1937)

Limerick

Waterford

Kilarney

Cork

MAPS by
Knowledge Quest, Inc.

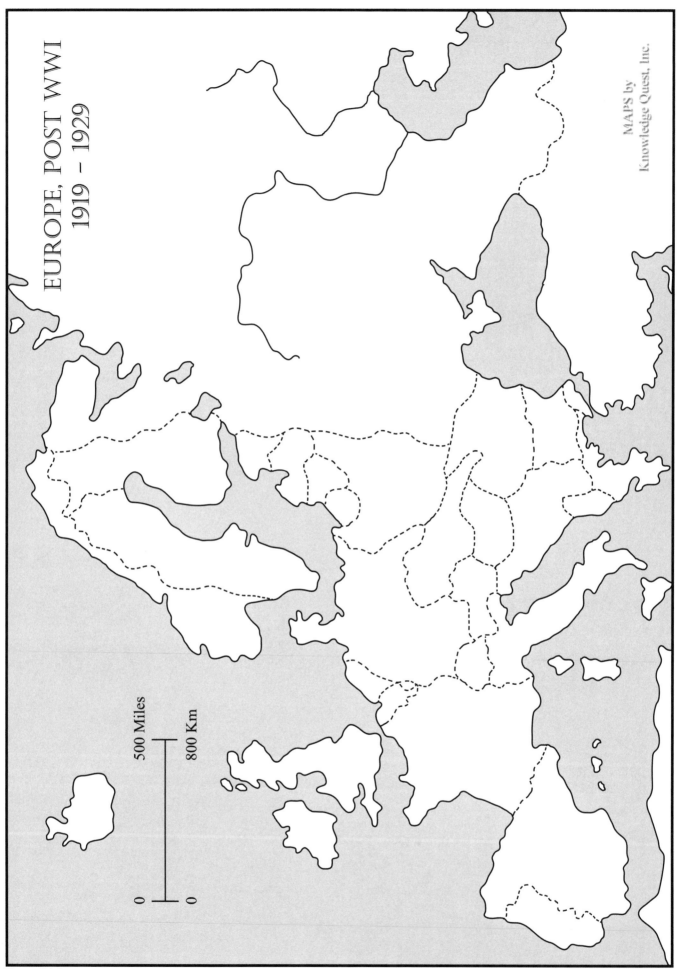

EUROPE, POST WWI
1919 – 1929

500 Miles

800 Km

MAPS by
Knowledge Quest, Inc.

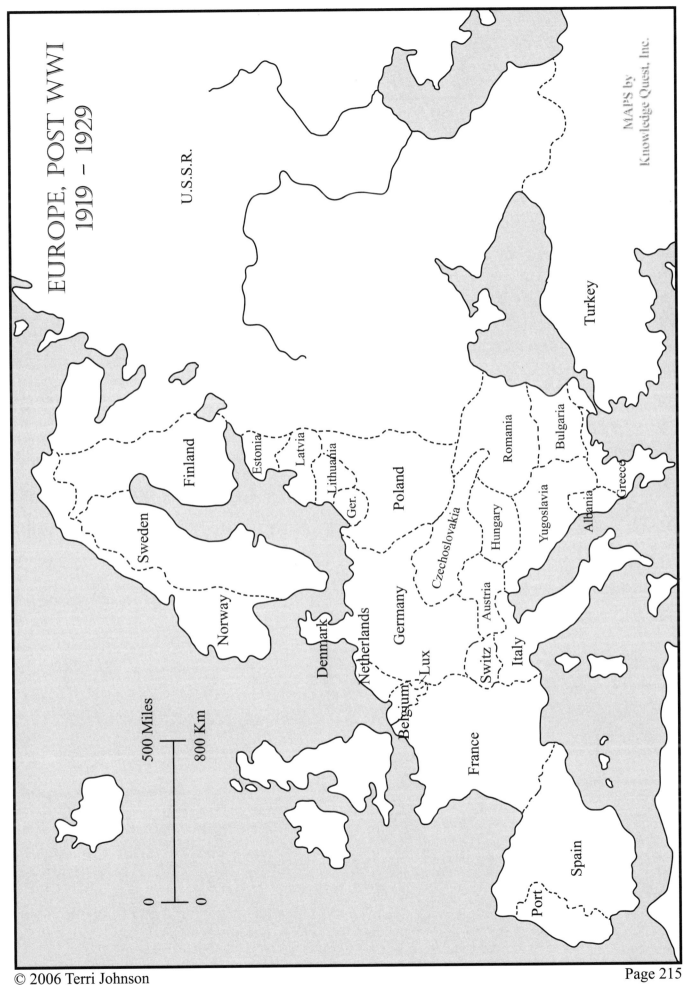

EUROPE, POST WWI
1919 – 1929

MAPS by Knowledge Quest, Inc.

U.S.S.R.

Turkey

Finland

Estonia

Latvia

Lithuania

Ger.

Poland

Romania

Bulgaria

Greece

Sweden

Czechoslovakia

Hungary

Yugoslavia

Albania

Norway

Denmark

Netherlands

Germany

Austria

Switz

Italy

Belgium

Lux

France

500 Miles

800 Km

0

Spain

Port

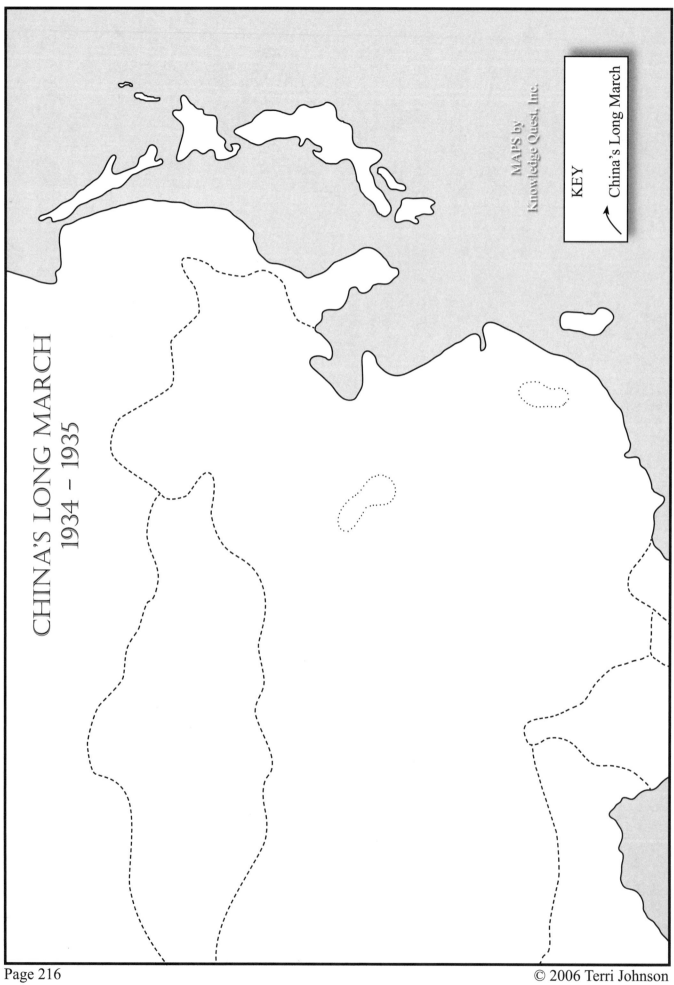

CHINA'S LONG MARCH
1934 – 1935

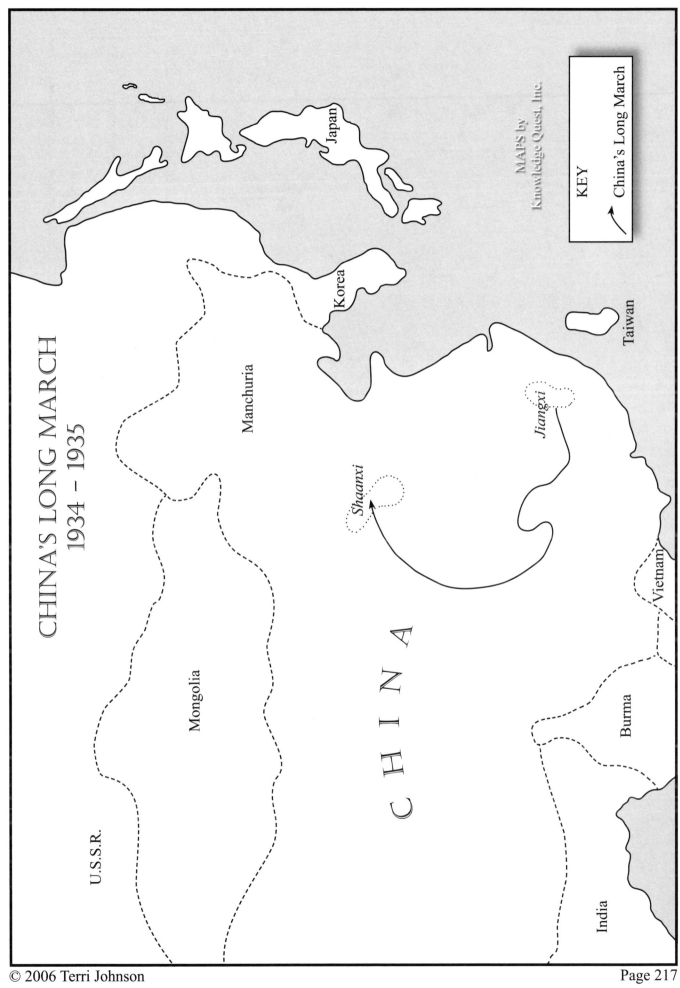

CHINA'S LONG MARCH
1934 – 1935

Japan

Korea

Taiwan

Manchuria

Jiangxi

Shaanxi

Mongolia

CHINA

Vietnam

U.S.S.R.

Burma

India

MAPS by
Knowledge Quest, Inc.

KEY

China's Long March

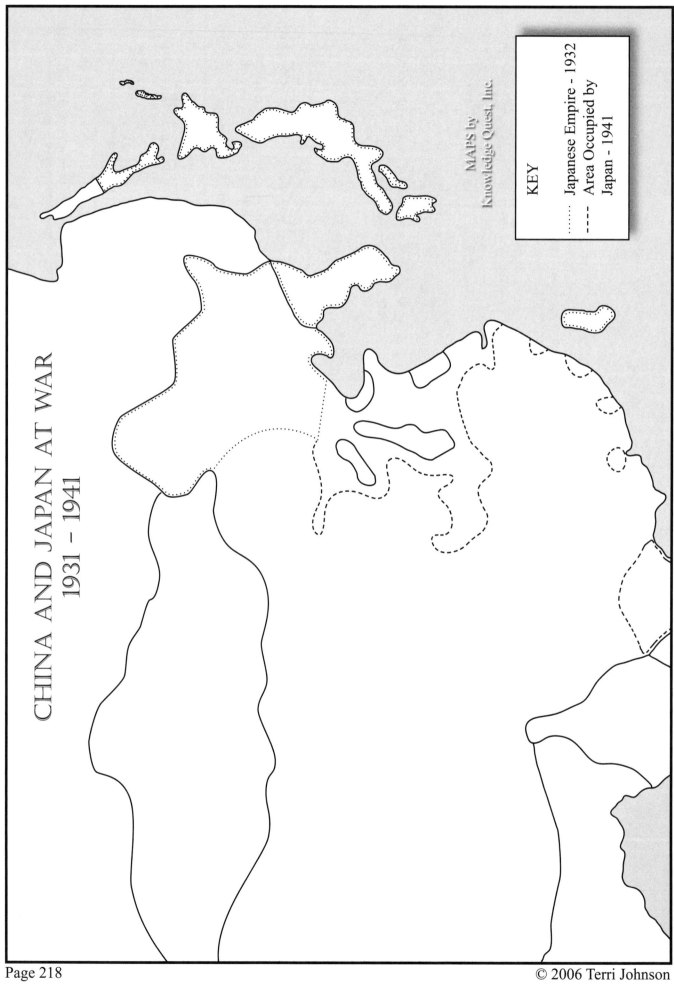

CHINA AND JAPAN AT WAR
1931 – 1941

MAPS by
Knowledge Quest, Inc.

KEY
.... Japanese Empire - 1932
- - - - - Area Occupied by
Japan - 1941

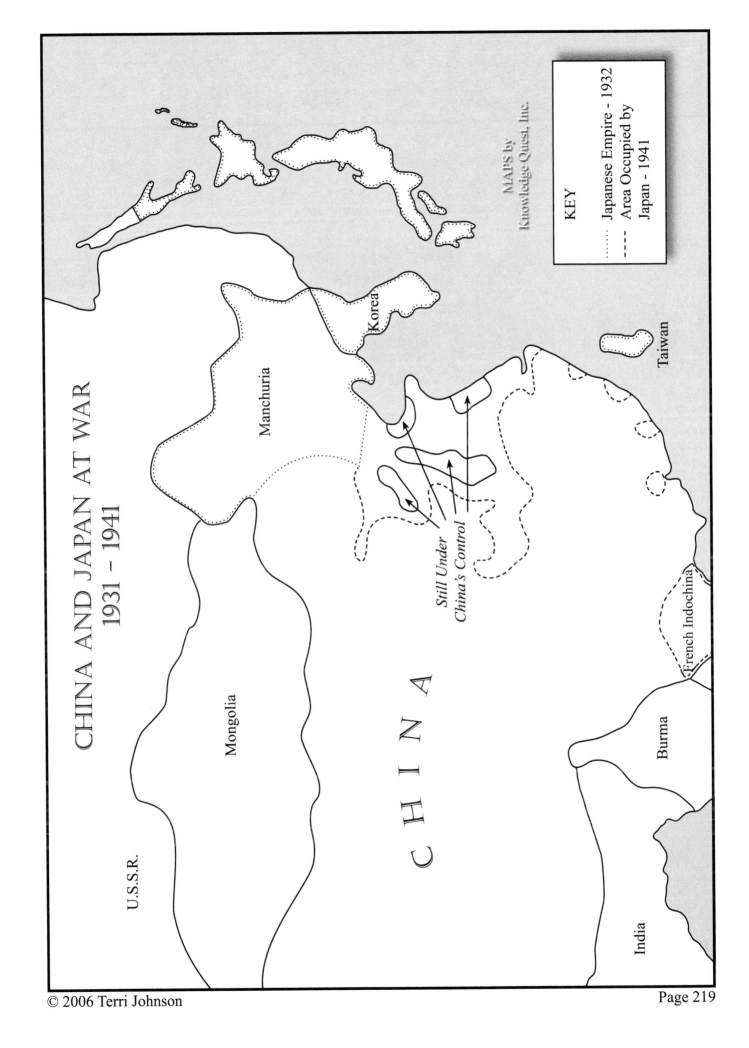

CHINA AND JAPAN AT WAR
1931 – 1941

KEY
Japanese Empire - 1932
Area Occupied by
Japan - 1941

MAPS by
Knowledge Quest, Inc.

U.S.S.R.

Mongolia

Manchuria

Korea

Taiwan

C H I N A

Still Under
China's Control

Burma

French Indochina

India

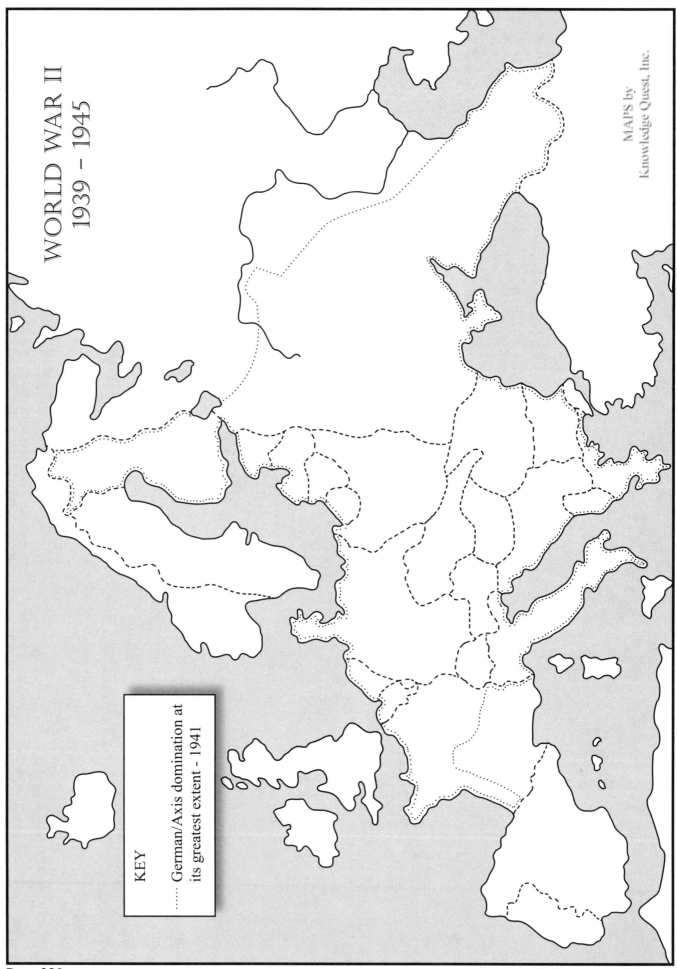

WORLD WAR II
1939 – 1945

KEY

······ German/Axis domination at
its greatest extent - 1941

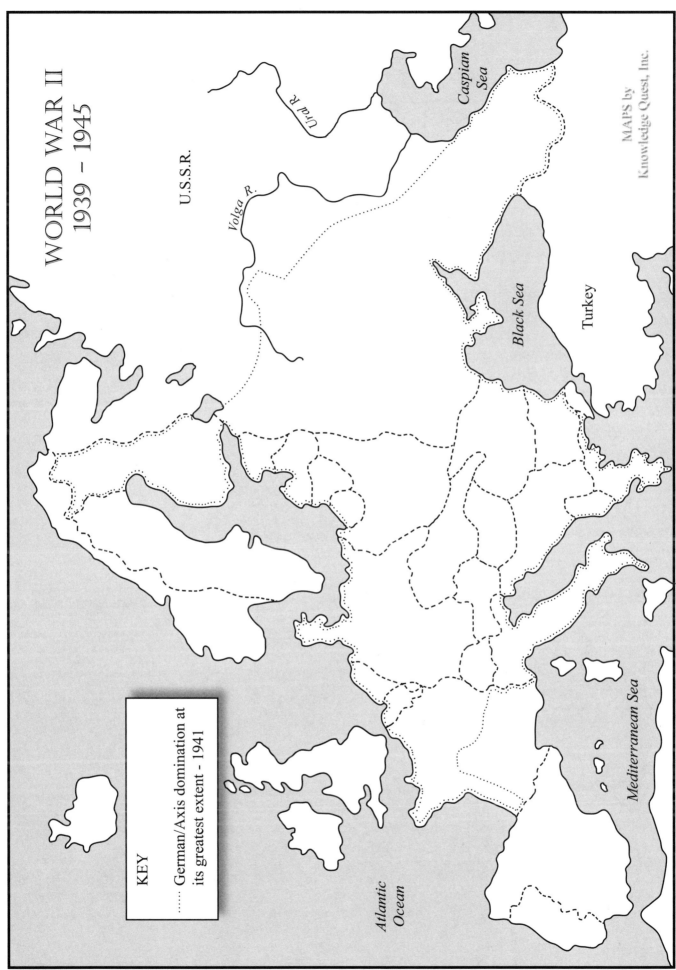

WORLD WAR II
1939 – 1945

U.S.S.R.

Ural R.

Volga R.

Caspian Sea

Black Sea

Turkey

Mediterranean Sea

Atlantic Ocean

KEY

.... German/Axis domination at
its greatest extent - 1941

MAPS by
Knowledge Quest, Inc.

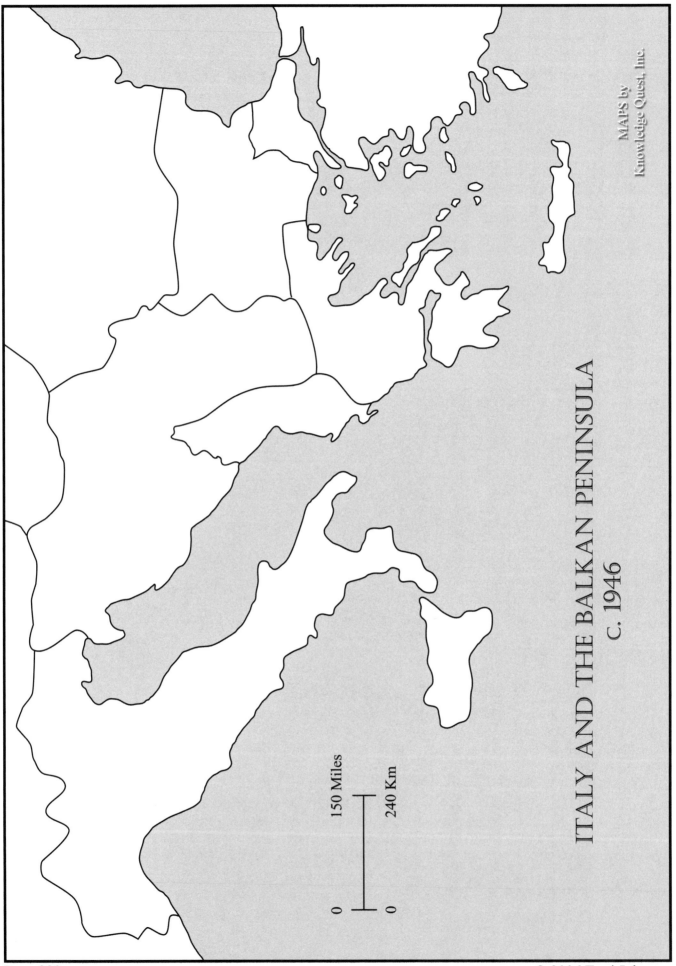

ITALY AND THE BALKAN PENINSULA

C. 1946

150 Miles

240 Km

0

0

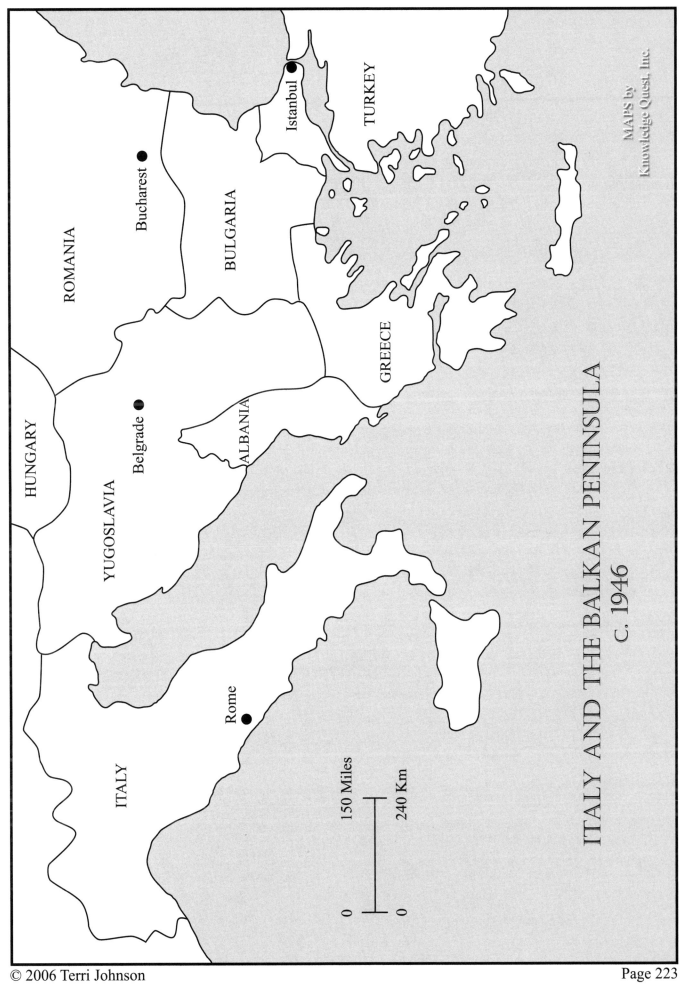

HUNGARY

ROMANIA

Bucharest ●

YUGOSLAVIA

Belgrade ●

BULGARIA

ALBANIA

Istanbul ●

TURKEY

GREECE

ITALY

Rome ●

150 Miles

240 Km

0

0

ITALY AND THE BALKAN PENINSULA
c. 1946

MAPS by
Knowledge Quest, Inc.

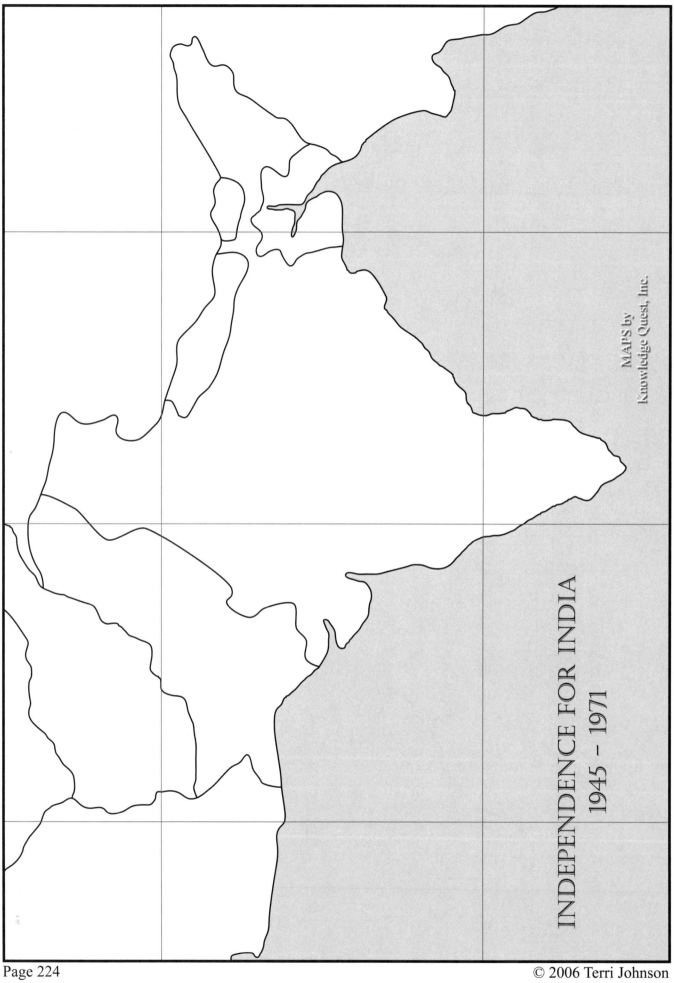

INDEPENDENCE FOR INDIA
1945 – 1971

MAPS by
Knowledge Quest, Inc.

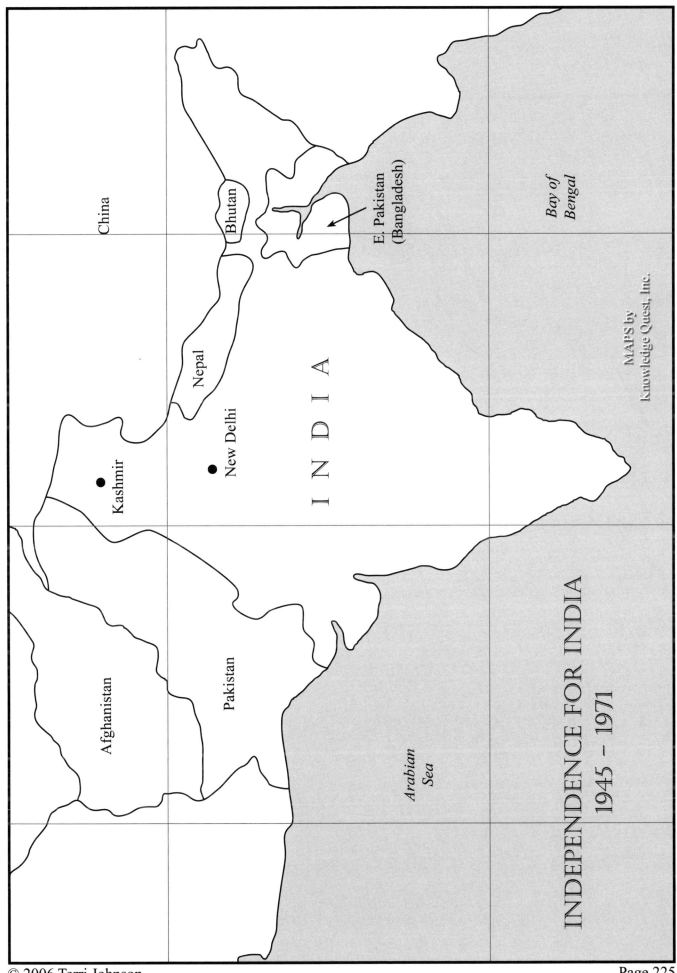

China

Bhutan

E. Pakistan
(Bangladesh)

Bay of
Bengal

Nepal

New Delhi

● Kashmir

I N D I A

MAPS by
Knowledge Quest, Inc.

Afghanistan

Pakistan

Arabian
Sea

INDEPENDENCE FOR INDIA
1945 – 1971

THE NATION OF ISRAEL
1948

THE NATION OF ISRAEL
1948

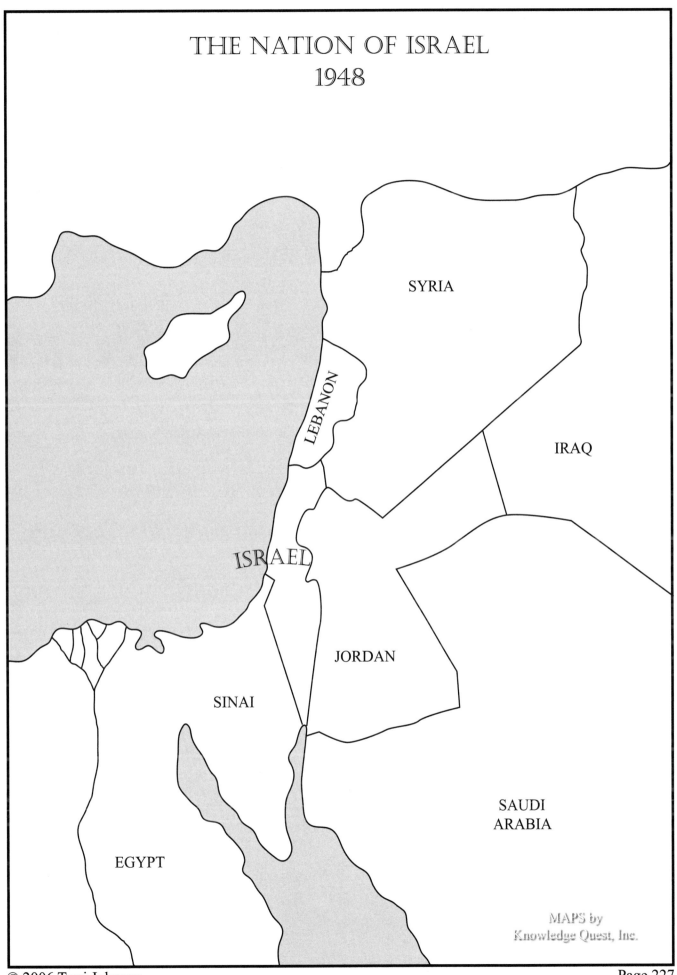

SYRIA

LEBANON

IRAQ

ISRAEL

JORDAN

SINAI

SAUDI
ARABIA

EGYPT

THE 50 UNITED STATES OF AMERICA

MAPS by
Knowledge Quest, Inc.

THE 50 UNITED STATES OF AMERICA

SINCE 1959

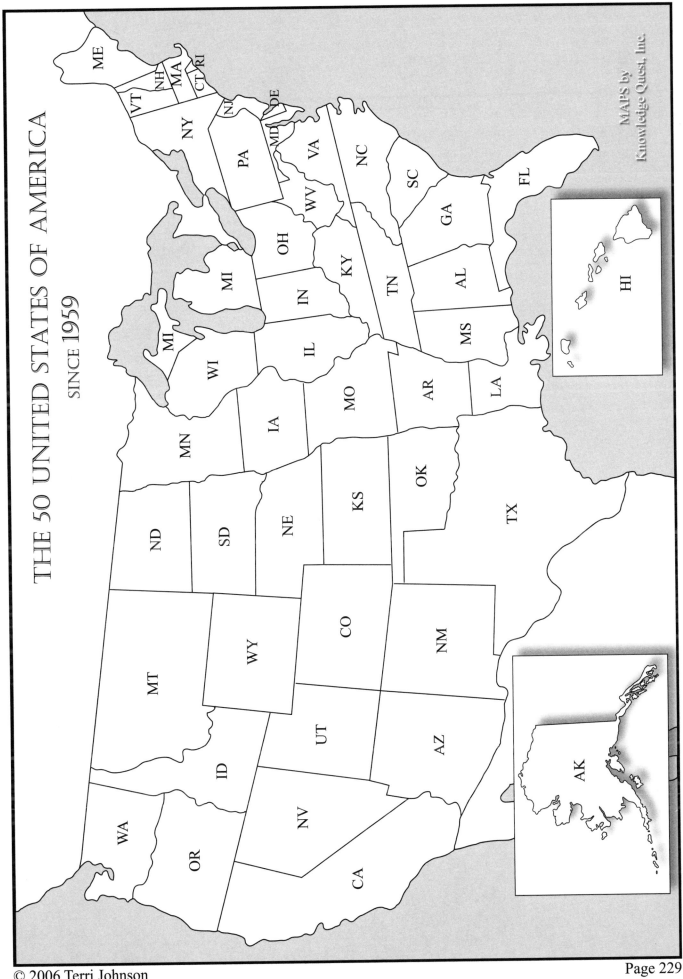

MAPS by Knowledge Quest, Inc.

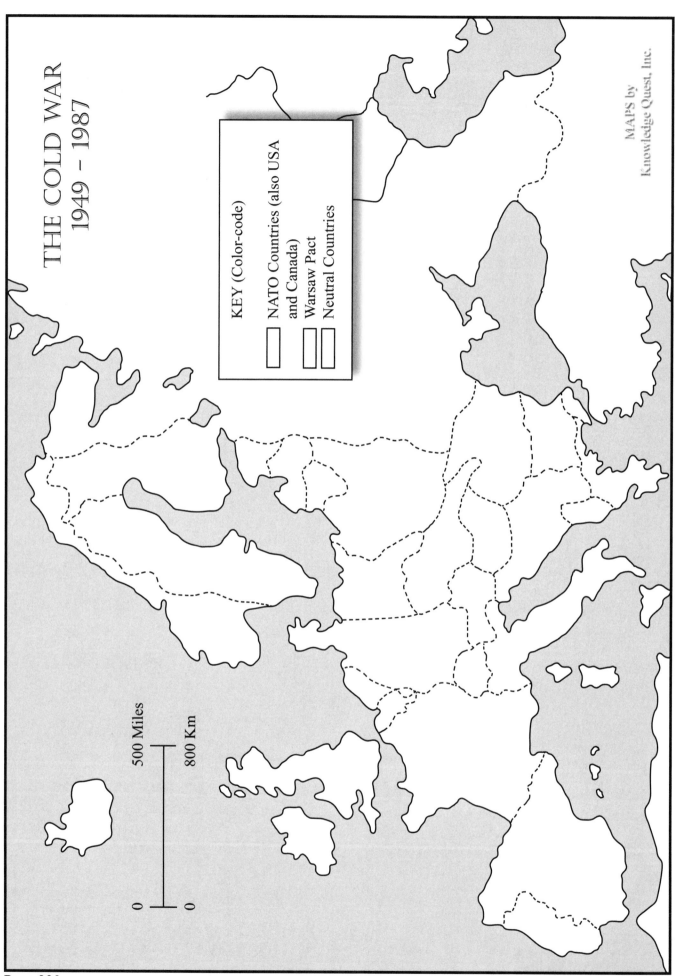

THE COLD WAR
1949 – 1987

KEY (Color-code)

NATO Countries (also USA and Canada)
Warsaw Pact
Neutral Countries

500 Miles

800 Km

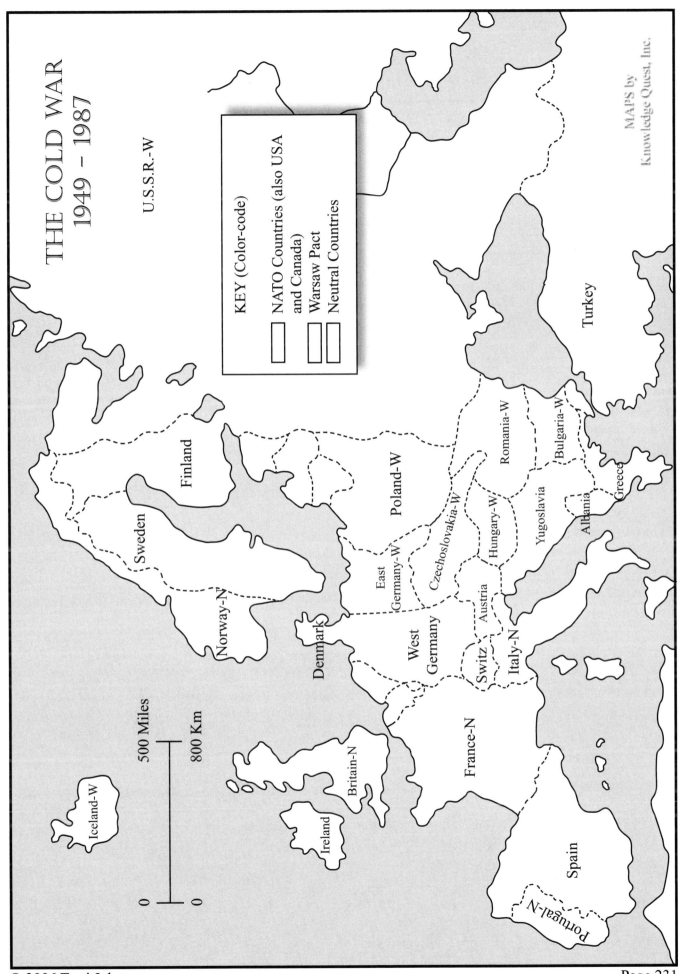

THE COLD WAR
1949 – 1987

U.S.S.R.-W

KEY (Color-code)

NATO Countries (also USA
and Canada)
Warsaw Pact
Neutral Countries

Finland

Sweden

Norway-N

Iceland-W

Ireland

Britain-N

Denmark

East
Germany-W

Poland-W

Czechoslovakia-W

West
Germany

Austria

Switz

Italy-N

France-N

Hungary-W

Romania-W

Yugoslavia

Bulgaria-W

Albania

Greece

Turkey

Spain

Portugal-N

500 Miles

800 Km

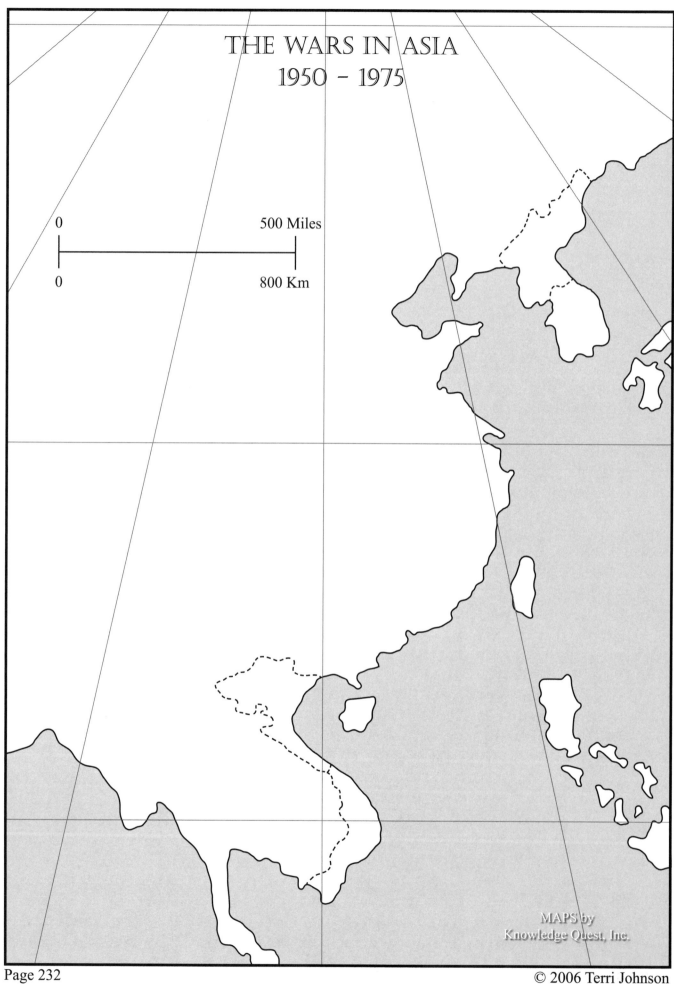

THE WARS IN ASIA
1950 – 1975

0   500 Miles

0   800 Km

MAPS by
Knowledge Quest, Inc.

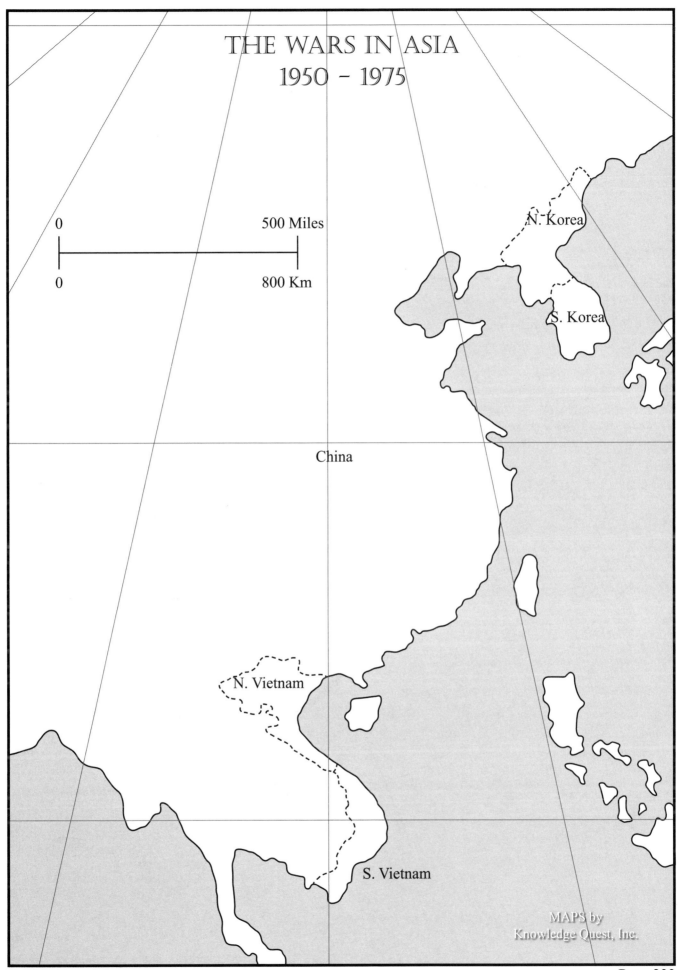

THE WARS IN ASIA
1950 – 1975

0   500 Miles

0   800 Km

N. Korea

S. Korea

China

N. Vietnam

S. Vietnam

MAPS by
Knowledge Quest, Inc.

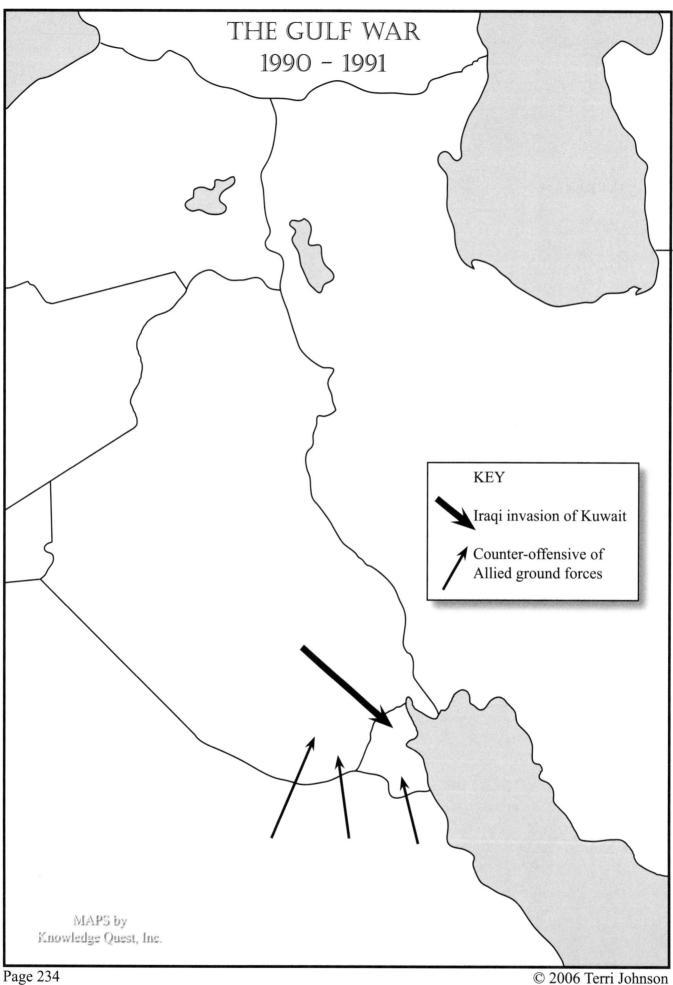

THE GULF WAR
1990 – 1991

KEY

Iraqi invasion of Kuwait

Counter-offensive of
Allied ground forces

MAPS by
Knowledge Quest, Inc.

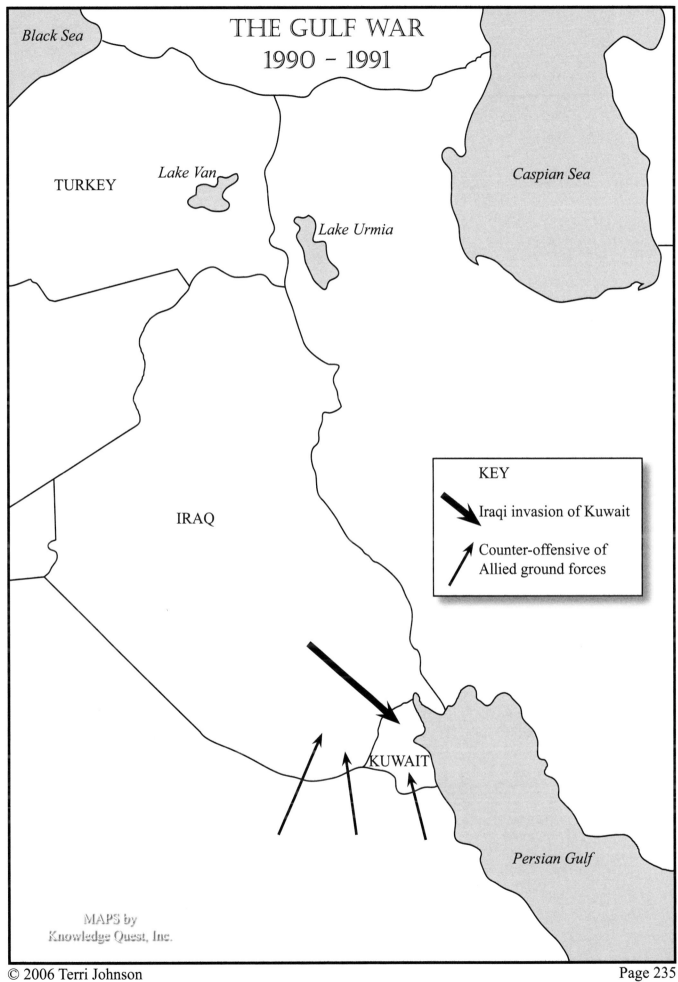

THE GULF WAR
1990 – 1991

Black Sea

TURKEY

Lake Van

Lake Urmia

Caspian Sea

IRAQ

KEY

Iraqi invasion of Kuwait

Counter-offensive of
Allied ground forces

KUWAIT

Persian Gulf

MAPS by
Knowledge Quest, Inc.

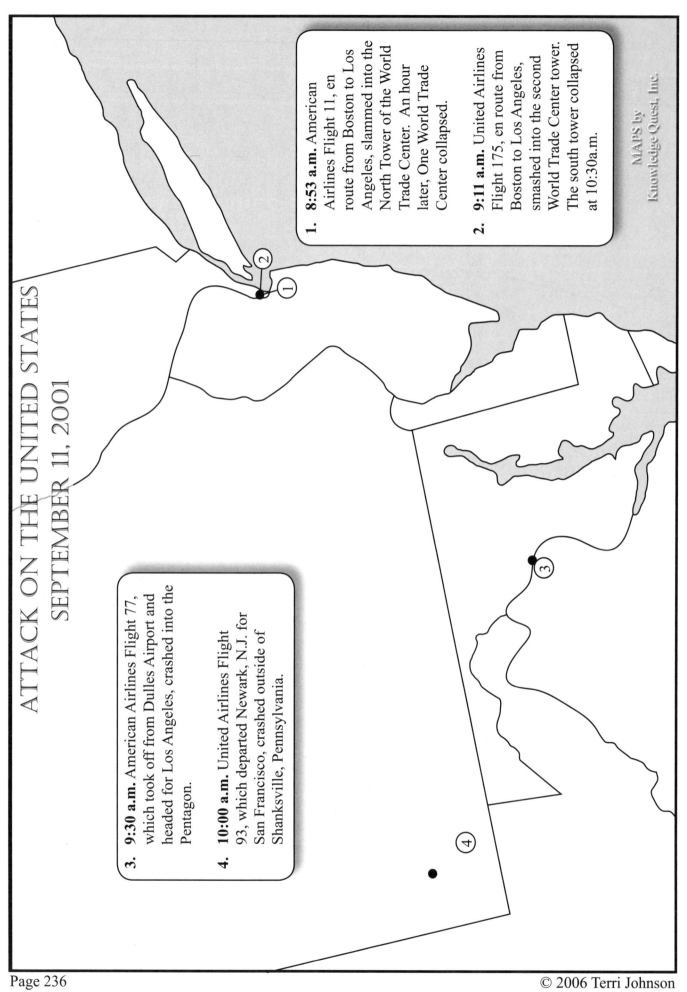

ATTACK ON THE UNITED STATES SEPTEMBER 11, 2001

1. **8:53 a.m.** American Airlines Flight 11, en route from Boston to Los Angeles, slammed into the North Tower of the World Trade Center. An hour later, One World Trade Center collapsed.

2. **9:11 a.m.** United Airlines Flight 175, en route from Boston to Los Angeles, smashed into the second World Trade Center tower. The south tower collapsed at 10:30a.m.

3. **9:30 a.m.** American Airlines Flight 77, which took off from Dulles Airport and headed for Los Angeles, crashed into the Pentagon.

4. **10:00 a.m.** United Airlines Flight 93, which departed Newark, N.J. for San Francisco, crashed outside of Shanksville, Pennsylvania.

MAPS by Knowledge Quest, Inc.

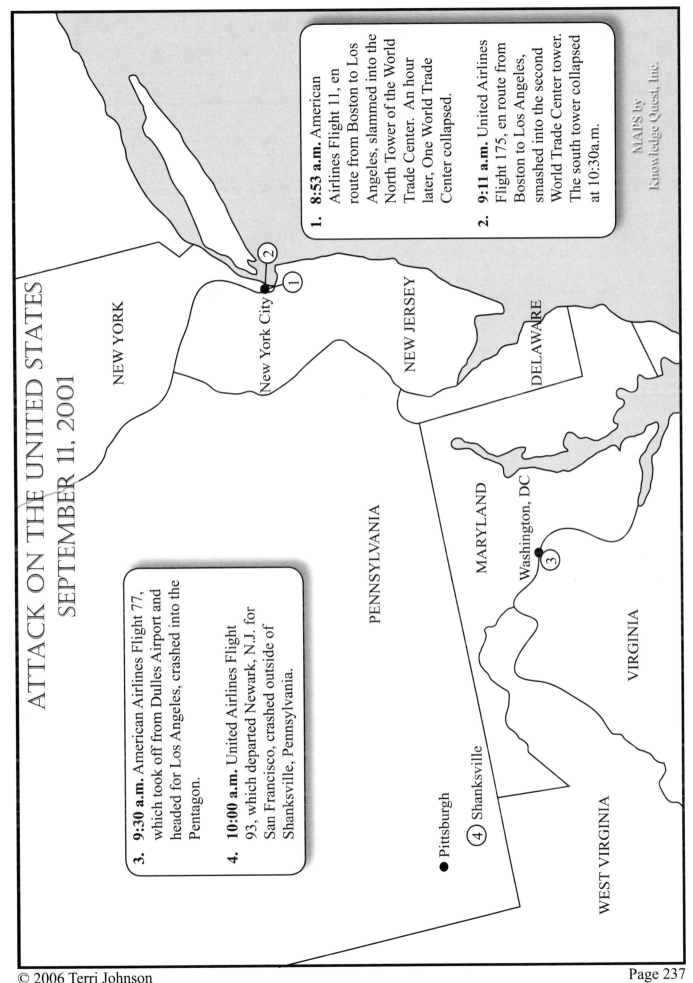

ATTACK ON THE UNITED STATES
SEPTEMBER 11, 2001

1. **8:53 a.m.** American Airlines Flight 11, en route from Boston to Los Angeles, slammed into the North Tower of the World Trade Center. An hour later, One World Trade Center collapsed.

2. **9:11 a.m.** United Airlines Flight 175, en route from Boston to Los Angeles, smashed into the second World Trade Center tower. The south tower collapsed at 10:30a.m.

3. **9:30 a.m.** American Airlines Flight 77, which took off from Dulles Airport and headed for Los Angeles, crashed into the Pentagon.

4. **10:00 a.m.** United Airlines Flight 93, which departed Newark, N.J. for San Francisco, crashed outside of Shanksville, Pennsylvania.

NEW YORK

New York City

NEW JERSEY

DELAWARE

PENNSYLVANIA

MARYLAND

Washington, DC

VIRGINIA

Pittsburgh

Shanksville

WEST VIRGINIA

MAPS by Knowledge Quest, Inc.

CONFLICT IN IRAQ
MARCH 20, 2003

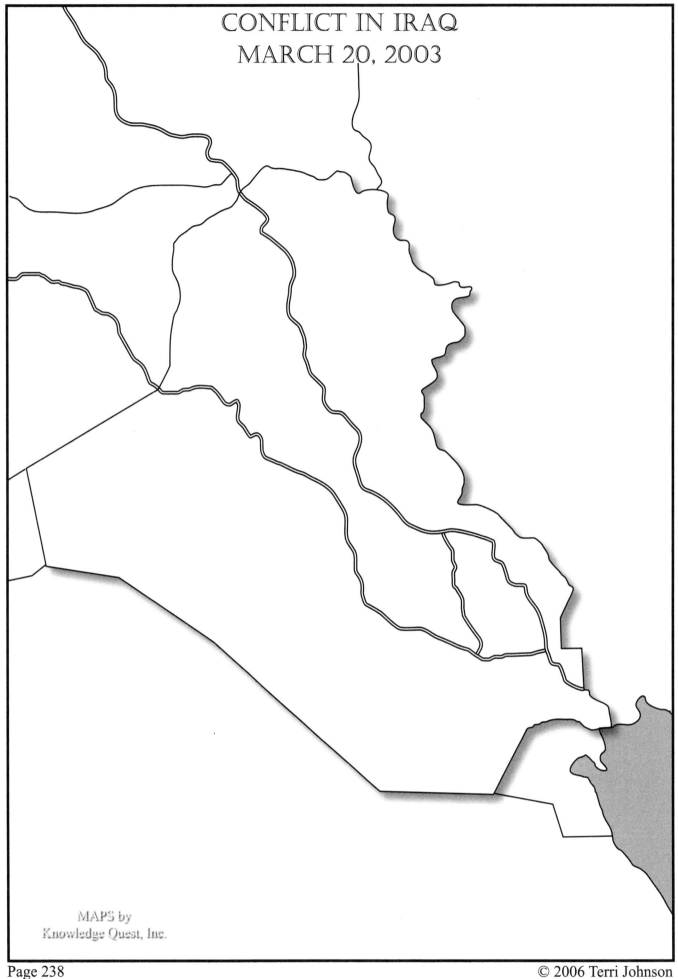

CONFLICT IN IRAQ
MARCH 20, 2003

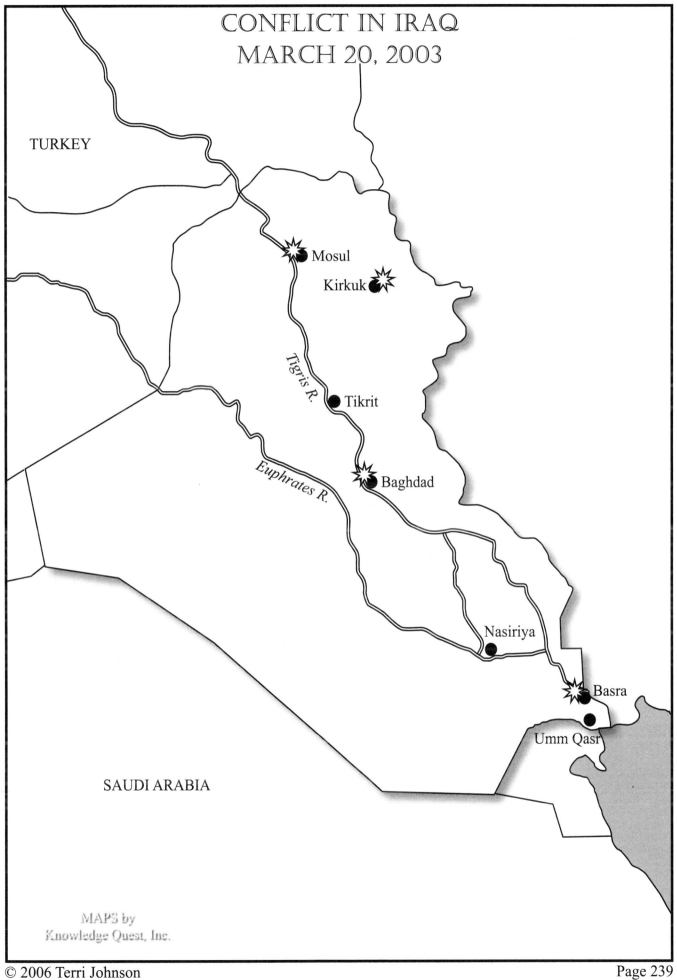

TURKEY

Mosul

Kirkuk

Tigris R.

Tikrit

Euphrates R.

Baghdad

Nasiriya

Basra

Umm Qasr

SAUDI ARABIA

MAPS by
Knowledge Quest, Inc.

KNOWLEDGE QUEST ORDER FORM

Please fill out this form and mail it along with check or money order
to Knowledge Quest, P.O. Box 789, Boring, OR 97009

Name

Address

City/State/Zip

Phone #   Email

Qty	Item #	Product Description	Price for each	Amount
	1001+	Blackline Maps of World History - The Ancients	$14.90	
	1002+	Blackline Maps of World History - The Middle Ages	$14.90	
	1003+	Blackline Maps of World History - The New World	$14.90	
	1004+	Blackline Maps of World History - The Modern World	$14.90	
	1110	The Complete Set of World History Maps + CD-ROM	$45.00	
	1011	The Complete Set - CD-ROM only	$29.95	
	1008	The Shaping of a Nation - American Map book + bonus CD-ROM	$29.95	
	1009	The Shaping of a Nation - CD-ROM only	$19.95	
	1031	Tapestry of Grace MapAids Year 1	$24.95	
	1032	Tapestry of Grace MapAids Year 2	$24.95	
	1033	Tapestry of Grace MapAids Year 3	$24.95	
	1034	Tapestry of Grace MapAids Year 4	$24.95	
	3020	Wall Timeline of Ancient History	$17.95	
	3021	Wall Timeline of Medieval History	$17.95	
	3022	Wall Timeline of New World History	$17.95	
	3023	Wall Timeline of Modern History	$17.95	
	3030	Wonders of Old: A Blank Timeline Book	$21.95	
	3031	Wonders of Old on CD-ROM	$19.95	
	3025	Timeline Category Stickers	$7.95	
	3005	Easy Timeline Creator	$29.95	
	3007	History Through the Ages - Creation to Christ	$19.95	
	3008	History Through the Ages - Resurrection to Revolution	$19.95	
	3006	History Through the Ages - Napoleon to Now	$19.95	
	3009	History Through the Ages - America's History	$29.95	
	3010	History Through the Ages - CD-ROM	$74.95	
	5011	Time Travelers - New World Explorers	$28.95	
	5012	Time Travelers - Colonial Life	$28.95	
	4001	What Really Happened in Ancient Times	$15.95	
	4002	What Really Happened During the Middle Ages	$15.95	
	4003	What Really Happened in Colonial Times	$15.95	
	4004	What Really Happened in Modern Times	$15.95	Spring '08
	4006	The Star Spangled State Book	$18.95	
	4007	The Star Spangled Workbook	$34.95	
	8011	Borderline - World Edition	$9.95	
	8012	Borderline - Europe/Middle East Edition	$9.95	
	8013	Borderline - Africa Edition	$9.95	
	8014	Borderline - USA Edition	$9.95	
	8015	Map Tangle by Borderline	$24.95	
	8016	Hop Off by Borderline	$24.95	
	Shipping for orders $10 - $30 is $5.10		Subtotal	
	Shipping for orders $30 - $100 is $9.25		Shipping & Handling	
	Shipping for orders over $100 is 9% of total		Total	

Orders are shipped USPS Priority mail. For an alternate shipping method (Media
or UPS), email: orders@knowledgequestmaps.com to request S&H rates.
Or you may call us at (877)697-8611
Checks should be made out to **Knowledge Quest, Inc.**

Name on credit card (Visa/Mastercard/Discover)

Credit Card#   Exp. Date